AMCHURCH COMES OUT

*The U.S. Bishops, Pedophile Scandals
and the Homosexual Agenda*

Paul A. Likoudis

Foreword by
Rev. Joseph F. Wilson

Published by
Roman Catholic Faithful, Inc.
Petersburg, Illinois

Printed in the United States of America

FIRST EDITION
May 2002

ISBN 0-9719558-0-8

Library of Congress Control Number: 2002103959

Jacket design by H. Ward Sterett

Roman Catholic Faithful, Inc.
P.O. Box 109
Petersburg, Illinois 62675-0109
Phone: 217-632-5920
www.rcf.org

Dedicated to all those who
helped me obtain my
Catholic education

FOREWORD

But seek first His Kingdom and His righteousness, and all these things shall be yours as well. [Mt 6:33]

+ + +

In my mind's eye as I begin this essay is the face of a seminarian, a Religious Brother who was a guest in our rectory a couple of years ago, a member of one of the most venerable Religious Orders in the Catholic Church, a centuries-old community with a long and proud tradition of scholarship and spirituality. The young man sitting before me was himself an impressive candidate. A trained engineer, he had been in the elite Green Beret special forces of the Army. He had left the military to become a priest. And here he was, telling me about the note tacked up on the community bulletin board by the superior of the formation house, instructing the Brothers and priests of the house that they were *not* to come to the house Hallowe'en party that year dressed in "drag" – made up like women.

It seems that there was some scandal given the previous year, as lay guests who were not quite attuned to the realities of Religious life today had been appalled to see consecrated Religious men appearing in drag or leather outfits accompanied by their boyfriends. This was one of the less disturbing stories this young man would tell me that afternoon.

Why I begin with that story in particular, why it should be on my mind, I am not sure; I suppose one has to start somewhere, but I am not in want of anecdotes and illustrations. In formation myself from 1977 - 1986, I do not need to borrow anyone else's stories. I watched as no fewer than three homosexuality "scandals" erupted over the years ("scandal" in the Church nowadays does not mean "something sinful has happened"; it means "somebody outside of the walls of this place found out about this and we had better contain it before our benefactors hear of it").

I squatted on the floor like an Indian as the priest professor celebrated a small group Eucharist in his living room, sitting on the couch with the coffee table as an altar, while a beautiful chapel with twenty minor altars languished downstairs. I saw the Liturgy regularly hijacked to make one point or another. I lived and tried to worship in places in which one could not open the altar missal or the lectionary or the breviary without "gender issues" and "inclusive language" being a concern, sat in class as a professor

i

opined that "Paul VI was, in my opinion, the greatest Pope of the twentieth century up to now and for the foreseeable future," a neat swipe at John Paul II. I was in the choir stalls of the seminary chapel as one priest prof, preaching on a Gospel text, referred sneeringly in an aside to "those of you who I know will be preaching about these texts as though they are historical fact." Of the same fellow, one of the other seminarians told me admiringly, "He is an awesome spiritual director. He prays using Buddhist scriptures."

I remember the first Mass of a newly ordained who had baked his own bread, but vastly overestimated the amount of bread needed for the congregation, with the result that there was a great deal left over. Someone had the bright idea of taking what was leftover and bringing it to a pond on the church premises and tossing it in, thereby, I suppose, turning the whole pond into the largest sacrarium in the world. The ducks, however, had another idea, paddling over and feasting on the Sacred Species. And history had been made – the first time since Pentecost that foul had been received into the full Communion of the Catholic Church (assuming, of course, that the whole ceremony had been valid, which mercifully, I doubt).

Then there was that memorable day when a Boston priest gave a workshop for the priests of the local diocese, and we seminarians were invited as well. It was on "Ministry to Homosexual Catholics," which apparently was this priest's area of expertise. It was a vile talk – "gays" are not accepted in parish life, the proof offered being that a "gay" couple could not come up to Communion holding hands as a "straight" couple could.

The priest made it clear from the outset: "One condition placed on me by my cardinal is that I may not say anything indicating that I don't accept the Church's teaching or that it needs to be changed. Therefore, I do *not* say that." This perverted, appalling nonsense was offered to us by our seminary as part of our formation for priesthood, and to the priests of the Dallas Diocese as ongoing formation. If one is tempted to wonder what would have happened if the bishop of the diocese had found out about this, may I hasten to assure that he was sitting in the front row center, laughing and thoroughly enjoying himself.

Yet another of the Dallas clergy, Rudy Kos, would later be the infamous clerical molester of well over a hundred boys. As for the Boston priest who gave us that workshop, he has been on the inactive list in the Kenedy

Directory for years...but has just surfaced on the pages of *The Boston Globe*. Fr. Paul Shanley is charged with the sexual abuse of teenagers during his years as a "street priest" in Boston, and will have his day in court.

Please pause for a moment now, and reflect on the fact that I encountered all of this appalling, perverted foolishness in the course of what the Church refers to as "priestly formation."

I don't offer these vignettes here because of a dearth of examples in this book – by the time you have finished this book, you will be weighted down with examples, I assure you! I offer these because they are *my* experience; I can vouch for them. They are but one priest's experience, and are by no means exhaustive; I have only scratched the surface of what I recall.

But this is Paul's book, not mine.

For fifteen years, Paul Likoudis has borne the burden and the heat of the day. He has reported on event after event, aberration after aberration. He has gone from the optimistic point where he expected that to bring these problems to light would mean to have them addressed, to the reality that these problems are public, that they have been for years, that they are known at the highest levels of the universal Church, and they are not addressed.

Paul began his began writing for *The Wanderer* in 1987; I was ordained a priest in 1986. In the years since, we have watched a terrible tragedy in the life of our Church continue to unfold and even gather steam, a tragedy which has been wholly unnecessary and, frankly, one which could certainly have been addressed many times over. That it has not been addressed – well, I cannot say that this is inexplicable, but the explanations which suggest themselves are very dark.

In 1992 Paul first used the phrase, "Amchurch," a shorthand to signify a deeply entrenched, influential, dissident faction within the leadership of the Catholic Church in our country – among the bishops, the heads of Religious orders, college and university administrators, chancery officials, prominent theologians, and seminary faculty (oh, the seminary faculties!!!). Their agenda diverges sharply from that of this pontificate and the teaching Church. I frankly do not see how the truth of his analysis can possibly be denied. Time after time we have seen new efforts initiated, corrective measures taken, and exhortations emanate from the Holy See which have been frustrated, stifled, or stonewalled by an entrenched elite in this country.

I think, for example, of the various documents issued in the name of the Holy Father clarifying liturgical praxis, even apologizing to Catholics of traditional sensibilities for the insensitivity with which they were often treated during the liturgical renewal, and asking the bishops for a "wide and generous application" of the Papal Indult permitting the traditional Mass – yet one hears from Catholics all over the country bemoaning the wretched, puerile state of the liturgy in their parishes, and characterizing the implementation of the Indult as anything but "wide and generous."

I recall, in the mid-1980s, the papally-initiated review of American seminaries and of American convents, entrusted to the supervision of Bishop John Marshall and Archbishop John Quinn, respectively, involving visitation teams of bishops, seminary educators and Religious. The Quinn report finding the state of American Religious life to be fundamentally sound and healthy was absolutely risible – the postconciliar period was to renewal of Religious life in this country what the Enola Gay was to urban renewal. As for the work of the Marshall committees, one finds fifteen years later that with a few exceptions, seminary life in our country is in a pitiful state: solid candidates still feel compelled to shop around for a bishop who will send them to a solid place of formation. The Church in the United States finds itself facing a dire crisis indeed.

As I complete this introduction, I have come across a report that New Ways Ministry is celebrating its twenty-fifth year with a convocation in Louisville in a few weeks. Founded by Fr. Bob Nugent, SDS, and Sr. Jeannine Gramick, SSND, who were formally silenced by the Holy See because they dissent from the Church's teaching on homosexuality, NWM seeks to promote the homosexual agenda throughout the Church. Conference speakers include two bishops (Gumbleton and Matthiesen), noted dissenters such as ex-priests Gregory Baum and Eugene Kennedy, Rosemary Radford Ruether and other prominent figures. It is interesting to note that over sixty sponsoring organizations of this dissenting event are listed – *most* of which are religious orders of men or women.

Fifty years ago, it would have been absolutely unimaginable that a religious order in the Catholic Church would sponsor or endorse theological dissent, but we have come a long way. The Congregation for the Doctrine of the Faith has directed the local bishop to inform NWM organizers that they do not have permission to celebrate Mass as part of the event because NWM does not promote the authentic teaching of the Church; one waits with bated breath to see if this monitum will have any effect.

Although American bishops have eagerly warmed to John Paul II's unprecedented innovations in such areas as ecumenism and collegiality, I simply cannot see how anyone can seriously deny that there is an Amchurch agenda which diverges sharply from, and stands in opposition to that of this pontificate and of the Universal Church on issues of sexual morality, where the Pope has unwaveringly supported Catholic traditional moral teaching. Paul Likoudis documented this in great detail in his marvelous article, "Love Among the Ruins," on the occasion of the silver jubilee of Pope John Paul II. There, set out meticulously in example after example, was a pattern of willful frustration of the goals and initiatives of the Vicar of Christ by those who stubbornly but, alas, successfully determined that they would be the architects of the future direction and character of the "American Church." The teachings of this Holy Father, his reflections, and his directives are there for all to read and ponder, quite accessible, a blueprint for renewal. They certainly set out a far more appealing agenda than the failed agenda of Amchurch, the decay of which is quite visible before our eyes.

Yet the directives go unheeded, the teachings unread. The utterly scandalous waste of the resources of the Church spent to promote the Amchurch agenda (the millions upon millions spent in wholly unnecessary sanctuary renovation – or conferences, workshops and Neo-Druidic retreats, and travel to and from such events) and the devastation which has resulted is a genuine tragedy.

This book is a well-crafted presentation of one perspective, an important perspective, on a disaster. The reality of that disaster should be obvious – yet, apparently, it is far from so for many. We have seen a sixty percent drop in Mass attendance in thirty years, our Religious communities are tattered, senescent remnants of their former vigor, our colleges and universities can no longer be expected to require a single course in Catholic theology, let alone uphold Catholic teaching and morality in campus life;

even our Catholic hospitals find creative ways to dispense contraceptives and make referrals for tubal ligations and other procedures condemned as immoral by the Church. Three generations have grown up in increasing ignorance of the Faith; two-thirds of our Mass-going Catholics cannot identify as the faith of the Church a simple declarative sentence expressing clearly and simply our teaching on the Eucharist.

Yet we still hear that tired, over-used word, "renewal," as though that has been what we have experienced over the past forty years. I hear it used of their communities by Religious who have not been to a profession in twenty-five years, by bishops who are training "lay ecclesial ministers" because they have no hope of staffing their parishes with priests since their gloriously renewed dioceses are so spiritually anemic there are no vocations stepping forward. I hear it used by people who audaciously refer to the vocation crisis as a "work of the Spirit" because it offers the "opportunity" to the laity to recover their own baptismal commitment through service to the Church (a sentiment aptly characterized by a correspondent as "blasphemy redeemed by stupidity," as though when we have prayed for vocations for the past thirty years we were praying to be delivered from the working of God the Holy Spirit).

But isn't it a good example of "the world turned upside down" that people who regard themselves as faithful Catholics would even think of saying that the shortage of priests is a blessing, a work of the Spirit, an opportunity for the faithful to exercise their baptismal charism.

How did we reach this point? Where did Amchurch come from? How can it have seduced so many, to the point where they willfully deny the dimensions of a catastrophe and speak instead as though it were "progress," a work of the Spirit? How did we arrive at this world turned upside down? How did we arrive at the moment when the unacceptable became desirable, the deviant became the norm? How can it be that the vilest sexual scandals, the most perverted violation of even innocent children by clergy, has become a staple of the evening news? How is it possible that we can be in the grip of such pathological denial that we look at this situation and dare to call it "renewal?"

I choose the term "pathological denial" deliberately. There is a deep-seated illness rampant in the Church today. That there are so many people who are able to look around them, disregard the evidence of decay and disorder, callously ignore the fact that countless souls are being harmed and led astray, and use the term "renewal" about what they see in the Church, is dismaying. It seems pretty evident to me that, if you were to be chatting with a bishop, and he were to describe to you with enthusiasm how he had gathered his tools, rolled up his sleeves and renovated his kitchen with the most satisfying results described in glowing terms, you could be quite certain that the ceiling had fallen about his ears and there had been a gas explosion which had leveled the whole neighborhood – the term "renewal" having acquired an elasticity which was unknown prior to December 8, 1965.

For those who love the holy Catholic Church, this book will make for painful reading. It chronicles a story which would literally be unbelievable had we not actually lived through it, a descent into Hell which would have been unimaginable fifty years ago. The priesthood we have loved, the Religious orders whose members taught our grandparents, the parishes and schools and universities established by earlier generations to teach us to seek first the Kingdom of God and His way of holiness, have in large measure been hijacked. The unacceptable has become the desired, the perverted has become the norm.

The liturgy of the Holy Sacrifice of the Mass is often celebrated in a way which reminds one of a cheap karaoke act, the Roman Rite standing out among the twenty-odd rites of the Catholic Church by the banality and vulgarity which often accompanies it. The few idealistic young men who present themselves for formation for priesthood today must be carefully guided and advised to choose among those bishops and dioceses which take seriously their responsibility to provide a sound formation, to send their men to a sound seminary – otherwise, they are in for a scandalous, disappointing encounter with all that is corrupt in the Church today, endangering not just their vocations, but often their very faith.

The story presented here is an ugly one, but it is one which everyone who loves the Church must read and take seriously. If the reader finds it surprising, then he cannot have been paying attention. Readers of *The Wanderer*, our nation's oldest lay-run Catholic newspaper, have been encountering these stories for years in its pages – indeed, this book is based by Paul Likoudis on his own reporting through these turbulent years.

For decades, *The Wanderer* has been derided as a journal for right-fringe kooks by those smiley-face Catholics who were determined to believe that they are living through a great age of "renewal" in the Church. Painstakingly chronicling scandals, describing New Age sexuality workshops given under diocesan auspices, analyzing the defects of catechetical materials, criticizing the assault upon the innocence of children represented by sex education classes – *The Wanderer* has assiduously and faithfully reported on the gathering madness, earning the derisive scorn even of those in the Church who profess loyalty to the Holy See but have convinced themselves that criticism is disloyal.

These eager imbibers of the postconciliar Kool-Aid need to look around themselves, and see the bitter fruits of the detour of the past forty years. For we have, indeed, wandered off the path. It was not the mind of the Fathers of the Second Vatican Council that, forty years later, we should find ourselves mired in clerical sex scandals, to the horror or titillation of the public. They did not intend that time-proven and sound methods of passing on the Faith from generation to generation be trashed, that the lifestyles of consecrated Religious be secularized, that the moral guidance of the Church's teaching be silenced to the point where most Catholics have never heard a homily on sexual morality.

It is time to wake up, push aside the tempting tumbler of the postconciliar Kool-Aid, and smell the coffee. For those willing, for love of the Church, to face reality, Mr. Likoudis offers a painstaking review of how we got to our present sad state of distress. He makes a persuasive case for his explanation of the tragedy, describing how, in an age of societal turmoil and sexual confusion, the Sacred Tradition of the Church became the target of those whose concept of freedom is license, who saw the opportunity to attain to positions of pastoral and administrative authority and who used their influence to implement a revolution against the traditional Catholic vision of holiness of life. As one lay theologian wrote to me recently, "Years of watching the situation carefully have convinced me that it really *is* all about sexual autonomy. People don't turn institutions upside down because they'd rather hear the Mass in English. You can do that without destroying buildings and the structure of religious life, and catechesis. You turn institutions upside down to support a 'complete change in teleological purpose' in your life – and eliminate unpleasant reminders that maybe your new purpose, sexual autonomy, isn't such a great idea."

This is painful reading, and the chronicling of it over these fifteen years has been costly for the author, who writes out of a genuine love of the Church. But this is a story which must be faced, for in our day the precious patrimony of our Faith has been compromised and betrayed; and for a world starving for the Truth, the light of the Catholic Faith has been obscured.

In our day, the unacceptable has become desirable, the unimaginable has become reality, the perverted has become the norm. If we would understand where we went astray, we must first retrace our steps; Paul has placed us all in his debt by enabling us to do that with his book. In His time, God will raise up the saints who will rescue His Church and leaven her with their holiness, as He has done in the past; in the meantime, we who love the Church must pause, pray, understand what has been allowed to fall upon her, and implore His mercy. And let us never, never, ever hear again, of anything that has transpired over the last forty years, that wretchedly over-used word "renewal."

Let us keep it for a better day, when it shall mean something.

And with it all, amid all of this sadness, let us hold to the joy of our Profession of Faith. I was raised by good Catholic parents to understand that Catholicism is far more than a set of rules to constrict life, or a list of things to be memorized and customs to be observed. Catholicism is a deep, and wide, and fruitful way of looking at all reality in light of the mystery of God made Man, Who died for us, and rose from the dead, and Who lives! To understand this is to understand everything; once one understands this, all things are transformed and seen in its light. May the Mother of the Lord Jesus, the Mother of the Church and our Mother obtain for us from her Son the grace while reading this troubling book to remember His words to us on the night He was betrayed: "I have said this to you, that in Me you may have peace. In the world you have tribulation; but be of good cheer, I have overcome the world." (Jn 16:33)

The Rev. Joseph F. Wilson
Priest of the Diocese of Brooklyn

ix

TABLE OF CONTENTS

"We cannot allow the Religious Right to confine our sexuality to the bedroom. Our sexuality must burst forth from the bedroom and leaven all of society."

— Fr. James Schexnayder,
founder of the National Association of
Catholic Diocesan Lesbian and Gay Ministries,
to the congregation at a Dignity Mass at
Dolores Street Baptist Church immediately following
the Sunday, June 28, 1992 San Francisco Gay Pride Parade.

INTRODUCTION

January 2002 was difficult month for the Catholics of Boston and Bernard Cardinal Law when, thanks to a successful lawsuit brought by *The Boston Globe*, the whole world learned that Church officials had repeatedly placed clerical sexual predators in Catholic parishes, and that there were upwards of 80 priests who were sexual abusers. The following month, Catholics in Tucson learned that Bishop Manuel Moreno also allowed priests, known by him to be pedophiles, to serve in various parishes. And within the next few weeks, bishops, archbishops and cardinals also admitted that they had sheltered clerical sexual molesters in neighborhood churches.

Revelation followed revelation, and what began as a sex abuse story became a homosexual network story. By April, Newark's Star Ledger (April 29, 2002) reported that a former Bishop of Camden, George Guilfoyle, the deceased defendant in a lawsuit filed by two brothers, was known as the "Queen of the Fairies" and that one of his top aides was known as his "pimp" who recruited "priests having a homosexual propensity." Guilfoyle, a native New Yorker who was bishop from 1968 to 1989, was, for 60 years, the "best friend" of former Atlanta Archbishop Thomas Donnellan, also a New Yorker who served in Atlanta from 1968 to 1987 and who was a promoter of Cardinal Law.

Thus, for the first time, Catholics nationwide learned about the standard operating procedure of the Catholic bishops for decades: the recruitment of homosexual priests, the re-assignment of recidivist sexual molesters in the clergy from parish to parish, diocese to diocese and a concerted strategy on the part of bishops to cover-up clerical crimes.

What was particularly offensive to Catholic sensibilities in this whole sordid affair, were claims from bishops that they "didn't know"; that "if we knew then what we know now" they would act differently; that they thought pedophilia[1] was "treatable," etc.

As far as back as 1957, a Boston priest, renowned for both his holiness and his pastoral care of troubled priests, had warned the American bishops, and Rome, of pedophile "devils" in the priesthood.

That priest was Fr. Gerald Fitzgerald, founder of the Servants of the Paraclete, a treatment center at Jemez Springs, New Mexico, and a chain of other centers in the United States and Europe. As Fr. Charles Fiore wrote in the April 15, 1993 issue of *The Wanderer*, just weeks after Archbishop Robert Sanchez of Santa Fe resigned after his molestations of young women were exposed, Fr. Fitzgerald knew pedophilia was incurable, and he warned against the use of his treatment center as a haven for pedophile priests.

"In two brutally frank letters written nearly 35 years ago," Fiore wrote, "the late Fr. Gerald Fitzgerald, founder of the Servants of the Paraclete, warned the late Santa Fe Archbishop Edwin V. Byrne in 1957, and a Paraclete superior in 1960, not to use the congregation's 'renewal and treatment center for priests and brothers' at Jemez Springs, N.M. – also known as its 'foundation house' – for the treatment of pedophile priests.

> The letters, reported in the *Albuquerque Tribune*, Friday, April 2, were filed in Albuquerque district court the day before as attachments to a motion by attorneys for the Paraclete congregation requesting reconsideration by a four-judge panel of restrictions on release of documents in pending cases having to do with sexually abusive priests treated at the facility…

---

[1]The author wishes to acknowledge at the outset of this work that there exists a difference between the use of the term *pedophilia* (sexual perversion in which children are the preferred sexual object) and that of *ephebophilia* (a sexual attraction to children or adolescents around the time of puberty or after). For the sake of brevity, the word *pedophilia* is used throughout this book to signify either attraction.

Fitzgerald, originally a priest of the Boston Archdiocese, founded the center, first called Via Coeli…in 1947, with $25,000 in seed funds donated by Francis Cardinal Spellman in New York…

In the letters released April 1, Fitzgerald, considered a compassionate, visionary priest of the 'old school,' is revealed as passionately opposed to the use of the retreat center for clergy sex offenders.

Writing September 18, 1957 to Archbishop Byrne, whose permission and blessing to begin the center in the Santa Fe Archdiocese earned his status as its 'co-founder,' Fitzgerald wrote that it would be best not to 'offer hospitality to men who have seduced or attempted to seduce little boys or girls.

'These men, Your Excellency, are devils, and the wrath of God is upon them; and if I were a bishop I would tremble when I failed to remove them to Rome for involuntary laicization. Experience has taught us these men are too dangerous to the children of the parish and neighborhood for us to be justified in receiving them here.'

In the second letter, August 11, 1960, written apparently to the Paraclete superior at Jemez Springs whose name is deleted, Fitzgerald urged him to immediately remove a pedophile priest from the Via Coeli facility, saying: 'Men who sin repeatedly with little children certainly fall under the classification of those who it were better had they not been born. He will hurt the Church; and he will hurt the community. Moreover, as a layman, the civil authorities will make short work of his activity and place him in the protective custody that his type merit…'

It has been reported previously, and his 1957 letter to Archbishop Byrne indicates, that Fitzgerald had purchased an island – its location was not revealed, but rumored to be located in the Caribbean – as a place for pedophile priests, who he evidently considered incurable…

This information is important because – contrary to statements by defenders of diocesan inaction, who now claim that little was known about the scope and severity of the clergy pedophile problem until recently — Fitzgerald's letter indicates that they, other bishops, and Rome certainly knew of the growing problem of priest sexual abusers, and the inability to cure them, more than 30 years before the warnings and media disclosures of the 1980s…

Fitzgerald informed Archbishop Byrne that he intended to speak with the Pope about 'this class [of priests]' saying 'they should ipso facto be reduced to laymen when they act thus.'

In 1965, Fitzgerald was called to Rome and ordered to sell the uninhabited island he had purchased in the 1950s as a permanent retreat for pedophile priests. In 1966, priests with 'psychosexual problems' were reintroduced into the treatment center at Jemez Springs…

What also happened between 1957 and 1966, I believe, was that homosexuals, pedophiles and other perverse persons in the priesthood rose to prominence in the Church, certainly in the United States and Canada, and began carefully plotting and promoting a sexual liberation agenda that would take Catholics by surprise, an agenda that first manifested itself in the new catechetical texts rushed into print during the Second Vatican Council. The immediate attacks were on Church teaching regarding masturbation, fornication, adultery and contraception and divorce; but by the middle of the 1980s, it became clear this was only the first stage, to be followed by the aggressive promotion of homosexuality, bisexuality and "transgenderism."

Popes since St. Pius X had foreseen the ascendant "new morality" preached by "modern" ethicists, and warned bishops, priests and laity to be vigilant and guard against it. For example, in an April 18, 1952 message to the International Congress of the World Federation of Catholic Young People gathered in Rome, Pope Pius XII addressed participants on the subject, "Moral Law and the New Morality", warning them that the "dangers besetting the faith of our young people are today extraordinarily numerous. Everyone knew this and knows it….Nevertheless, we feel that few of these dangers are as great or so heavy in foreboding as those which the 'new morality' creates for faith….

"This [new morality] would be the death of faith," said Pius XII, and he offered these young Catholic activists two directives that would not only be ignored, but would be perverted: to teach children how to pray, and to teach them to be proud of their faith. Though always serene, Pius understood what each of his predecessors in the century knew: there was a broad movement in the Church, largely forced underground by Pope Pius X's condemnation of Modernism, that would take up the decadent Victorians' cause of "free love" to deconstruct all of the Church's doctrines.

This loose and hidden movement would emerge in the United States in the late 1950s and early 60s, and coalesce under the leadership of the late Joseph Cardinal Bernardin, who, reported Fr. Andrew Greeley in his autobiography *Confessions of A Parish Priest*, blasted Pope Paul VI's 1968 encyclical *Humanae Vitae* as "that goddam encyclical."

Long before Pope Paul VI's New Mass and the turning-around of the altars, long before most Catholics were aware of the pending moral revolution glamorized by Hollywood films and Haight-Ashbury's hippies, Catholic school children – particularly adolescents – were being groomed for the sexual revolution via the major catechism publishers, such as Sadlier.

Typical of these early works was *To Live Is Christ,* which deconstructed Scripture and Church teaching on everything from sin to salvation, encouraged rebellion against every form of authority, especially of parents and Church tradition, promoted self-absorption and secular notions of social justice, and promised a new stage of mankind where both individuals and society would attain "self-fulfillment" and perfection.

In the preface to *To Live Is Christ* (Chicago: Henry Regnery, 1965), Brothers J. Frederick, FSC and H. Albert, FSC, (both of whom left their Religious order before the second edition of their text was published) wrote that Vatican II and the new awareness the Catholic Church had reached of itself demanded a new way of thinking about the Church, and that every settled belief, custom and practice had become irrelevant as a result of the Council.

INTRODUCTION

This book, produced by the Archdiocese of Chicago's Confraternity of Christian Doctrine, was expected to reach an audience of 400,000 Catholic students in schools across the country in its first year.

In the first pages of the preface, teachers are advised:

"Because Catholic Christianity (through the impact of the Second Vatican Council) is passing through a crisis of deeper understanding and better practice, your students tend to be confused about what is essential to our faith and what is changeable (italics in original). No doubt you are confused, too. This state of affairs will not end with the Council, but will continue past the end of your lifetime. Perhaps because we live in the age of 'the knowledge explosion,' there will never again be pat answers or eternal customs…"

On May 22, 1965, before either the liturgical or catechetical revolutions had manifested themselves in the vast majority of Catholic churches and schools, the New York *Journal-American*, which dubbed itself "New York's Largest Evening Newspaper," published on its front page a full-page report on the dramatic changes coming to Catholic catechesis under the headline, "Ecumenical Progress in New Catholic Textbook by Nuns," and in larger block letters: "The Jewish Background of Jesus."

How, one wonders looking back, did the release of a new Catholic catechism rate a news story the equivalent in stature of the attack on Pearl Harbor or the assassination of John F. Kennedy?

Perhaps it was the author's connections.

The report by Alfred Robbins touted the catechism series *The Lord Jesus* by Immaculate Heart of Mary Sisters M. Elizabeth and M. Johnice, published by the then-Michigan firm of Allyn and Bacon.

Sisters M. Elizabeth and M. Johnice were the co-founders and co-directors of the Pius XII Center in Monroe, Michigan, established as the "official" U.S. associate of Lumen Vitae, the catechetical center in Brussels, founded by the Jesuits in 1957 to disseminate a progressivist agenda in the Church.

The Lumen Vitae center at the time was playing a major role in Quebec's "Quiet Revolution," promoting Liberation Theology in Latin America, and laying the groundwork for the catechetical and liturgical revolutions in the United States.

The Monroe Center's consultants included: then-Jesuit Fr. Bernard Cooke (who remains active on the Call To Action circuit while teaching "Christian sacramental practice" at the University of San Diego); Fr. Edward Burkhardt, director of religious education, Archdiocese of Detroit; Rabbi Marc Tanenbaum of the American Jewish Committee; and Alice L. Goddard, executive director, Department of Curriculum Development, National Council of Churches.

Buried deep in Robbins' breathless prose on this "truly revolutionary textbook series – which may reach ten million Catholic pupils in the next ten years" – is a statement from Thomas Gilshannon, the supervisor of the "Come Lord Jesus" series at Allyn and Bacon, that the project began in 1960, when "it became evident that a revolution was about to take place in Catholic religious education."

"Familiar with the work of Sisters Johnice and Elizabeth at the Pius XII Center," Robbins continued, "Gilshannon contacted them and they agreed to the project. In 1961, the Sisters invited Rabbi Marc Tanenbaum, regarded as an authority on Christian-Jewish relations, and he offered to help."

Rabbi Tanenbaum lavished praise on the series, which was revolutionary in more ways than one; perhaps most notably because of the original, very modernistic, art produced by Lutherans, Alice and Martin Provencen, designed to deliver a psychological jolt to the typical Catholic child of the time, a kind of "double-whammy" to the text.

This artwork, observed the National Federation of Laymen, shortly after it was released, depicts Jesus, His Blessed Mother and the Apostles "in a grotesque and deformed manner. Strangely, the children consistently appear pleasant throughout." But in Book 1, "an illustration of Jesus, the Good Shepherd, bending over his sheep...is a monstrous-looking, wild-eyed character with a huge nose and claw-like hands. This image of the loving Savior could only leave a child with repugnance and fright. He would find it impossible to believe that this creature was the Son of God."

A dissenter way back then

In a book aimed at Catholic high schoolers, *What Do We Really Believe?* (1968, published by the National Center of the Confraternity of Christian Doctrine), Fr. Richard McBrien (the infamous dissenting Notre Dame theologian, then Dean of Studies at Pope John XXIII National Seminary for Delayed Vocations) opened his tirade against the Church with a criticism of Pope Paul VI's lament that many theologians are distorting the Catholic faith, with a condescending assertion that the Holy Father doesn't understand the difference between theology, doctrine and faith.

In the first chapter of the book, he lampoons the "anti-Modernist" era of the Church (the 20th century up to Vatican II), dismisses the notion that the Church has anything "to fear from people who make errors in theology," and proposes that the Church has nothing to fear from theologians who want to deconstruct the Church's dogmatic statements in the same way that Protestant Bible scholars deconstructed Scripture in the 19th century.

He rounds out the chapter by parodying and mocking the faith of the parents of his intended audience.

Chapter Two is titled "What Kind of God," and facing the page of text is full-page black and white photograph of Santa Claus. In Chapter Four, "Jesus is Lord," McBrien suggests that Catholics do not have to believe that Jesus rose from the dead. The book ends by suggesting there are "problems" with the Church's teaching on transubstantiation, and a call to Catholics to become socially involved in the wars on poverty and racism and the other causes of the day.

The imprimatur on this book was provided by Bishop Henry J. O'Brien of Hartford, Connecticut.

Another book in the series was by Fr. Gerard Sloyan, *How Do I Know I Am Doing Right?*, (1966) with an imprimatur by Archbishop Karl Alter of

Cincinnati. The premise of the book is that "the whole Church has a problem of fidelity to Jesus," and too many Catholics give "blind obedience" to the Church's teachings on morality "as a substitute for forming their own consciences."

"The question is," writes Sloyan, "has the Church itself got moral teaching straight? For the most part the Church has been a good guide, but one not entirely free from ambivalence in its teaching on morality."

For Sloyan, the Church has been too obsessed with sexual morality; but that is changing under the impulse of post-Vatican II theologians who take a more "nuanced" approach. On the other hand, it has not taken a firm enough approach on such matters as capital punishment, racism, poverty and war, but that, too, is changing.

In the Christian Brothers' *Living With Christ* series, one finds such lines as:

- "Wouldn't it be better to drop the idea of God until we see which way the world will go? So an idea of God that fits the needs of today would depart from the Church's official teaching, wouldn't it?"

- Doesn't the history of the western world suggest to you that Christianity has failed? That the Church has been mainly concerned with power and wealth?"

Teilhardian revolution

In the euphoric early 1960s, a tremendous press campaign told the world that the Church was changing, transforming its liturgy, jettisoning its traditions, exchanging its strict morality for an ethos of self-fulfillment.

Behind this ethos, expressed in the majority of catechetical texts produced in the early 1960s, was the evolutionary thought of Teilhard de Chardin, a Jesuit priest condemned as a heretic by Pope John XXIII.

In a Sadlier text, *Growth in Christ* (1966), by Brother Andrew Panzarella, FSC, one reads towards the end of 400-plus page book devoted mostly to pop-psychology theories offered as a substitute for solid Church teaching the following:

INTRODUCTION

"[Teilhard's] theory of evolution is not without its flaws, but it stands out as the prophetic vision of the twentieth century…

"What is really new in Teilhard's theory of evolution is the idea that evolution is moving towards a goal. Evolution is not just haphazard change but well ordered change moving toward the goal of the fulfillment of the universe, when all things – material, living, social and cultural – come under man's control so that man can fulfill himself as the master and summit of creation. If there is a divine plan visible in the history of the universe, it is a plan to bring all things to fulfillment under the hand of man. Evolution has reached a point where it is now under man's control…

"Mankind is building the kingdom of God. We are participating in God's creative activity by marshaling the elements of the universe into new forms, so that all forces – material, social and cultural – nourish an emerging mankind. We participate in God's redeeming activity by ceaseless war against the forces of evil – in our physical world, in our biological and psychological organisms, in our social structures, and in our culture," and the book is full of lines as:

- "In adolescence a person rejects many childish religious notions on the basis of his experiences of life. This is a good and necessary part of religious growth."

- "Is a person religious if he keeps various religious practices and assents to various religious beliefs but does not take a stand on social issues? Can a person be religious if he does not go to church but is involved in social issues?"

- "Genetics…can also be constructive in determining what human beings will be like. A century from now doctors may be able to control the sex, the looks, and the intelligence of the children to be born. Whether or not we like the idea of giving doctors control over what each person will be like, we have to face the fact that genetics is rapidly moving toward this objective. And it may offer some wonderful advantages."

- "The ideal Church, as described for us in the New Testament, is a community of men sealed in fellowship by love. It is hard for Catholics to understand this because our Catholic parishes do not always offer us an experience of community with other people. We know only a few of the people in church with us on Sunday…[M]uch more is needed before we achieve the ideal of the New Testament…The Church today is a rapidly changing organization. The rapid changes are leading some people to a maturer faith and leaving others dismayed. The Church itself is in the process of maturing. But not everybody is prepared to mature with it…

"What Christ left behind was an infant Church; it has been and is going to continue to mature…People who cannot get over the shock of having their superstitious idea of the Church destroyed are becoming bitter and hostile. They think that the Church is going to ruins…"

Come to the Father

In February 1967, many Catholic newspapers across the country ballyhooed in full-page spreads publicity generated by Paulist Press for its new *Come to the Father* series – "'the catechism of the 70s,' a totally new concept in religious education…

"The bold new program which has been hailed as a 'ten-year leap forward in catechetics' is now being piloted in one third of the dioceses of the country," declared the publicity.

"*Come to the Father* is the result of collaboration between a team of 30 trained catechists, theologians, psychologists, sociologists and teachers who began their efforts in 1961 in Canada.

"As the program developed, it was constantly tested; by the fall of 1964 a small group of schools put it into use for a full year. Only a year later, in Canada, it was being used by 125,000 students in 6,000 classrooms.

"Because of the excellent results it is now receiving in the U.S., *Come to the Father* is being made available for immediate adoption.

INTRODUCTION

"*Come to the Father* is presented as 'the first comprehensive catechetical program to reflect the renewal brought about by Vatican II' by the Paulist Press, which is responsible for its development in the U.S.

"The *Come to the Father* program is a complete departure from the traditional question and answer approach to religious education. It is not a religion textbook; nor is it conceived or planned as simply another subject to be studied."

What readers of the Catholic newspapers back in February 1967 did not know from reading their Catholic press was that *Come to the Father* was the subject of vigorous protest in Canada by parents because of its anti-dogmatism, anti-intellectualism, ersatz ecumenism, rejection of all tradition and blind trust that technology was going to make the world a better place.

Neither did they know that one of the top "experts" working on this text for the Canadian bishops, Fr. Kenneth Martin, would – forty years later – be accused of molesting minor boys back in the 1960s. Brought to trial on the charges in 2001, he was subsequently acquitted, the judge essentially ruling that his victim couldn't remember the exact dates the abuse occurred.

This catechism series, predictably, did not teach the Ten Commandments, the precepts of the Church, the Real Presence of Christ in the Blessed Sacrament, the Sacrifice of the Mass, Original Sin, the Immaculate Conception, the Virgin Birth, the Assumption of Mary into Heaven, the divinity of Christ, the infallibility of the Pope, the hierarchical structure of the Church, and most of the sacraments. Strange omissions for a "catechism."

As this revolution has played out over the past quarter century, I have been a close observer, with much of that time spent in the Catholic press.

In late November 1978, just a month after Pope John Paul II was elected to the papacy, I was on my first day of work as an artist-illustrator at the National Catholic News Service, NC News, located at the U.S. bishops' national headquarters in Washington, D.C., when an odd-looking fellow dressed in skin-tight pants and chest-hugging shirt approached me and asked if I would like to have lunch with him. I politely declined, telling him I brought my lunch to work. I would later learn that the man, John Willig, worked in the Office of Public Affairs and Information at the National Conference of Catholic Bishops/United States Catholic Conference, where he had access to all the financial information of every diocese in the country. Willig, who would later die of AIDS, was president of the Washington, D.C. chapter of Dignity, an association of gay activists who work for a change in Church teaching on homosexuality.

That was the beginning of my education as a Catholic journalist. I had just turned 24. In the 23 years since, especially since 1987 when I began reporting for *The Wanderer*, the oldest independent lay-run Catholic newspaper in the United States, it has become obvious that the most important issue facing the Catholic people in this country is the rise of a broad-based, exceedingly aggressive homosexual movement, and that the "movers and shakers" in the Catholic Church in this country – bishops, priests, religious, academics, journalists, publishers and laity – have become co-conspirators in a revolutionary campaign to disorient men, women and children from the moral law and natural law as it applies to human sexuality.

In the past 15 years, many Americans have learned that the Catholic Church in the United States, as well as in Canada, Europe and Australia, has a serious problem with sexual predators, especially pedophiles and pederasts, within its ranks. Not a diocese has been spared the anguish and embarrassment of seeing its priests hauled before a judge and exposed in the media. But most Catholics are completely oblivious to the fact that the public outing of these clerical sexual perverts serves a very valuable function for the sexual revolutionaries in the Church: they demoralize faithful Catholics and deconstruct the traditional understanding and practice of the Faith.

The evidence is now irrefutable that an influential and very powerful coterie within the Catholic Church – well-embedded and well-protected by the Roman Catholic hierarchy and their peers in the police, the courts, legislatures and the media – is successfully advancing a sexual liberation agenda that will not end until every social stigma attached to any sexual activity, no matter how bizarre, has been erased. Since the first high-visibility priest-pedophile case broke before the public with Lafayette, Louisiana priest Gilbert Gauthe in 1984, there have been close to a thousand similar cases involving tens, if not hundreds of thousands of victims, costing the Church an estimated $1 billion – though some speculate that figure is far too low. And through all of this, the leadership in the Catholic Church in the United States has pursued a homosexualizing agenda in its grammar and high schools, colleges and seminaries, its social service agencies, initiatives in art, architecture and liturgy, catechetics, and pastoral ministries at the diocesan and parish levels.

When I began working for *The Wanderer* in 1987, I had no idea how the Amchurch's sexual liberation agenda would play out, how Church agencies were honeycombed with homosexuals with the queen bees choreographing each successive move. I naïvely assumed that the exposure of sexual perverts would prompt episcopal action to root out the abusers and to institute strict reforms to remove potential threats, especially in seminaries. But in the 15 years since I reported on my first sexual abuse case in the priesthood, sexual scandals have become more egregious, the legal tactics more bare-knuckled, the payoffs larger, while Amchurch's leaders only accelerate their educational agenda to advance the cause of sexual liberation.

This book is based on reports I have written for *The Wanderer* over the past 15 years, with some additional information from other sources. It is intended as a review of where we, as Catholics, have been over the decade of the '90s, when "Amchurch Came Out," and, unless the Catholic people are roused from their slumber, sluggishness and sloth, where we are likely headed.

This reporter firmly believes that the Catholic Church was established by Christ and is protected by Him; but it must be recognized that for a variety of complex social reasons, cliques of "devils" – to use Dostoyevsky's term – managed to come to power in the Church, and have used their power and the Church's resources *to destroy her from the inside*, to wreck her credibility, to sully her image, to make her appear ridiculous in the eyes of the world and in the minds of the faithful. In the end, they will be on the losing side of history, but the damage they will have wrought will be enormous.

CHAPTER ONE

The Ferrario Case

Background

Between the time when a young man, David Figueroa, accused Honolulu Bishop Joseph Ferrario of sexual abuse at a press conference in Baltimore in 1989 during a meeting of the National Conference of Catholic Bishops and Steven Cook's charge four years later that Joseph Cardinal Bernardin of Chicago – the most powerful and influential churchman in the United States – had sexually assaulted him while a seminarian in Cincinnati, it became obvious to this reporter that a clique of homosexual pedophiles and pederasts had control of the episcopal appointment process, and that clerical pedophilia was endemic, deep-rooted and multi-generational.

After the 1984 "Gauthe case," when Fr. Gilbert Gauthe admitted under oath he had sexually abused 37 young male parishioners, one of the first major exposés supporting the "theory" that a web of pedophiles had infected the Church was published by the Phoenix *New Times*. In the October 25-31, 1989 issue, reporter Terry Greene's "Let Us Prey" detailed the cases of Frs. John Maurice Giandelone, Joseph Marcel Lessard and George Bredemann, all of whom had a long history of sexually molesting minor males.

Four paragraphs in Greene's report set the theme for numerous subsequent newspaper reports over the coming decade, and could be applied in every high-profile case involving clerical sexual abuse:

"A *New Times* investigation reveals that in each of the three local cases, the diocese buried its head in the sand by ignoring early warnings that the priests might be pedophiles – adults who crave sex with children.

"After their arrests, none of the three priests were fired, although all were immediately suspended from parish work until they'd completed psychological treatment. Two still are priests today; one eventually quit the priesthood.

1

"In all three local cases, the priests had worked hard to befriend the parents to gain their trust and access to their children. When caught, all three initially denied having sexual relations with their victims. And numerous people, clergy and lay, defended the priests. In some instances, the victims' families – not the priests – were ostracized by their fellow Catholics.

"Diocesan officials spent more time and money on the offending priests than on the victims…"

With Greene's report, many Catholics learned for the first time of a "secret" paper written by Louisiana attorney Roy Mouton and Fr. Thomas Doyle, O.P., for the U.S. bishops titled, "The Problem of Sexual Molestation by Roman Catholic Clergy: Meeting the Problem in a Comprehensive and Responsible Manner," which estimated the problem of pedophile priests would cost the Church in this country $1 billion over the decade from 1985 to 1995.

Perhaps the most disturbing and unbelievable – at the time – part of Greene's report was information that a former diocesan official "left the priesthood because he was angered by what he saw as Bishop [Thomas] O'Brien's toleration of corruption, including homosexual acting-out by some priests…

"[The priest] says he was 'suspended' by O'Brien after an argument. 'I told the bishop a couple of years ago that I was fed up with him and all the garbage that he was keeping quiet,' [he said]. He claims he told the bishop that he would start telling police about criminal behavior by priests. 'I told him I could no longer carry out my vow of obedience to him…The bishop told me I'd lost my faith. Essentially he fired me. I had already decided to quit.'"

Bishop O'Brien, incidentally, ordained Bredemann, despite the protests of people who knew Bredemann and had warned the bishop that Bredemann could not be trusted around children.

"George Bredemann came to St. Teresa's Parish in Scottsdale in 1980, after he was recruited by Fr. Jack Cunningham, the former vocations director for the diocese. Bredemann became good friends with Monsignor James McMahon, the pastor of St. Teresa's.

"Davern, the diocesan chancellor," continued reporter Greene, "admits that there were several letters in Bredemann's file recommending that he not become a priest...A few nuns at St. Teresa's also recommended the priest not be ordained..." O'Brien then ordained Bredemann in 1983.

Greene also revealed another pattern that would be duplicated numerous times, and one that raises suspicions that some bishops did have a concerted project to deconstruct the Catholic Church with their clerical pedophiles: the assignment of known sex offenders to Catholic schools, youth ministries and Boy Scout chaplaincies where they would have access to children.

Four years later, on September 8, 1993, under the headline, "Sins of the Bishop," Phoenix *New Times'* reporter Michael Lacey suggested that Bishop O'Brien had neither learned anything nor understood the problem of depraved priests preying on young men – at least the way most reasonable people would.

Lacey's report concerned Fr. Wilputte Alanson 'Lan' Sherwood, who had been sentenced to ten years in prison a week earlier, on August 27, 1993, and who had, essentially, convicted himself by evidence he had created: diaries and home movies in which Sherwood chronicled his sexual exploits with 22 minor males.

"Before handing down the terms of confinement," wrote Lacey, "Judge Cheryl Hendrix viewed a videotape of Reverend Sherwood performing oral sex on a 14-year-old child. But Sherwood's superior, the man responsible for the priest's astounding record of depravity, Bishop Thomas J. O'Brien, did not get so much as a stern lecture from the judge, let alone the jail sentence he so richly deserves for his gross negligence. Make no mistake. Reverend Lan Sherwood was the perpetrator, but Bishop O'Brien was the facilitator.

"When Sherwood was arrested in the mid-80s for deviant acts, the Bishop gave him five Hail Marys as a penance and then released him into the community, where the priest prowled the Valley's freeways looking for hitchhikers to prey upon. The priest would engage in another seven years of aberrant sexual behavior before he was brought to justice. Bishop O'Brien should be held accountable ..."

Over those seven years, Sherwood was arrested time and time again. One time, after police nabbed him for committing lewd acts in an adult book store, O'Brien claimed, as Lacey put it, "a priest getting busted for masturbating in an adult bookstore was not unusual."

After Sherwood's sentencing, O'Brien held a press conference in which he delivered a line that would become a mantra for the U.S. bishops, one they would use right up to the present day, as evidenced by Bernard Cardinal Law's statement in January 2002 when the matter of clerical pedophilia in Boston made banner headlines across the nation:

"I believed my response was appropriate [at the time]," said O'Brien, adding: "If you asked me what I would do today faced with a similar situation, in the context of 1993 and considering what we know about this type of behavior, my actions might well be different."

That, snarled Lacey, "is a crock."

Another signpost

Another signpost along the way indicating how the story of clerical homosexuality and pedophilia would develop was a December 10, 1989, feature in the *San Francisco Examiner's* Sunday magazine, *Image*, which featured a glossy, front-cover photograph of Fr. Bob Arpin headlined, "Living in the Light: Bob Arpin, Catholic priest with AIDS."

"Fr. Bob Arpin," wrote Elizabeth Fernandez, "is a devout Catholic priest. He is gay and he has AIDS. And he's not content to stand by silently while his Church persecutes him and his gay brethren."

Fernandez is observing Fr. Bob as he leads a prayer service, reciting a "litany of indictments" against the Catholic Church:

"I forgive the Church and all religious people for their bad example, for their hypocrisy, for their lack of faith. I forgive the Pope, bishops, priests, nuns, brothers, all of those who hold positions of leadership in the Church. For their double standards. For their fear of the truth. For their distortion of the Gospel. For their use of guilt control. For their hardness of heart."

Arpin, who has since died of AIDS, was the first Catholic priest to "come out" – in 1978, and Fernandez happily informed *Image* readers that he was not the only San Francisco priest to have AIDS; but what was most interesting in her report was the news that Arpin was on loan to the San Francisco Archdiocese "from a diocese in Massachusetts," a state which, as the years rolled on, seemed to produce an exceptionally large number of homosexual and pedophile priests, including the monstrous Fr. James Robert Porter, Fr. David Holley and Fr. John Geoghan who abused hundreds of minor males in numerous parishes and dioceses as their superiors shuttled them off, one step ahead of the law, so to speak, to continue their abuse in some other place. The problem of clerical pedophilia in both Canada and the United States was not yet a blip on the radar screen for most American Catholics, but the U.S. bishops must surely have been aware of a looming crisis, for between 1982 and 1990 nearly 400 Catholic priests in this country and Canada had already been reported to Church and civil authorities. Among the most notable:

In March 1990, Massachusetts priest Fr. Robert E. Kelly was sentenced to prison for five-to-seven years for sexually molesting an eight-year-old girl at least 100 times in 1983.

In October 1990, Fr. James Arimond, a priest of the Archdiocese of Milwaukee, who was one of the most outspoken advocates of homosexuality in the state of Wisconsin, was charged with sexual assault on a minor male, convicted and jailed. For years, Catholics in the archdiocese had written letters to Archbishop Rembert Weakland protesting Arimond's homosexual proselytization in workshops, on radio and television, in letters to the editor, and in his promotion of theological dissent. Weakland typically responded by calling his critics' letters insulting.

When three teachers at Mother of Good Council Parish School wrote to Weakland in July 1984 expressing their concerns that Fr. Dennis Pecore was involved in scandalous activities with students at the school, and asked him to do something "before this turns into a full-fledged scandal," Weakland wrote a letter to one of the teachers, threatening to sue him for libel.

The teachers then wrote to the papal nuncio. Two months later, Weakland fired the three teachers from their positions. In January 1987, Pecore was finally charged and pleaded guilty to second-degree sexual assault. The archdiocese tried to keep the terms of the civil suit settlement secret but the Milwaukee *Journal and Sentinel* filed suit and the judge ordered the terms of the settlement released. Pecore's abuse cost Catholics in the archdiocese $595,000.

5

Fr. Arimond, along with Fr. Dennis Pecore, were prominent AIDS activists and AIDS educators, and at the same time these priests were in the news, the archdiocese began disclosing that its priests were dying of AIDS.

On March 18, 1989, the Canadian Press reported that noted French Canadian Catholic TV evangelist Pierre Lacroix was freed by Quebec Court of Appeal Justice Yves Bernier two days after he began serving a two-year prison sentence ordered by Justice Jean Bienvenue, who found Lacroix guilty of conducting a "marathon of gross indecency" at his "Marathon of Love" rallies.

In March 1989, the famous "singing priest" of Newfoundland, Brendan Foley, was charged with committing sexual assault on boys between 1982 and 1985, the eighth Newfoundland priest to be charged up to that point.

In March 1989, the Archdiocese of Atlanta paid out $358,000 to families of three altar boys sexually abused by British priest Anton Mowat, and sent Mowat to a treatment center in England.

On April 14, 1989, the Billings *Gazette* reported that former priest John Bauer, then 52, was being sought as a fugitive after law enforcement became aware that he was producing child pornography in Mexico. For seven years, while he was still a priest, Bauer was working in group homes in Helena, Montana.

In December 1989, Fr. Bruce Ritter, founder of Covenant House, a "safe place" for street kids, was accused of sexual abuse.

In September 1989, parents of children abused by Newfoundland priest Fr. James Hickey filed a lawsuit against Archbishop Alphonsus Penney for negligence. Penney would subsequently resign his office, becoming the first North American prelate to resign due to a sexual misconduct scandal.

After Penney's resignation in August 1990, I interviewed noted Canadian Catholic author Anne Roche [Muggeridge], a native of Newfoundland, who insisted that Penney was guilty of little more than naïveté; but she offered this insight into the problem:

"For years people in Newfoundland have known what was going on. For a long time, people knew that one priest had been keeping most of his [pornography] collection and giving it to boys. There were priests and boys engaged in organized vice, and everybody knew it.

"Newfoundland is a very queer place – no pun intended. It's half-Catholic and everybody knows everybody. It's like a small town…It's very stratified socially, and the professional classes protect each other. The upper-class cops and judges protect the upper-class Catholics. People cover up. It's very corrupt, but it doesn't seem like corruption."

Muggeridge also predicted that the radical apparat of nominal Catholics who run the Newfoundland chancery would take advantage of Penney's resignation to accelerate their homosexual agenda for the Church, explaining: "The nuns and lay people in the chancery are very sympathetic to homosexuality. They are a part of that faction in the Church that feels homosexuality is okay. They approve; they think homosexuality is all right. They don't see anything wrong with homosexuals teaching in the schools or the seminaries. They think the worst thing that could happen is homophobia.

"This radical apparat," she continued, "you have to understand, wants to break the power of the priests…It all seems so extraordinary, that it is happening in the Church I grew up in."

Nearly ten years to the day after he resigned, in July 2000, Penney was found liable for failing to stop Fr. Kevin Bennett, accused of committing hundreds of sexual assaults against altar boys over a 20-year period from the 1960s to 1980s, after he had been informed of the abuse.

Novel strategy

At the same time as these and many similar stories were erupting with increasing frequency in the secular press, the U.S. bishops, going through the motions of devising policies and procedures to deal with the escalating problem of clerical pedophilia, actually embarked on a novel mission: they would devote enormous resources to indoctrinate the Catholic people to accept homosexuality.

That is how, this reporter would argue, their national guidelines for sex education, which they would approve during their 1990 plenary meeting in Washington, *Human Sexuality: A Catholic Perspective for Lifelong Learning*, must be understood.

The late Auxiliary Bishop of New York, Austin Vaughan, made a valiant, heroic effort to send the document, which called for "cradle-to-grave" sex education for the Catholic people of this country, back to Dolores Leckey's

7

Laity and Marriage and Family Life Committees at the NCCB/USCC for further work. Vaughan voiced a number of concerns about the document, but two issues especially irritated him: the document was produced by a secret committee, and he believed that the laity, who were not consulted, had the right to know who produced it. Most importantly, he insisted, the bishops had no competency to speak as sex educators.

One of the serious problems with the document identified by the laity immediately upon its release was that it seemed to "open the door" to Catholics accepting homosexuality, a worry supported by what several bishops said on the floor of their plenary meeting.

During the debate on the sex education document, a number of key bishops expressed their fear that homosexuals would be "hurt" if the document affirmed the Holy See's statement, *On The Pastoral Care of Homosexual Persons*, issued by the Congregation for the Doctrine of the Faith in 1986. Among those bishops who wanted no mention of the document – not even in a footnote – were Joseph Cardinal Bernardin of Chicago, who said he found himself "on the horns of a dilemma" because he wanted to respect Vatican teaching but he also wanted to be sensitive to homosexuals. San Francisco Archbishop John Quinn worried that if the bishops referred to the Holy See's statement, it would cause "untold harm," and homosexuals "would find it offensive." The retired Archbishop William Borders of Baltimore, whose archdiocese was the home base for two of the leading homosexual agitation-propaganda (agit-prop) activists in the country, Sister Jeannine Gramick, SSND and Fr. Bob Nugent, SDS, warned that any reference to the Holy See's 1986 document "will cause a real hurt to take place." (The full discussion on this issue was reported in *The Wanderer*, Nov. 29, 1990, by this reporter who was covering a plenary assembly of the U.S. bishops for the first time.)

Coming into focus

My education as a Catholic journalist moved into high gear when members of the Coalition of Concerned Catholics of the Diocese of Albany invited me to meet with them in January 1991. Convinced that Bishop Howard Hubbard of Albany, then entering his 15th year after being appointed by Pope Paul VI in 1977, was engaged in a deliberate program to deconstruct the Catholic Church, these Catholics gave me boxes of documentation illustrating their plight, and they wanted Catholics around the country to learn of their predicament.

Over 11 weeks, beginning in March 1991, *The Wanderer* published the series "Agony in Albany" an in-depth exposé of the process of ecclesial deconstruction on every front, including liturgy, education at every level, clerical discipline, and Hubbard's apparent commitment to establishing some sort of New Age religion in the diocese, along the lines described by novelist Irving Wallace in *The Word*.

In describing Hubbard's meteoric rise from a young street priest to bishop in a mere 14 years, Albany priests and laity also told how a fellow student and graduate of the North American College in Rome, Fr. C. Howard Russell, chancellor of the diocese, began a policy in the late 1960s of recruiting homosexuals from outside the diocese to come to Albany to join the priesthood. Russell, who was very close friends with both Hubbard and fellow Albany priest, now bishop of Rochester, Matthew Clark, eventually left the priesthood; but not before changing the face of the diocesan priesthood.

"Almost every priest brought in during this period," a priest told me at the time, "has turned out to be a homosexual" – and created scandal.

At the time "Agony in Albany" was in preparation, Hubbard himself defended his decision to ordain homosexuals, telling Tim Beidel of the Albany *Times Union* (Feb. 22, 1991): "I believe the Church has a responsibility to all its members...I don't think gays or anybody else should be excluded from the ministry. Indeed, I think we have a responsibility to reach out to them with sensitivity and compassion..."

In the ten years since then, many of the few priests ordained by Hubbard have created some sort of sexual scandal or another, including the sexual abuse of minors, attempted abuse of minors, leaving the priesthood to "marry" another man, publicized their contraction of AIDS, *etcetera, etcetera, etcetera*. Perhaps the defining moment of Hubbard's episcopacy was the revelation by *The Wanderer* (Feb. 3, 2000) that one of his priests, Fr. Dennis Brennan, with "Hubbard's understanding and guidance" was undergoing a sex-change operation, and Brennan had already legally changed his name to Denise.

As of this writing, "Denise" is often seen at church functions.

The Brennan story was one of the few *Wanderer* reports that the secular press found newsworthy, and subsequently the *New York Post*, on February 15, 2000, ran a big two-page spread by Frederick U. Dicker along with a photograph of Brennan, dressed as a woman, emerging from a local grocery store.

Precisely how totally corrupt "Catholic education" has become in Hubbard's diocese, as well as that of his close friend Bishop Clark, was powerfully illustrated by an obituary that appeared in the Albany *Times Union* on June 2, 2001.

Here's the story: "Fr. Charles (Chuck) Francis Farrelly, born November 9, 1953, died Thursday May 31, 2001 at his residence after a brief illness…Fr. Farrelly was ordained on February 19, 2000 at Christ The Light American Catholic Church in Albany, where he was associate pastor. He attended St. Bernard's Seminary in Rochester, graduated from St. John Fisher College in Rochester, and from Christian Brothers Academy in Albany…

"Survived by his loving, longtime companion, the Most Rev. Timothy A. DeTraglia…and his loving dog Gracie May…

"Interment will be in Our Lady of Help Christian Cemetery. Donations may be given to Christ the Light Catholic Church…"

Now here are the details the obituary avoided: Bishop Howard Hubbard ordained DeTraglia in 1981. Albany priests knew that DeTraglia was living a notorious homosexual lifestyle while at St. Bernard's, then under the direction of Bishop Matthew Clark.

Even as a Catholic priest, DeTraglia was up-front about his homosexuality, and was featured in the local press as a person "living with HIV." At his last assignment, before opening his schismatic church (another of Hubbard's accomplishments as Bishop of Albany) he announced to his flock at St. Clare's Catholic Church in Colonie that he was leaving the priesthood to marry. But he didn't tell his flock he was marrying a man.

Such has been the progress of gender dysphoria in the Diocese of Albany.

Ferrario

The case involving Bishop Joseph Ferrario and David Figueroa is extremely important for a number of reasons; but the chief reason is that it showed how tough bishops could and would play when confronted with charges against themselves. As we will see, Ferrario abused every weapon in his arsenal of ecclesiastical authority to batter his accusers.

10

During the Ferrario case, I was in close touch almost on a daily basis with Joseph O'Connor and Patricia Morley, two devout Catholics who with others were working around the clock to persuade the Vatican to remove Ferrario, a cause they had been working on since Ferrario's appointment as an auxiliary bishop on the island ten years before.

Journalist Jason Berry provides the key details in his groundbreaking work, *Lead Us Not Into Temptation* (Doubleday, 1992), a masterful work on clerical pedophilia that is nonetheless flawed because Berry's liberalism prevents him from considering the possibility of a conspiracy on the part of the hierarchy to promote the secular agenda of sexual libertinism; rather he blames the Church's policy of celibacy for attracting perverts to the priesthood. Nevertheless, and importantly, Berry does connect Ferrario to his friend and powerful protector Archbishop John Quinn of San Francisco, and thoroughly documents the inability of Ferrario's predecessor, Bishop John Scanlan and key laity in Honolulu to have him deposed – even after they had failed to block his appointment as Bishop of Honolulu.

Ten years later, Ferrario is enjoying his retirement on the golf courses of Maui and Figueroa is dead of AIDS. The courageous Morley is also deceased. O'Connor, publisher of the monthly *Catholic Lay Press,* and Morley, host of a weekly radio talk show, worked over the years to expose Ferrario as a pervert, as did Figueroa on Geraldo Rivera's national talk show on NBC. The U.S. bishops rallied around their brother, the major newspapers in Hawaii completely ignored the story, as Berry reported, out of fear of losing advertising revenue, and Ferrario continued his rampage against the Catholic priests and people of Hawaii, ruthlessly gutting churches in the name of liturgical renewal, promoting liturgical abuses, and every other sort of scandal, and, generally, acting like a vicious buffoon. He even went so far as to excommunicate his critics, forcing Rome to tell him to back off. Finally, Ferrario "resigned" in 1993.

Ferrario personifies the abusive personality that, tragically, came to prominence in the American Church in the years just before, during and after Vatican II. Aside from the claims made by Figueroa, laid out in a sexual abuse lawsuit filed against Ferrario in Federal Court on August 8, 1991, which claimed Ferrario had sexually abused him in Hawaii and California over a ten year period beginning when Ferrario was pastor of St. Anthony Church in Honolulu and continuing after he was named bishop, nothing more exhibits Ferrario's abusiveness than his attempt to

11

excommunicate Patricia Morley, John O'Connor, Morley's son Christopher and two others affiliated with Morley's radio program.

Ferrario was named an auxiliary bishop in 1978 and bishop in 1982. By 1985, Catholics on the island were traveling to Rome with some regularity to report on various aspects of his egregious misrule, such as his punitive actions against good priests, his tolerance and promotion of liturgical abuses, selling-off of Church properties, the recruitment of homosexuals into the priesthood and the favoring of homosexual clergy for important positions, the gutting of churches, and the closing of schools.

In March 1985, even before David Figueroa went public with the sex-abuse charges, Ferrario had hatched a scheme to excommunicate his critics, soliciting the opinions of canon law experts Fr. Michael Hughes, OMI; Fr. Francis Morrissey, OMI; and Fr. James Provost.

For nearly six years, Ferrario's tribunal of the Diocese of Honolulu carefully charted out its process to excommunicate his critics, and over the multi-year process, Ferrario consulted with Apostolic Nuncio Archbishop Agostino Cacciavillan and Cincinnati Archbishop Daniel Pilarczyk, then president of the National Conference of Catholic Bishops. The canonical charges against Morley, O'Connor, et al. consisted of claims these Catholics were "disruptive" and "disobedient," publicly incited hatred and contempt of Ferrario, and engaged in "plots against the Church."

Finally, in May 1990, the diocesan tribunal prepared a document to formally begin the process of excommunicating Morley and O'Connor if they did not cease exposing Ferrario in public.

In April of 1991, Morley announced on her radio program that Figueroa had passed a lie detector test that validated his charges against the bishop, and revealed that another local priest, Fr. Art O'Brien, ordained by James Cardinal Hickey for the Archdiocese of Washington, would be charged for sexually abusing a 14-year-old boy. O'Connor reported that Cardinal Hickey had transferred O'Brien to Mobile, Alabama, after scandal arose at his parish in Bowie, Maryland, and, two years later, was transferred to Honolulu. One month later, on May 2, 1991, O'Connor, Morley, et al. were excommunicated.

As for O'Brien, at the time the "ex-communicated" made the revelations, he was a member of the diocesan Liturgy Committee, then under a barrage of criticism for promoting "disco" Masses.

On August 8, 1991, a federal lawsuit was filed against Ferrario by Maui attorney James Kreuger and Jeffrey Anderson of St. Paul. Minnesota, the latter of whom told *The Wanderer* (August 22, 1991) that he was prepared to tell the court he had evidence that not only had Ferrario abused Figueroa, but that he had abused others as well. The lawsuit against Ferrario also named two other island priests who were accused of sexually abusing Figueroa, Fr. Joseph Henry and Fr. Tony Bolger.

According to the lawsuit, after Ferrario was appointed pastor of St. Anthony's Church, Figueroa went to him to complain that he had been sexually abused by Fr. Henry. "Defendant Bishop Joseph Ferrario," the lawsuit declared, "failed to refer the plaintiff for proper counseling and therapy and failed to inform the plaintiff that he had been the victim of wrongful conduct by Fr. Henry. Instead, defendant Bishop Joseph Ferrario purported to provide counseling to the minor plaintiff at his office at St. Anthony Church. In the course of providing counseling, defendant Bishop Joseph Ferrario regularly…sexually molested and exploited" Figueroa. The lawsuit also alleged that Ferrario had abused Figueroa while visiting him at St. Patrick's Seminary in Menlo Park.

(The lawsuit was rejected by the federal court in Hawaii and appealed to the Ninth Circuit Court of Appeals in San Francisco, which also rejected it on the grounds the statute of limitations had expired.)

One month later, on September 10, 1991, Archbishop Cacciavillan, Archbishop Quinn, and a host of bishops from the Pacific islands flew into Honolulu to help Ferrario celebrate the 50th anniversary of the Diocese of Honolulu. Catholics on the islands were wondering what there was to celebrate, since Ferrario had alienated perhaps three-fourths of Hawaii's Catholics, driven it $9 million into debt despite his wholesale selling off of Church properties, and his abusive treatment of priests and even his predecessor, Bishop Scanlan, whom he exiled from Hawaii, was legendary.

But some Hawaii Catholics were thrilled with Ferrario's initiatives, notably the gay community, who publicly praised Ferrario, stating: "[O]ur bishop has changed the Roman Catholic Church in Hawaii's position on Gay Catholics…"

On June 28, 1993, three years after the diocesan tribunal produced its excommunication document against Morley, O'Connor, et al, and more than two years after that excommunication was declared in public, Archbishop Cacciavillan informed the "excommunicated" six that he had received a letter from the Congregation for the Doctrine of the Faith stating that Ferrario's letter of excommunication was "null and void" – but that they could be punished with an interdict for creating a "grave nuisance."

The practical effect of that threat was that Morley, O'Connor, et al. were still shunned by their Catholic friends, calumniated in the press and even refused Communion.

After six months of appealing to the Holy See for a copy of the letter Cardinal Ratzinger of the Congregation for the Doctrine of the Faith sent Cacciavillan, Morley finally received the copy, in which Ratzinger stated that the Hawaii six "did not, in fact, commit the crime of schism…[and] it is clear that the Decree of the Bishop lacks the condition on which it is founded."

In his accompanying cover letter, Cacciavillan informed Morley, et al. that his threat – i.e. that Ferrario could place them under interdict – was "not in the Decree, as you may notice, [and] was simply intended as a reflection and suggestion to the Bishop."

In the words of Patricia Morley, "Cacciavillan and Ferrario conspired to discredit us in the eyes of the public." O'Connor told *The Wanderer* (March 31, 1994) that he had no idea how events "could have ever come to the point that an archbishop falsifies a document to protect someone else.

"Clearly, Cacciavillan was trying to protect Ferrario, to cover for him. He had no business sitting on the original document for so long, and he had no business stating the congregation said Ferrario could punish us with interdict when the congregation said no such thing…

"People still call us outcasts," he continued. "We took copies of the decrees to all the newspapers, the radio and television stations, and they all just refuse to publicize it. The diocese even refuses to publicize in its newspaper the fact that we're Catholics in good standing."

This three-year tragedy is compounded by the fact that during this same period, O'Connor was publicizing in his *Catholic Lay Press* details of clerical molestation and drug dealing by island clergy, and Ferrario had enraged thousands of Catholics and non-Catholics on the island by deciding to "renovate" Our Lady of Peace Cathedral.

In an attempt to get his good reputation back, O'Connor filed a lawsuit against the Diocese of Hawaii, Ferrario and his canon lawyer, Fr. Joseph Bukoski, III, in federal court, in which he alleged that: "(1) he was wrongly excommunicated from the Roman Catholic Church; (2) the allegations leading to his excommunication were false; (3) appellees published the fact of his excommunication and made false statements about him; and (4) appellees engaged in acts that violated his rights to freedom of the press, freedom of speech, freedom of worship, and freedom to associate with others." Additionally, O'Connor claimed Ferrario et al. had defamed him; that contrary to the state's fair business practices acts, had engaged in efforts to put his newspaper out of business; and that the diocese was engaged in criminal activities.

The federal District Court that heard O'Connor's suit rejected it on the grounds that to rule on it would violate the separation of Church and State. O'Connor appealed to the Ninth Circuit Court in San Francisco, which sided with the lower court, declaring on November 23, 1994:

"Because each count of O'Connor's complaint can be adjudged only in accordance with standards of church doctrine, church law, or church governance, such claims cannot be adjudicated by a civil court without abridging the free exercise clauses of the state and federal constitutions.

"When viewing O'Connor's complaint in a light most favorable to him, we can conclude only that the acts alleged to have been committed by the appellees are shielded from civil review. Thus, O'Connor can prove no set of facts upon any of his claims that would entitle him to relief in civil court, and the circuit court did not err when it dismissed his complaint with prejudice.

"Consequently, we hold, that under the first amendment to the United States Constitution and article I, section 4 of the Hawaii Constitution, civil courts have no authority to resolve disputes that turn on matters of church doctrine, practice, policy, or administration or that cannot be decided without resolving underlying controversies over such matters. When faced with such claims, civil courts must dismiss them."

O'Connor appealed that ruling to the U.S. Supreme Court, which declined to accept it.

A Post Script

On May 25, 2001, Hawaii's *Catholic Herald* published a report on the joyous celebration in Honolulu of Ferrario's 50th anniversary as a priest. Reporter Patrick Downes wrote:

"The friends and extended family of retired Bishop of Honolulu Joseph A. Ferrario filled the Co-Cathedral of St. Theresa, May 18, for a joyous twilight Mass to celebrate his 50th anniversary of ordination to the priesthood.

"Bishop Ferrario presided at the liturgy, joined by the present Bishop of Honolulu Francis X. DiLorenzo, Bishop Daniel F. Walsh of Santa Rosa, 49 priests and 13 deacons. Bishop Walsh, a friend of the retired bishop since he was his student at St. Joseph Seminary in Mountain View, California, preached. 'Tonight we celebrate this goodness and love of the Lord in a very concrete way,' Bishop Walsh said. 'We are celebrating the generous response Father Joe gave to that call (to the priesthood) and continues today to give to that call...

"'Through his ministry he brought renewal to the Church in Hawaii...His dedication was acknowledged when he was called to be a bishop.' Bishop Walsh mentioned the difficult periods of Bishop Ferrario's administration calling them the 'thorns' that 'help us share in the passion of Christ...It was his deep and abiding faith and personal love for Jesus that made his ministry blessed and so fruitful,' he said..."

Sex education

The year Ferrario attempted to excommunicate Morley, O'Connor, et al., the lid on the Church's cauldron of secret sexual abuse seemed ready to blow off.

In January 1991, in Washington, D.C., Fr. Thomas Chleboski, then 31, ordained in 1987 by Archbishop James Hickey, was arrested and charged with nine felony counts involving sexual abuse and other sexual offenses, the second time in six months charges were filed against the young priest.

According to the lawsuits, which named Archbishop Hickey and St. Mary's Seminary in Baltimore as co-defendants with the priest, Chleboski began abusing minor males when he was still a seminarian, continued as a deacon, and, of course, as a priest. At the time he was ordained, the Archdiocese of Washington already had a three-year-old "comprehensive program" designed to protect Catholic children from sexual abuse and a policy for handling cases of clerical pedophilia.

In a statement issued after Chleboski pleaded guilty, the Archdiocese declared: "It has only been within the past 15-20 years that our society has begun to learn more about pedophilia and the disturbing incidents of child sexual abuse that occur throughout all professions in our society and also within the family where 80-85 percent of all pedophilia occurs. The Church, like the rest of society, is struggling with how best to deal with cases of pedophilia in a responsible and compassionate way…"

What was interesting about Chleboski is that he had been dismissed from a seminary in Ohio because of his sexual problems (Hickey had been bishop of Cleveland) and then accepted by Hickey for the priesthood in Washington.

What was particularly ironic about Hickey's ordination of Chleboski is that he should have known better, since just one year earlier, in September 1986, he was hit with a lawsuit involving Fr. Peter McCutcheon, who had just pled guilty to molesting three youths. In this case, reported Paul Duggan of the *Washington Post* (Sept. 24, 1988), "in pre-trial proceedings, Fr. McCutcheon…repeatedly refused to give permission for psychologists and fellow clerics to testify in the lawsuit about counseling sessions they had with him in the early 1980s, about the time McCutcheon was committing the assaults.

"Circuit Court Judge Stanley B. Frosh had ordered McCutcheon to release those counselors from what they view as their professional obligation to remain silent about the sessions. Because McCutcheon has defied the judge's order, Frosh yesterday found him guilty in 'default.' The ruling means that a jury in the lawsuit will be instructed to consider McCutcheon liable for negligence, clergy malpractice, assault and other misdeeds listed in the plaintiffs' complaint."

McCutcheon, ordained in 1979, like many other clerical abusers, was a graduate of St. Mary's Seminary in Baltimore. Found guilty, he was sentenced to 25 years in prison, a sentence later reduced to one year, and five years probation, and treatment at the Servants of the Paraclete treatment center in Jemez Springs, N.M.

In May, in New Orleans, Catholics learned of the lawsuit against laicized priest Dino Cinel, who shot more than 160 hours of videotape depicting his sexual trysts with young boys and animals.

Cinel, 49, who surrendered to police on May 28, was serving as a "distinguished professor" of Italian culture at the City University of New York, was a native of Italy who came to the states in the late 1960s, and had been involved in homosexual relationships with young men in New York, San Francisco, Montreal, New Orleans and other cities. Upon arriving in the United States, then-Fr. Cinel found work in Manhattan at the Center for Migration Studies, which was linked with the United States Catholic Conference, took courses at both Georgetown University and the Catholic University of America in Washington, and then entered a doctorate program at Stanford University. In 1979, when he was hired to teach history at Tulane University in New Orleans, he resided at St. Rita's parish rectory, where he heard confessions and celebrated Mass.

St. Rita's was a block from archdiocesan headquarters. In 1982, he met Chris Fontaine, a man described by his attorney as mildly retarded, and began a two year affair with Fontaine. The affair included smoking marijuana as a prelude to sex, and producing 51 pornographic videos. After the pornography was discovered in 1988 while Cinel was on vacation in Europe, and brought to the attention of New Orleans Archbishop Philip Hannan, Cinel was advised to stay abroad and become laicized. In return, Hannan promised Cinel he would not be prosecuted. Unfortunately, his victims did not also agree, and pressed charges against him after they learned their sexcapades were circulating in the international pornography market.

In his deposition, Cinel detailed his homosexual past, beginning when he was a student at a boarding school in Rome, the Institu Scalabrini, when he was seduced by his superior at about the age of 13 or 14. Cinel described the superior "as an older priest, an eminent priest, a friend of the Pope's."

Cinel arrived in New Orleans with an April 23, 1979 letter of introduction to Archbishop Philip Hannan from San Francisco Auxiliary Bishop Francis A. Quinn, future bishop of Sacramento, one of the Amchurch's most active promoters of homosexuality. Quinn, who supported and personally celebrated Dignity Masses, wrote the letter on official archdiocesan chancery office stationery.

18

On August 14, in Chicago, a lawsuit was filed against Fr. William Cloutier, ordained in 1975. According to the complaint filed for his client, written by St. Paul attorney Jeffrey Anderson, "During this sexual abuse, defendant Cloutier counseled the plaintiff that these sexual activities were normal for young males, that experimentation was the only way a young male could learn about sexual expression, that he had brought other boys to [his] cabin and done this, and that this sexual contact was a normal act of passage for a young man." The complaint also alleged that the priest "brandished a handgun."

In the October 31, 1991 issue of *The Wanderer*, Eric Bower reported from Chicago that parishioners of St. Odilo's in Berwyn were outraged when they learned that Fr. Robert E. Mayer, who was known as "Satan" when he was a seminarian at St. Mary of the Lake in Mundelein and had left a "trail of human carnage" as he went from parish to parish, was appointed to their church.

"The trail of human carnage," wrote Bower, "left behind by Fr. Mayer includes reports of drug abuse, attempted suicides, ruined reputations, loss of faith, public scandal, and ridicule of the young boys he 'befriended.'"

The parishioners' outrage was particularly directed at Joseph Cardinal Bernardin, who appointed Mayer to St. Odilo's while, at the same time, claiming he was instituting reforms to protect Catholic children from pedophile priests.

Parents learned of Fr. Mayer from their children, to whom he was showing pornography and instructing them in the intricacies of homosexual sexual acts. One mother told Chicago Auxiliary Bishop Raymond Goedert at a public hearing: "We trusted you and believed the bishops when they said that our kids needed sex education. We had no idea that the pastor would use the rectory to conduct his sex education classes to abuse our kids. We trusted you and you betrayed us."

Ironically, when *The Wanderer* reported Mayer's formal indictment for sexual abuse in the December 19, 1991 issue, a companion story on the front page, datelined Buffalo, declared: "Educators In Catholic Schools Urged to Teach Sex With Religious Fervor." Sister Therese Chmura urged Catholic educators to "give their blood, sweat and tears" to the cause of sex education as she announced to Catholic teachers that the Church in Buffalo would use the Diocese of Albany's *Christian Approach to Human Sexuality* in its schools – a program that had been widely and seriously critiqued for years for its promotion of androgyny and bombardment of elementary school-age children with college-level biology relating to the excretory and reproductive systems.

From August 25 through September 1, Dignity, a national association of Catholic gay activists, held its national meeting in Washington D.C., attracting some 500 participants from across the country. In his presidential address, Dignity's Kevin Caligari asserted that Dignity had entered a "growth process," and would have a "stronger presence" in the Church. One homosexual, speaking of the U.S. bishops, said, "We must get these daddies to come out."

The November, 1991 issue of *San Diego News Notes* carried an interview with AIDS caregiver Jim Johnson conducted by reporter Tim Ryland, in which Johnson proclaimed that San Francisco Archbishop John Quinn and Los Angeles Cardinal Roger Mahony are "prisoners" of their homosexual clergy. Speaking of Cardinal Mahony's chancery, Johnson said: "Cardinal Mahony is surrounded by homosexual priests. The first three priests to run the AIDS ministry here have all been homosexual. One of them had an affair with a friend of mine, a business associate in the AIDS industry who was a drug pusher. So the whole thing has been more like a soap opera than a Catholic outreach."

Of the Archdiocese of San Francisco's AIDS ministry, Johnson said: "It is not an AIDS agenda. It is a homosexual political agenda."

For the November 14 issue of *The Wanderer*, this reporter revealed that seminarians at Mt. Angel Seminary in Portland, Oregon, were very upset about a requirement that they study a text called *Our Sexuality*, by Robert Crooks and Karla Bauer (Benjamin-Cummings), which provided graphic instructions, including illustrations, for masturbation and homosexual sexual acts, and even advised seminarians that if they were not comfortable with their sex, they could have it changed.

Bishops against Rome

One year after Ferrario attempted to excommunicate Morley, O'Connor et al., and was receiving praise from Hawaii's homosexuals for being so supportive, the Holy See's Congregation for the Doctrine of the Faith released its letter, *Some Considerations Concerning the Catholic Response to Legislative Proposals on the Non-Discrimination of Homosexual Persons*, which advised the bishops of North America to oppose homosexual rights legislation – even if such legislation exempts the Church from the new law's provisions.

This 1992 document, signed by Cardinal Ratzinger, said that laws which prohibit homosexuals from adopting children, from jobs as teachers or coaches, from military recruitment, and which deny equivalent family status to homosexual unions, do not constitute unjust discrimination.

The letter, which declared that homosexuality is an "objective disorder," was sent to all the American bishops through the NCCB's general secretary, now-Bishop Robert Lynch of Tampa-St. Petersburg, on June 25; but it was kept secret from the nation's 55 million Catholics until a brief notice appeared in the *New York Times* by Peter Steinfels on July 15. By the time most Catholics learned of the document two days later via the Associated Press, they were reading propaganda supplied by New Ways Ministry, which called the letter "an embarrassment" to U.S. Catholics and "seriously flawed."

John Gallagher, of New Ways Ministry, told this reporter that he received notice of the letter on July 6. Meanwhile, the late Archbishop Thomas J. Murphy of Seattle, one of only two bishops to address the letter publicly, dismissed it as "an internal memo" from a Vatican office to the U.S. bishops. Archbishop Rembert Weakland of Milwaukee complained the letter "poses many theological and practical problems," and doubted whether it would be "helpful" in the United States.

The Holy See's letter could not have been more timely, with homosexual activists ratcheting up their agit-prop in favor of special rights legislation for homosexuals across the country, city by city, state by state, and except for the negative statements of Weakland and Murphy, the U.S. bishops made no effort, singly or collectively, to apply the document to any of the cases which demanded application.

Shape of things to come

In 1993, former Jesuit priest Robert Goss explained the role of "small faith communities" and the "new biblical scholarship" in institutionalizing the homosexual agenda in the Church.

His book, *Jesus Acted Up* (Harper: San Francisco), subtitled, "A Gay and Lesbian Manifesto," provided incontrovertible evidence of the link between dissident theologians and the rise of a militant homosexual movement in the Church, one committed to overthrowing the Church's 2,000-year moral and doctrinal tradition.

In his heavily-annotated book, Goss, who left the priesthood after he fell in love with another priest, personified the theological training he received. With advanced degrees in Scripture studies from the Jesuit Weston School of Theology and Harvard University, he breezily showed how such contemporary Catholic scholars as Hans Küng, Raymond Brown, Andre Guindon, John Dominic Crossan, John Meier, James Drane, Paul Hollenbach, Xavier John Seubert, Mary Hunt, Rosemary Radford Ruether, Leonardo Boff, Jon Sobrino, and dozens of others – many of whom remain "in good standing" with the American hierarchy – are dismantling orthodox theology while reconstructing a new "queer theology" that affirms the sexual experiences of homosexuals, lesbians, and bisexuals.

Though all of these scholars write from different perspectives and have different agendas, Dr. Goss, a student of the French "father of deconstructionism," Michel Foucauld, who died of AIDS, showed how each in his own way is demolishing Catholic teaching on Jesus and His Church in order to rework Catholic moral teaching into an "inclusive," "non-patriarchal," "non-sexist," "liberating" form of Christianity which can celebrate gay and lesbian sexuality – indeed, which affirms it as superior to "culturally imposed" heterosexuality.

The "fundamental identity" of God's children as heterosexual, insists Goss in numerous passages, is "based on an erroneous reading of Scriptures and a faulty view of sexuality based on natural law" (p. 13).

The starting point for the dismantling of traditional Christian moral teaching begins with the new biblical scholarship which denies or calls into question the orthodox belief that Jesus was conceived by the Holy Spirit and born of a virgin.

"This notion," writes Goss, "was transformed into the antisexual rhetoric as Christianity evolved in the Hellenistic world." As Christianity spread through the Greek world, Jesus was divinized and made asexual. This was essentially a political ploy to shore up the collapsing world of patriarchy, the family, and the Church. For nearly 2,000 years, Christ's maleness and the maleness of God were used "to justify rampant ecclesial and social misogyny."

Now, led by feminist scholars, the meaning of Christ is being "widened" to "include feminist social practice," and Christ is no longer male but female, Christa, a symbol of erotic power which "will transform a world that includes our own personal lives in relation."

Following feminist theology comes "queer criticism" which "radically questions contemporary heterosexual or past asexual constructions of Christological discourse. It unpacks sexual oppositions that have been glossed over in totalizing truth claims of Christian discourse. It uses feminist reconstructive practice against misogyny as part of its discourse. It employs its own critical-practice against homophobia, but it also constructs queer bodies, queer selves, and queer sexuality. In feminist and queer critical practice, the erotic self is embodied over and against the apathetic self. The recovery of bodily connectedness and the affirmation of the erotic goodness of the body provide a corrective to the Augustinian severity that has long dominated Christian discourse..

"Queer criticism recognizes [C]hristological discourse as historically constructed through misogyny, antisexuality, and homophobia. A queer Christology starts with Jesus' practice and death and reconstructs the claims of Easter within queer critical practice."

As bizarre and noxious as these ideas may strike the reader, his views resonate deeply with many bishops, priests, religious, chancery bureaucrats and Catholic school teachers, as we will see in the next few chapters. Thus, when Bishop Matthew Clark, several years after Goss' book came out, celebrated a Mass for lesbians and gays in Rochester, he processed up the aisle behind a statue of "Christa," the female Jesus, the "symbol of erotic power."

In chapter 4, "A Queer Biblical Hermeneutic," Goss provided a thorough review of the "new biblical scholarship," and how it supports a "queer Christology" and a rationale for homosexuality; first by arguing that there is nothing in the Bible which can be used as a "text for terror" against homosexuals once those passages – i.e., in Genesis, Leviticus, or the Epistles of St. Paul – are understood in light of contemporary exegesis.

But "it is not enough to dismantle homophobic biblical interpretations. Biblical texts can enhance the queer battle for truth and the struggle for liberation. A queer critical reading of the Scriptures transforms texts into

23

narratives of resistance, releasing powerful motivational elements in our struggle against homophobic oppression."

In chapter 5, Goss urged that gay activists accelerate their confrontation with Church leaders. "Critical confrontation of ecclesial oppression is an essential strategy in queer Christian practice," and crucial means to do that would be, he wrote, through "small faith communities."

Incredibly enough, within six years, the entire National Conference of Catholic Bishops put its authority behind a "pastoral plan" to turn parishes into "welcoming communities," along the lines specifically called for by Goss:

"Base communities become nurturing alternative forms of community practice that challenge homophobic power relations in churches and in society...It is time to create hundreds and thousands of gay/lesbian affirming base communities of faith that practice God's justice. It is time to break the grip that homophobia/heterosexism exercises upon the discourse and practice of churches. It is our moment to radically challenge churches to practice God's solidarity with the oppressed...Gay and lesbian believers must no longer submit to the belief that their relationships do not reflect God's love and justice. Making love and doing justice have become synonymous for gay and lesbian people."

CHAPTER TWO

The Kos Case, Or
Friends In High Places

With its February 8, 1996 issue, *The Wanderer* became the first national publication to break the news that the National Conference of Catholic Bishops (NCCB) had been named as a defendant in a lawsuit involving clerical sexual abuser Fr. Rudy Kos and two other priests in Dallas, and was facing charges it engaged in a decades-long civil conspiracy to protect known sexual abusers. The "Kos case" would become one of the biggest clerical pedophile stories of the decade, not only because of the historic, record-setting judgment against the Church at the end of the affair, but also because of a series of sordid revelations indicating that Church officials went out of their way to recruit and protect sexually deviant priests.

Before looking at the Kos case in depth, there was a similar case of potentially equal import in Seattle, and headed for trial, where attorney James Bendell (who eventually became counsel for Roman Catholic Faithful, the Midwest watchdog group which would cause much distress for more than one corrupt bishop) was representing plaintiffs sexually abused by Fr. Paul Conn. Among the defendants in the case were the Archdiocese of Seattle and the Catholic University of America's seminary, the Theological College and its Sulpician rector, Fr. Albert Giaquinto.

What Bendell wanted to determine was if Catholic officials can be held legally accountable for the recruitment, training and ordaining of men to the priesthood who are known to be pedophiles. His pleadings were comprehensively reported in *The Wanderer* of May 2, 1996, "For Archdiocese of Seattle, It's Hard To Confess Wrongdoing."

Conn, ordained in 1985, was recruited to the priesthood in Seattle by Fr. David Jaegher, the archdiocese's director of seminarians, himself an accused child abuser, who was one of the Seattle area's most prominent homosexual rights activists. Furthermore, Conn was screened and evaluated by Sr. Fran Ferder, who has a decades-long record as a dissenter from Catholic moral teaching, and who sincerely believes in the superiority of homosexuality and bisexuality over heterosexuality. For ten years before Bendell filed his lawsuit against the archdiocese, in 1994, lay Catholics had complained to former Archbishop Raymond Hunthausen, and to the Vatican, that Ferder and her colleague, Fr. John Heagle, were corrupting the morals of priests and seminarians, and thousands, if not tens of thousands, of lay faithful by promoting her bizarre sexual theories at major religious education conferences, clerical workshops and seminars for religious.

Unfortunately, shortly after *The Wanderer* filed its report in mid-1996, Bendell's clients made an out-of-court settlement with the archdiocese, so the full details Bendell sought on the recruitment, training and ordination of known pedophiles remain hidden. Bendell did, however, uncover enough information to establish that the archdiocese knowingly trained and ordained a priest with known psycho-sexual problems, and that immediately upon his ordination Conn began sexually abusing altar boys; also, incredibly enough, the archdiocese appointed him to serve along side as a "supervisor" for another clerical pedophile, Fr. James McGreal!

To tell the truth

During the two-plus years *The Wanderer* covered the Kos case, it was the lone voice in the Catholic press, even though the facts of the case would seem highly newsworthy because of their scope. In addition to the conference as a civil entity being named as a defendant, top NCCB officials, including General Counsel Mark Chopko and then-current General Secretary – now Bishop – Daniel Schnurr, and former General Secretary – now Bishop – Robert Lynch, were accused of providing false testimony under oath, and other legal improprieties in their efforts to protect the NCCB from the lawsuit.

Attorneys pursuing the case against the NCCB asked the Dallas District Court to impose severe sanctions on Chopko, Lynch and Schnurr, as well as other NCCB attorneys, in order to compel them to "tell the truth," to stop making false statements to the court, and to desist its "harassment."

At the time *The Wanderer* broke this story, the lawsuit against the NCCB was in its third year, and was stalled in the Texas Supreme Court as the NCCB sought to evade the lawsuit on First Amendment grounds that it constituted a violation of religious freedom.

NCCB attorney Mark Chopko told *The Wanderer* that if the Texas Supreme Court did not dismiss the NCCB from the lawsuit, it would pursue its claims in the United States Supreme Court.

The bone of contention was an order by Dallas County District Court Judge Anne Ashby to release conference documents subpoenaed by attorneys Sylvia Demarest and Windle Turley, who were representing clients claiming they were abused by three Dallas priests, documents the attorneys claimed demonstrated that the NCCB had formulated a specific policy to assist dioceses in the cover-up of clerical sexual abuse 20 to 30 years ago.

The NCCB attorneys did not deny that the documents existed, but, surprisingly, that they were "protected" – not only that, they claimed the episcopal conference should be exempt because it had nothing to do with Catholic life in the United States!

"There was an extensive system set up by the NCCB to cover-up the fact that Catholic priests were abusing children," Sylvia Demarest told this reporter. "The allegations in the case say the bishops conspired together to make sure no priest was prosecuted, that no victims sued, and that the public remained unaware of their activities. That system included accepting the transfer of priests when it was necessary to get them out of their home community, and reassigning them, with access to children, without making any effort to control their behavior.

"The bishops had this network of 'safe houses' – so-called treatment centers – where they could place these perpetrators until an assignment was available."

The first line of defense set up by attorneys representing the NCCB was to claim that since the NCCB did not do business in Texas it could not be sued there, a procedural tactic to avoid answering the lawsuit.

"Then they claimed the NCCB has no power within the hierarchy of the Church to make policies, and they are asserting that because they do not want anyone to call them to task for failing to protect children when they knew what was happening," Demarest explained.

"In fact, in their legal papers, they say lay Catholics are 'strangers to the Bishops' conference,' and since the conference had no relationship with them, there was no duty to protect them, even from known danger.

"What lay Catholics need to know," Demarest added for emphasis, "is that the Catholic bishops of the United States are telling a judge they are not the shepherds of the Catholic flock, and they have no duty to protect them from a danger they knew about and, in fact, they created."

Attorneys for the NCCB/USCC countered in their legal briefs that the episcopal bureaucracy does not direct Catholic activities, that it is not part of the Catholic hierarchy, that it does not have authority over or control individual Catholics or even dioceses, and has no influence over Catholic schools, hospitals or treatment centers – all of which, said Demarest, are patently false statements.

Furthermore, attorneys for the NCCB said in sworn depositions that NCCB/USCC statements are not binding on any Catholic, an assertion Demarest found preposterous.

"You can go into any Catholic Church in Texas and find the NCCB statement on political responsibility; we provided documentation that shows the NCCB claims to speak for American Catholics when it goes to the Supreme Court, when it lobbies in Congress, when it sets policies for the Catholic people to follow in schools and hospitals, when it disseminates policy statements and tells the Catholic people how to act, and that it raises money from the Catholic people in every diocese. So it is absurd for the NCCB attorneys to claim they do not communicate directly with the Catholic people, that it has no relationship with them.

"The fact is, there is a relationship, and it is one of trust, guidance and caring. That's what their pastoral statements are all about," she added.

Legal wrangling

The plaintiffs represented by Demarest and Turley claimed they were abused by Frs. Rudy Kos, Robert Peebles and William Hughes, all of whom lived together in North Dallas' All Saints rectory, and that Kos and Peebles were known to diocesan officials as long-time child sexual abusers.

In fact, the Diocese of Dallas knew from Kos' ex-wife that he was a pedophile before he was admitted to Dallas Holy Trinity Seminary (while Archbishop Michael Sheehan, a long-time friend of the late Joseph Cardinal Bernardin, was rector) to study for the priesthood.

The sexual abuse case itself is typically tragic, though exceptionally sordid. The plaintiffs' lawyers argued that two Dallas bishops, then-reigning Bishop Charles Grahmann and his predecessor, Thomas Tschoepe, knew their priests were habitual child abusers, but continued appointing those priests to parishes where they could have access to fresh victims. Turley and Demarest decided to include the NCCB in their legal action when they realized the NCCB was at the heart of the continuing sexual abuse scandal plaguing the Catholic Church in the United States.

"It was not part of our original plan to include the NCCB," Turley told this reporter at the time, "but we decided to include it when we learned the diocese was following directives sent by NCCB officials. We also realized that this terrible problem of the sexual abuse of children by Catholic priests would never end as long as the NCCB continued engaging in a conspiracy to cover-up clerical criminal activity."

The documents the NCCB was fighting to protect, he claimed, would show the NCCB sent out policy edicts or guidelines to keep this matter under wraps and locked up from professionals and laity for years. In other words, there was an orchestrated plan to conceal this ongoing problem.

"We know this material exists, and trial judge Anne Ashby has ordered the NCCB to produce the documents."

After Ashby ordered NCCB officials to turn over documents, the NCCB asked the Texas Supreme Court in March 1995 to issue a *writ of mandamus*, claiming Ashby's order violates the Church's religious freedom, as well as the "attorney-client privilege."

This extraordinary writ was necessary, NCCB attorney Mark Chopko explained to *The Wanderer*, because the lower court did something egregiously wrong. "In our case, that means the discovery order against the conference – the production of documents – and the claims on which they are based – are impermissible, so we have asked the Texas Supreme Court to rule in our favor by either dismissing the conferences entirely from the litigation or substantially narrowing the scope of the case and the discovery against us."

Turley and Demarest responded to that claim by saying they do not dispute the Catholic Church's right to formulate religious policies, and the discovery they seek is limited to the secular issue of child sexual abuse.

"Chopko and Lynch," said Turley, "exemplify the attitude that prevailed in the past, that they are above the law, that the Church will take care of itself, in its own way, even if its conduct is unlawful under secular law. They are stonewalling, clear and simple.

"That's why we had to request the court to impose sanctions on them because the law clearly provides if a party to litigation or their attorneys deliberately or recklessly impede the progress of the litigation, or have lied or concealed material wrongfully, then the court can take certain actions against them; those sanctions may range from a fine, to striking defense arguments, or to entering judgment against them for a range of sanctions. That would be for Judge Ashby to determine."

In an interview with this reporter, Chopko said the NCCB fought Judge Ashby's order to release documents because the plaintiffs' request was "very broad," and constituted "a fishing expedition to determine whether the conference acted correctly as a religious entity in dealing with issues of clergy misconduct.

"One of the areas that the plaintiffs want to explore," he continued, "is the change in Church law which the Holy Father announced in 1994. Leading up to that change were a number of meetings, draft proposals, etc., all of which go to the internal practice of the Catholic Church, which are not subject to review by any civil court in the United States."

That, he said, is "black letter constitutional law. We have offered to make available all the public files of the conference but we will not make available any of the internal deliberations."

Other documents which plaintiffs want, he said, are correspondence between him and bishops and their diocesan attorneys, which he said are protected by the attorney-client privilege. Some the court has protected, but others have been rejected. Chopko also described the allegations made by the plaintiffs against him and other NCCB officials that they provided false testimony as "completely spurious.

"It illustrates the egregious nature of the claim and illustrates another reason why the claims against the conference are an attempt to scrutinize the internal workings of the Catholic Church...I would be the first person to say not every case of clerical sexual abuse has been properly handled. But I don't think there is anything nefarious or sinister about the conduct of the bishops. The ideas of treatment in the '60s and '70s were different than what we have now. Catholic clerics were not treated differently in terms of treatment and work recommendations than others who had similar problems.

"In terms of how the bishops' conference has dealt with it, this was never on the agenda until 1985, and that was because bishops wanted to have a briefing on the Gauthe case in the Diocese of Lafayette, Louisiana. They wanted to know all the implications, pastoral, legal, etc., and over the next six years, almost all of the communications between the bishops and the conference were in these areas – which leads to an important factor.

"Under Church law and practice, the supervision, assignment, training and ordination of clergy is only in the hands of individual diocesan bishops, and this is a power which the bishops jealously guard. There would be no formal way for the bishop of Fort Worth to influence the decisions of the bishop of Dallas and vice-versa."

In order to move their clients' case forward, rather than fighting for years in the Texas Supreme Court and, quite possibly, the United States Supreme Court, Demarest and Turley eventually dropped the NCCB from their lawsuit – but not before briefs were filed, and it is important to examine in detail the defense NCCB counsel made.

The briefs asserted the "conferences have no responsibility for ministering to individual members of the Church" and there is no "legal or ecclesiastical relationship with individual members of the Church." Moreover, the conferences exist solely "for the benefit of the bishops and no relationship with the conferences is created by virtue of an individual member of a given Catholic community referring to himself or herself as 'Catholic.'"

That claim was necessary because Demarest and Turley charged the conferences have a fiduciary relationship with the Catholic people "grounded upon the duty of good faith, fair dealing, and the duty to act with the highest degree of trust and confidence."

Demarest told this reporter the conferences' arguments were "spurious" because, "there is a legal relationship between the NCCB and the Catholic people, which includes a fiduciary relationship, because the NCCB and USCC are dependent on the Catholic faithful for their livelihood. Nobody in the organizations would get paid without the offerings made by the faithful. Their whole ministry is to lay Catholics, and I think a jury would find their arguments ridiculous."

Demarest contended in her brief that the bishops, through their conference, established a uniform policy to deal with their pedophilia crisis.

"This uniform position and approach was designed to keep the abuse secret, avoid prosecution of priest offenders, prevent or minimize claims for damages, avoid pubic exposure of the sexual abuse of children by Catholic priests, protect the reputation of the Catholic Church and thus insure the continued financial contributions of the Catholic laity. This conspiracy included spoilation of evidence and is ongoing."

She explained to this reporter: "It's too much to be a coincidence. No matter which diocese you go into, whether it is urban or rural, whether it is in the north, south, east or west, you have a certain number of perpetrators, and all the offenders and victims are treated the same way. Because the bishops knew there was a problem, and enough of a problem to set up treatment centers, we will argue they had a duty to assist the victims and prevent further victimization. They were spending a fortune on treatment centers. Since 1976, they paid for at least 1,000 offenders at the Servants of the Paraclete in Jemez Springs, New Mexico, at $50,000 a pop. That could be as much as $50 million in just one institution. Plus, we have clear evidence of cooperation among bishops to place these abusers in assignments. But they didn't help the victims."

In the March 1995 *writ of mandamus* filed by NCCB/USCC attorneys, in which they asked the Texas Supreme Court to vacate District Court Judge Anne Ashby's order to turn over official documents to attorneys representing the victims of sexual abuse, the bishops' attorneys declared:

"The most basic fact" about the conferences, "is that (they) are not in any chain of command. The conferences are off to one side; they have no operational responsibilities; and their statements on various issues – except when provided by Church law – are not binding on anyone…The conferences had no control over wrongdoing priests, no control over the bishops and dioceses, and no relationship to the victims. To sue the conferences for the wrongdoing of a parish priest in the Diocese of Dallas is nonsensical. It is like suing Notre Dame University for the wrongdoing of that parish priest in Dallas."

The assertion that the NCCB has no relationship with the Catholic people, explained NCCB General Counsel Mark Chopko "is a technical legal point.

"The liability posited against the conferences is that we had an affirmative obligation to find out about clergy sexual abuse and affirmatively warn individual Catholics that their priests might be potential sex offenders. For that assertion to be true, it requires a lot of facts to fall into place, including a 'special relationship' to exist between plaintiffs and the conference, which exists for the bishops.

"That special relationship," Chopko continued, "would have to be a fiduciary relationship, which under the law exists only when there is a special level of trust and intimacy between two people, such as an attorney-client relationship, a doctor-patient relationship or even a clergy-penitent relationship. The plaintiffs assert the conferences have a relationship with each individual member of the Catholic Church that would be legally analogous to, say, the attorney-client relationship.

"When we say the conferences are strangers to individual Catholics, we are talking about 'strangers' in terms of the law. As a practical matter, however, most Catholics do not know what the conferences are. Only one person connected to the case in Dallas had ever heard of the conferences. Most Catholics relate to the Church in their parish and parish activities, and to a lesser extent the diocesan Church."

The Peebles case

Supporting the plaintiffs' view that the NCCB/USCC set a unified national policy for dioceses to protect clerical criminals is the strange case of Fr. Robert Peebles, ordained for the Diocese of Dallas in April 1977. Shortly after his ordination, the diocese learned of his dangerous sexual proclivities, and by 1980, the diocese was receiving reports that he was sexually abusing minors.

In 1982, Peebles was, however, judged "spiritually, morally, intellectually and emotionally (qualified) to represent our denomination" in the chaplains' corps by the military vicariate.

As a chaplain in the United States Army Reserves and the regular Army, Peebles used his position to ingratiate himself with minor boys, and continued abusing them. In June 1982, he was put on "temporary leave" from the Dallas Diocese and sent to an orientation session for Catholic chaplains at Spring Lake, New Jersey, and then began an assignment at Fort Polk, Louisiana, where he continued abusing young boys.

In March 1984, now at Fort Benning, Georgia, Peebles sexually abused a young boy, was turned over to military police, and a court martial was instituted for conduct unbecoming an officer, taking indecent sexual liberties with a child under the age of 16, and attempted sodomy.

With proceedings underway, and with a four-star general seeking to put Peebles in Leavenworth Prison, the Diocese of Dallas began working to prevent his prosecution by the military and bring him back to Dallas.

How it happened very few people know – including the four-star general who wanted Peebles prosecuted to the full extent of the law – but Peebles was allowed to resign from the military on the promise that he would receive extensive counseling and long-term treatment.

In May 1984, just two months after his arrest for attempted sodomy, Peebles was serving as assistant pastor of St. Augustine Church in Dallas. The fact that he was a sex offender was never made known to either the pastor or parishioners.

A year later, Peebles was appointed pastor of St. Augustine's. In August 1986, he resigned his position after abusing three more boys, and the Diocese of Dallas was able to shield Peebles again – for the third time – from prosecution on the promise that he would receive treatment.

The Diocese sent Peebles to St. Luke's treatment center in Suitland, Maryland, and began his laicization process. The diocese also provided money for Peebles to earn a law degree from Tulane University and living expenses while going to school. Today Peebles is practicing law in New Orleans.

To Sylvia Demarest, it was "absolutely astonishing" that Peebles could avoid prosecution by the military unless the U.S. bishops had a mechanism in place to protect its criminal clerics and help them avoid prosecution.

"What the Peebles case shows," she added, "is that sexual abusers are protected by a system that felt it was better to let criminals go free than to expose the problem of pedophilia in the clergy. At the time, the Catholic hierarchy possessed enough information to implement policies and procedures that would have prevented this incident. And yet, in this case, they have taken the position that even though they are the shepherds of the flock of Catholic faithful they have no duty to protect the flock from known danger."

"If that's the case, then all Catholics should ask themselves: *is this what we really expect?*"

Revelations at the trial

Four weeks into Kos' highly-publicized eleven-weeks-long civil trial in June 1997 (the first of the three priests to be tried), which focused largely on Kos' admission to Holy Trinity Seminary, the Dallas *Morning News* ran a story commemorating the 20th anniversary of the local Gay and Lesbian Alliance.

Buried mid-way into the report on how the alliance's founder Don Baker pushed the homosexual agenda on the Dallas community, reporter Brooks Egerton casually mentioned that Baker now lives in Boston with his partner of ten years, Fr. Mike Hartwig, "a Roman Catholic priest and former academic dean at Holy Trinity Seminary in Irving."

At the time of the trial, Kos was living *incognito* in San Diego under another name, and the Diocese of Dallas was claiming that it should not be held financially or legally liable for Kos' crimes, for which he had already been found guilty.

"The trial's very embarrassing for both the clergy and the laity. It's a great tragedy, but it exposes the long pattern of corruption and planned deconstruction," one priest told this reporter.

Over the course of the trial, all Dallas learned how top diocesan officials, including former seminary rector Michael Sheehan, now Archbishop of Santa Fe, knowingly admitted a known pedophile to the seminary. (When Kos applied to the seminary, Kos' ex-wife told tribunal officials that she divorced him because he had a "problem with boys"). Sheehan also rebuffed priests who warned seminary officials that Kos was an aggressive homosexual while he was attending Holy Trinity, and then rejected warnings that Kos, now ordained, was abusing minors.

"This trial shows neglect, neglect, neglect," a priest told this reporter, "but it also shows how a small clique determined to 'liberalize' the Church were able to destroy a great institution."

Among the highlights of the first four weeks of the jury trial:

- Judge Anne Ashby threatened former vicar general Monsignor Robert Rehkemper, who had run the diocese for the past 20 years, with contempt of court if he didn't answer plaintiffs' attorney Sylvia Demarest's questions in a straightforward manner.

Rehkemper, 73, who was responsible for supervising Kos at the seminary and who was supervisor of all clergy in his role as vicar general, said he never investigated allegations of sexual abuse against Kos because he never received "actual proof" of the activity.

He also testified he was not aware of the Diocese of Dallas' own sexual abuse policy, nor of national guidelines – a laughable assertion, countered a Dallas priest, because Rehkemper brought in Monsignor Michael A. Jamail, vicar general in Beaumont, to talk to the seminarians about pedophilia and the expense pedophile priests are costing the Church.

(Curiously, Rehkemper was also present – with Rudy Kos – at a mandatory priest's study days retreat at the seminary, when the subject was "profile of a pedophile.")

- Among those testifying against Kos was a then-31-year-old man who lived with Kos for two years at the All Saints rectory while he was a teenager, and claimed Kos had abused him hundreds of times.

Kos claimed he had legally adopted the young boy, whom he had begun abusing when he was ten and a patient at the Methodist Medical Center, where Kos worked as a nurse before going into the seminary.

The "adoption" – though it never really took place – and strange living arrangement, was even the subject of positive news story in the diocesan newspaper, the *Texas Catholic* – which actually promoted the arrangement.

- One of Kos' victims, then 25, testified that Kos abused him while he was on a weekend "leave" from the Servants of the Paraclete treatment center in Jemez Springs, N.M., where Kos took a 14-month sabbatical in 1992 for "treatment" of his pedophilia problem.

- Two priests, Fr. Robert Williams and Fr. Daniel Clayton, testified they kept detailed logs of the time Kos spent in inappropriate behavior with boys in their rectories, from the day they arrived, and made frequent efforts to air their concerns to diocesan officials, who turned a deaf ear.

As early as 1986, Fr. Clayton testified, he began sending "alerts" to Monsignor Rehkemper, warning him that Kos was spending too much time with boys in his room, but Rehkemper took no action.

Clayton also wrote a stern letter to Kos, demanding that he stop entertaining boys in his room. Kos wrote back: "You do not lead a life I desire to emulate. I reject your letter as full of tripe and unfounded."

- Monsignor James Harris of Laredo testified that he went to seminary officials after a seminarian complained that Kos had "made a pass" at him, and Rehkemper responded simply that Kos "had been investigated" and dismissed the allegation.

- Noted canonist Fr. Thomas Doyle, a former Vatican Embassy lawyer, a paid expert witness for the plaintiffs, testified that diocesan officials failed to investigate Kos when they had good reason, and that Kos should never have been admitted to the seminary, nor ordained. He accused the diocese of "shameful" practices in the whole Kos affair.

Also revealed was the fact that Kos was probably ordained illicitly, because he received an invalid annulment (granted by now-Archbishop Thomas C. Kelly, O.P. of Louisville in 1976 while he was assistant general secretary of the National Conference of Catholic Bishops) in a judicial process marked by serious deficiencies and conflicts of interest.

While the trial ostensibly focused on Kos and his misbehavior, the real picture that came into focus was the total arrogance and neglect of Monsignor Robert Rehkemper and his methodical plan to deconstruct the Diocese of Dallas and especially Holy Trinity – once considered the orthodox flagship seminary in the South.

In 1976, Kos applied to Holy Trinity, then under the firm orthodox direction of Monsignor Gerald Hughes, its founding rector, who rejected him on the grounds of "instability."

In 1977, after Hughes' ousting by vicar general Rehkemper, Kos reapplied and was admitted by Holy Trinity's new rector, Monsignor Michael Sheehan, a Dallas priest recently returned from service in Washington where he was an aide to Bishop Joseph Bernardin at the NCCB.

Kos' admission to Holy Trinity was emblematic of the changes at the seminary, according to two priests who were seminarians at the time.

"Rehkemper wanted to make sure Hughes' seminary (established by Dallas Bishop Thomas Gorman, who created Holy Trinity as part of his 'master-plan' to make the University of Dallas the great center of Catholic education in the Southwest) was deconstructed. He oversaw the deconstruction.

"To me," added the priest, "his purpose in life was to make sure it was deconstructed. In my view, Sheehan was viewed as someone who had 'grown' and would liberalize it. Rehkemper was living at the seminary when Kos was there, and he certainly knew what all of us knew about him.

"In fact," the priest continued, "Kos was a 'known quantity' before he was ordained. People in the community knew his reputation from his work as a nurse at nearby Methodist Medical Center – and they were scandalized that he was accepted by Holy Trinity."

Now, said the priest, Rehkemper "sounds like Hillary Clinton.

"For years, he presented himself as the smartest man around. Well, if he's so smart, why can't he remember anything? He wants to be known as the most astute vicar general in history, but in court he's denying he knows anything."

Kos' admission to Holy Trinity seminary was the subject of several days of trial proceedings. Plaintiffs attorneys' argued that the new directors were accepting any warm body who applied, just to keep the seminary full, and Kos was an ideal student since he was already degreed and would therefore cost less to make a priest.

The diocese maintains Kos was admitted because he "appeared qualified."

In court testimony on May 21, Fr. Don Fischer, who was vocations director for the diocese when Kos applied, said: "I remember being very excited about presenting him (Kos) to the seminary. He was intelligent and seemed extremely mature. I thought he was an excellent candidate."

In his letter of recommendation to Bishop Thomas Tschoepe, Fischer wrote: "His background, rather than being a hindrance, seems to have helped prepare for his decision to enter the seminary."

Fischer, said one priest, is another of the "deconstructionists" who, at the time, was serving on the diocesan building commission. His most "notable" accomplishment – other than pushing for Kos' admission to the seminary – was the demolition of St. Bernard of Clairvaux Church in Dallas. Under the guise of "renovation," he gutted a beautiful early '60s church in perfect condition, rearranged the entrance, sanctuary, and obliterated the baptistry.

During his 11-year service as a priest of the diocese, Kos served in three parishes, abusing children in each place. From 1981-84 he was at All Saints, with Fr. Greg Kelly (current vocations director for the diocese, and best friend of Fr. Bill Hughes, who also faced a trial for pedophilia), and Monsignor Raphael Kamel, now deceased.

From 1985-87, he was with Fr. Daniel Clayton at St. Luke's in Irving; and from 1988-1991 he was at St. John's in Ennis, with Robert Williams.

Under Sheehan, and his successor Fr. Charles Elmer, "the seminary was transformed into something else," a Dallas priest told *The Wanderer*. "The seminarians lost the sense that they were representing something greater than themselves, and instead of the traditional disciplines and devotions, we had drummed into our heads the notion that we had to be 'good to ourselves to avoid burnout.'

"Our focus became 'what can we do on our time off?' Well, we didn't get 'burnout'; we got rust-out." After Sheehan was assigned to Immaculate Conception parish in Grand Prairie so that he could get some "parish experience" before being named bishop of Lubbock, he was replaced by Fr. Elmer, the former "economo" or "spending overseer" at the North American College in Rome.

"Elmer was Rehkemper's best friend," a priest said, "and he was the Willy Loman of seminary rectors. During his years, the quality of seminarians 'turned south,' and he made the seminary look like an ad for destruction. I never saw so many sociopaths in one place in my life – and I know what a sociopath is.

"Rehkemper's 'fair-haired boy' was Michael Hartwig, who had studied at the North American College, and was appointed vice-rector. He certainly was on the fast-track, and probably would have been named a bishop had he not 'married' Don Baker, a leader of the gay community in Dallas.

"Hartwig had plenty of money; he always had the newest car, the finest clothes and CDs. When he abandoned his vocation to 'marry' the president of the Dallas Gay and Lesbian Activists' Alliance, he invited the seminarians to his 'wedding.' That gives you an idea of what was happening to Holy Trinity."

CHAPTER THREE

Reaching The Kids, Or
Making The Pubic Public

At the same time the Kos saga was running in Dallas, some distraught parents from the Tucson area contacted me, seeking publicity in *The Wanderer* for an outrageous, totally invasive and very secret "AIDS curriculum" imposed on all Catholic elementary schools in the Diocese of Tucson, a program designed by the University of Arizona/National Institutes of Health.

Here was another lesson on how the "green light" given by the U.S. bishops' 1990 document on sex education paved the way for the sexual abuse of children, and that in the cultural and political elites' campaign to promote the homosexualization of the American population, Catholic leaders would offer their school children as guinea pigs for experiments intentionally designed to break down modesty, decency and a child's natural antipathy to sexual perversion.

Ironically, the Tucson AIDS curriculum story appeared in *The Wanderer* just a few weeks after the Holy See's Pontifical Council for the Family issued its definitive statement on the highly controversial subject of classroom sex education, *The Truth & Meaning of Human Sexuality* – a document parents, at the time, thought would support their demands for a ban on the sordid and vile sex indoctrination programs endemic in Catholic schools. As time would show, however, this document was a dead letter as soon as it arrived in this country as far as the U.S. bishops and their bureaucrats were concerned. Indeed, had not an advance document been given to *The Wanderer* from a source inside the Vatican before its formal release, it most likely would never have received any publicity at all here.

The March 31, 1996 issue of *The Wanderer* broke what should have become a national scandal and *cause celebre*. Under the headline, "Catholic Schools Supply Subjects for Government's Sex Researchers," this reporter disclosed a highly secret $1,240,299 grant from the National Institutes of Health to University of Arizona researcher Dr. William Crano for an intensive three-year sex survey and "values clarification" program involving all children attending Catholic elementary schools in the Diocese of Tucson.

In his application letter to NIH, Dr. Crano wrote: "We have been allowed access to a heretofore shielded sample, and given the freedom to employ treatments as progressive as any used anywhere in the country, in any type of school system, public or parochial."

With the blessing of Bishop Manuel D. Moreno, a protégé of Roger Cardinal Mahony of Los Angeles, Crano would have access to thousands of human "guinea pigs" to test theories on how to desensitize Catholic children to sodomy and the homosexual lifestyle.

One of the key aspects of the program, Dr. Crano said in his application, was the assumption that if the government could change the attitudes of Catholic school students towards homosexuality, those students would, in turn, change their parents' attitudes.

"For example," he wrote, "consider the possibilities...that effects on children's AIDS knowledge/attitudes might impact on their parents. We can study this possibility by determining whether the systematic effect of an intervention on children is mirrored by congruent changes in their [non-treated] parents. Variations in children's and their parents' AIDS knowledge/attitudes across time may help us understand the secondary or ripple effects of our treatments on untreated groups."

Crano was allowed access to 2,453 Catholic school children in Tucson's 16 Catholic schools, as well as students in the neighboring Diocese of Gallup.

"Tucson attorney and Catholic activist Sheila Parkhill, who opposed the NIH-funded research project on Catholic children, pointed out to this reporter that in this AIDS curriculum almost every appearance of the word *pubic* was misspelled as *public*.

One example appeared in Lesson 4 of *Human Sexuality* for fifth graders: "The area between the legs of boys and girls is different and is called the genital or *public* area."

"That's a very revealing Freudian slip," observed Parkhill, "but it illustrates the view of the sex researchers conducting the study and the diocesan officials who permitted it: they believe the most personal, private and intimate affairs are *public*."

Sheila Parkhill's conclusion is further supported by the Diocese's ambitious program to saturate young Catholics with sex. In some Catholic schools in the Diocese of Tucson, she told *The Wanderer*, children from kindergarten through eighth-grade are submerged in three *different* sex education programs per year: the National Catholic Education Association's (NCEA) AIDS Curriculum; the *In God's Image* sex education program authored by dissenter and pro-homosexualist Patricia Miller; and the NIH/UA sex experiment conducted by the bitter ex-Catholic Dr. William Crano.

"When do the kids have time to study other subjects?" Parkhill asked rhetorically.

Even if they should have the time, another major question remains: are young school children immersed in the details of sex, disease and death capable of learning anything else?

The University of Arizona's $1.24 million NIH-funded HIV/AIDS education research project raised dozens of other crucial and very disturbing legal, ethical and invasion of privacy questions – questions which parents asked Bishop Manuel Moreno, questions he and his officials refused to answer.

Deep Secrecy

One of the biggest questions parents raised was: Why the deep secrecy of the NIH/UA project and what was the Diocese of Tucson's role in coordinating the project?

The AIDS research project came into public view only after a diocesan school board member, worried about the diocese's engagement in an inappropriate government-funded research project, discussed her concerns the previous September with two friends, Tom and Sheila Parkhill.

On September 25, 1995, the school board member and the Parkhills went to the University of Arizona Speech Building, which housed Dr. Crano's Department of Communication, and requested all documents related to the project.

They picked up, along with curriculum guidelines for the three-part, four-year research program, a series of letters written in August and September and sent to Catholic parents by UA researcher Edwin J. Dawson, Ph.D. (a former seminarian), informing them the "comprehensive health and HIV/AIDS education program for the diocesan elementary schools" was already underway in the Catholic schools, and asking parents to complete "informed consent and waiver" forms.

There was also a "Dear Parent or Guardian" letter dated September 20 (1995) from Sr. Ruthmary Powers, HM, the diocese's superintendent of Catholic schools, informing them the NIH/UA HIV/AIDS research project had the "blessing" of Bishop Moreno, writing: "several years ago the Catholic Schools Office of the Diocese of Tucson and the University of Arizona began a collaborative project to develop a program for teaching elementary age students about the various aspects of HIV/AIDS...This program began with the endorsement and blessings of Bishop Moreno, as in all aspects, it complies to the Catholic teachings in the presentation of information on this subject."

Powers assured parents that "this project is good for our schools and our children," and she told them – as had Dr. Dawson – the UA research project was based on the NCEA's AIDS curriculum.

Furthermore, she told them that Janet Haas, the Diocesan Health Coordinator and long-time diocesan AIDS educator, was working on the UA project, along with Dr. Ronald Starcher, the former Superintendent of Schools for the Diocese.

What was so astonishing about the letters the Parkhills found on file at the university is that they didn't know any parents of children attending Catholic schools – including themselves – who had received the letters.

Just as the Parkhills learned of the vast scope of the project, they began hearing from other parents whose children had told them of surveys they were given in school, which probed children's attitudes about AIDS and other health matters, their relationships with God and their relationships with their parents.

Kelly and Barbara Copeland, parents of a third-grader attending St. Joseph's school in Tucson, however, did receive Dawson's letters, along with the consent form.

But when they learned their child would be involved in the NIH/UA research project, they told the school's principle and their son's teacher that their son was *not* to be involved in the Human Growth and Wellbeing Project.

Imagine their surprise, then, when Barbara Copeland picked up her eight-year old after school one day and he started asking his mother questions about AIDS.

Barbara immediately asked his teacher what his son was talking about, and learned that a university graduate student had read an AIDS questionnaire aloud in a class from which her son was supposed to be excused.

When she complained to Sister Ruthmary Powers that their parental rights had been violated, Sister Powers flatly responded that their son's participation in the program was mandatory.

Moreover, if she didn't like it, she should remove him from St. Joseph's – a school both she and her husband had attended.

Organizing & Informing

As parents began to learn more about the NIH/UA AIDS Project implemented in Tucson's Catholic schools, they also began to organize.

With the leadership of the Parkhills; Dr. Lazaro Hong; Dr. Andrew Stopko, a licensed psychologist; Kelly Copeland and Leticia Munozcano, the parents formed the Holy Family Society and began earnest efforts to inform as many Catholic parents as possible about the AIDS program, and to convey their concerns about the program to Bishop Moreno.

In their communications to other parents and to Bishop Moreno, the Holy Family Society raised the following questions:

- Why, if parents have, as Vatican II and Pope John Paul II affirm, "the original, primary and inalienable right to educate" their children, were they not consulted, advised or informed about the NIH/UA AIDS Project?

- Why weren't parents informed of the true nature and explicit content of the materials before their consent was obtained?

- Would Church authorities sanction a sex instruction program that utilizes a computer-delivered program that provides detailed, explicit sex instruction, and a peer-delivered sex instruction program to young children?

- Where did Dr. Ronald Starcher, the Diocese of Tucson's non-Catholic Superintendent of Schools, obtain the authority in the Fall of 1992 to promise University of Arizona researchers "all the students from grades

3-8, in every parish elementary school of the Diocese of Tucson (2,500 family units)" to be used as human subjects in an experimental research project, "the first of its kind in the United States"?

- Who reviewed the NIH/UA AIDS project for compliance "in all its aspects...to the Catholic teachings in the presentation of information on this subject," as Sister Powers told parents?

- Who gave Janet Haas, the diocese's "health consultant" and long-time diocesan AIDS educator with a bachelor's degree and a nursing degree the right to evaluate the material to ensure its conformity with Catholic doctrine?

- If Bishop Moreno supported the project from its inception and "endorse(d) the direction this research is taking," as Dr. Starcher told researchers Crano and Michael Burgoon, why didn't he inform parents of Catholic school children of the project?

- Was it ethical for diocesan officials to promise the AIDS researchers complete and unfettered access to its elementary school children "for the coming years" when it was unknown what the effects of the research would be on the children?

- Was it moral for Bishop Moreno and his officials to promise researchers that they would not be "constrained in terms of approach or topic selection" when teaching 8-to-12 year-olds about various sex topics?

The Holy Family Society also alerted both the parents and Bishop Moreno that there were some troubling legal and ethical aspects of the research project.

- One of the lead members of the research team, Dr. Thomas Moon, professor and chief of the Arizona Cancer Center, was a co-principal investigator of the National Institutes of Health Women's Health Initiative, which supports abortion, birth control and sterilization. Another investigator, Michael Burgoon, a University of Arizona professor of communications, was using his paid position in the Pima County Superior Court System to collect data for the AIDS project from the county's jury pool. The diocese's "health consultant" Janet

Haas has an extensive background in secular sex education with the University of Arizona.

Most troubling of all was the lead investigator and project originator, Dr. William Crano, whose field of expertise is social psychology. Crano, report Tucson Catholics, is an ex-Catholic who cannot cover up his disdain for the Catholic Church.

- The Human Growth and Wellbeing Project would be illegal in the state's public schools.

State board of education guidelines: forbid teaching sex as a separate course; limit sex instruction to a maximum of six lessons per year; prohibit co-ed sex instruction; forbid any tests, psychological inventories, surveys or examinations containing any questions about the student's or his parent's beliefs or practices in sex, family life, morality, values or religion; require public meetings with parents at least one week before any classroom instruction; and require parents to see all sex instruction materials.

The state guidelines also forbid the teaching of any abnormal, deviate and unusual sex acts and practices.

- The "informed consent" forms submitted by the University of Arizona researchers to Catholic parents were invalid, since the parents were not informed their children were being used for a research project as live "human subjects." Parents were not made aware of the details of the research, nor of the physical, psychological or social risks of the research.

Furthermore, federal and state laws and the university's own "human subjects" research guidelines mandate that informed consent implies full knowledge of all aspects of the research, and parents were not provided with any written and audio-visual materials that their children would be exposed to in the classroom.

- The NIH/UA AIDS project in Tucson's Catholic schools also violates federal statutes which prohibit the use of taxpayer funds for Catholic programs. If the NIH/UA program is based on the NCEA AIDS curriculum, say opponents, how can the Federal Government finance a "Catholic program"?

- The NIH/UA AIDS project is "culturally insensitive," because its explicit, graphic content is offensive to Hispanics and Native Americans.

The majority of parents of students subject to the program in the border town of Nogales, Arizona, for example, are Mexicans who do not speak English and accept traditional morality. The University of Arizona asserts Hispanics are at a higher risk of contracting AIDS because of their "lack of knowledge about the disease, attitudes towards homosexuality and bisexuality and an apparent lack of sympathy toward people with AIDS. All of which may be ameliorated if proper educational principles are applied."

If this sounds as if researchers *want* to introduce AIDS into the Hispanic community, consider researchers' rationale for introducing a program to dispel "homophobia" among Native Americans.

The grant application to the NIH states: "There is a dearth of empirical HIV research devoted to Native Americans...(T)he incidence of AIDS cases in the Native American population is comparatively low...(159 reported cases in 1990 – Rowell, 1990) ...Luna (1989) suggests that HIV will spread rapidly in the reservation population, *once introduced*..." (page 55, Grant Application).

What purpose?

The Holy Family Society also asked other parents, and Bishop Moreno, what purpose the intensive AIDS program served.

Why, for example, if University of Arizona researchers acknowledged that "the average age of first sexual intercourse for young women is 16.2 years and 15.7 years for young men," does the sex research target pre-adolescents beginning at age 8?

Why, if AIDS is the 10th "leading cause of death" according to the U.S. National Center for Health Statistics, after heart disease, cancer, stroke, accidents, pneumonia, diabetes, etc., are children not bombarded with information on those other causes of death?

Why, if according to *Sex in America, A Definitive Study, 1994*, only 1.4 percent of women and 2.8 percent of men think of themselves as homosexual, is there a comprehensive indoctrination of children in the homosexual lifestyle?

47

Why, if there is abundant evidence proving that sex education promotes promiscuity, increases teen pregnancy, abortion and sexually transmitted diseases, is this sex research project being imposed on Catholic children?

Why do the NIH/UA researchers encourage children, beginning in third grade, "to talk freely with us, without fearing that we will tell someone else" about their most intimate thoughts, feelings and beliefs on personal and private matters?

Why is family defined for third graders as "a group of people that belong together"?

The parents highlighted other serious problems with the program, including the presentation to children of medical and biological misinformation via the peer counseling and computer games designed as part of the NIH/UA experiment regarding the spread of AIDS, sexual reproduction and pregnancy.

Stonewalled

In early October, 1995, as the controversial program became better known among Catholic parents, members of the Holy Family Society, as a group and as individuals, began requesting a meeting with Bishop Moreno to discuss their concerns.

While the growing controversy about the program forced Moreno to temporarily suspend it while his "damage control" committee studied it to ensure it complied with Church teaching (something Sister Powers had assured parents had already been done years earlier) he did finally schedule a meeting for Halloween evening with four parents in the Holy Family Society.

Then he notified the parents a day before the scheduled meeting that it was canceled.

Repeatedly, Moreno refused to meet with parents; he failed to respond to their letters; and he prohibited parents who opposed the NIH/UA research project from expressing their views to his "damage control" committee studying the project.

After the Holy See's Pontifical Council for the Family released its long-awaited sex education document in December, 1995, parents again started writing to Moreno, showing how the NIH/UA AIDS Project violated every guideline for sex instruction provided in *The Truth & Meaning of Human Sexuality*.

As usual, Moreno did not respond to those concerns, except to assure parents that "we are following Catholic teaching and sound moral principles," and he began filling his *Catholic Vision* diocesan newspaper with articles supporting sex education and the use of condoms to prevent AIDS.

In the aftermath of the publicity generated by *The Wanderer*, the parents in Tucson suffered the predictable consequences. High profile critics such as Dr. Lazaro Hong, a Cuban refugee who had experienced Castro's totalitarianism, was fired from his position as a member of the school board of St. Cyril's in Tucson, and forced to withdraw his children from the school.

"I see more and more of this all the time. It's one of the signs of the times," he told this reporter.

After months of trying to obtain all the materials relevant to the research project, and seeing her Freedom of Information requests denied, Sheila Parkhill was accused by one of the project researchers, Dr. Michael Burgoon of stealing the material at a parents' meeting on the NIH/UA AIDS Project at St. Cyril's Church.

When she later wrote to the University attorney objecting to Burgoon's attack on her, she received a curt reply from the University's lawyer, Thomas Thompson, stating: "I respectfully decline to make myself a potential witness in any dispute between you or those you may represent, and Dr. Burgoon, or the University of Arizona, or both."

Nor would the NIH give Parkhill "internal review" documents she requested under the Freedom of Information Act which would explain why government researchers were given permission to conduct research on Catholic school children.

In addition to withholding documents and other sources, Parkhill charged, NIH/UA researchers violated their own grant application, in which they stated that "Some issues (e.g. dangers of unprotected anal intercourse) probably will not be discussed, owning [*sic*] to the age of the sample, not religious instruction" (i.e., restrictions from Catholic officials).

49

As Parkhill discovered, after she located the "assessment" tests teachers gave students after each lesson, to ensure they were learning the material, not only were 8th graders learning about "anal sex," they were also learning about bestiality!

In the course of seeking expert opinion on this travesty, I interviewed psychiatrist Jeffrey Burke Satinover, M.D., who publicly charged that it was "criminal" for Bishop Moreno to allow the Catholic children of his diocese to be used as "human subjects" for sex research.

Dr. Satinover, an expert on homosexuality and sex education and the author of the recently published *Homosexuality and the Politics of Truth* (Baker, 1996), said there is "substantial documentation showing that programs designed to dispel homophobia actually increase homosexuality."

Homosexuality, he said, "is not pre-determined. If you reinforce it, it will become more widespread. It's like stealing. If you tell a child every day for four years that it's okay to steal, would you be surprised if he starts stealing?

"If you normalize homosexuality and homosexual practices, you will increase the number of people who practice it, and we know the number of people who have the various physical illnesses and diseases that result from anal intercourse will increase.

"Regardless of whether or not a condom is used – and studies show that AIDS education and 'safe sex' programs do not increase condom use – you will have more and more young people with 'gay bowel syndrome' and other diseases.

"The NIH/UA AIDS Project," he continued, "is designed to normalize the homosexual subculture. The idea and the implementation are criminal. The entire project is designed to guarantee that the practices of the homosexual lifestyle become accepted and widespread.

"Epidemiologists, even in the homosexual community," Satinover revealed, "are expressing concern that multiple studies show that 30 percent of 20-year-old homosexuals will be dead of AIDS by the time they are 30. This program will not only lead to an increase in homosexual activity and AIDS, but it will inevitably lead to a dramatic rise in early sexual intercourse, higher rates of pregnancy, an increase in abortion and more venereal diseases."

Finally, Satinover offered this somber warning: "In ten years, the train of government-funded research will be heading in a different direction, and no one will be around to study the 'subjects' of this research for a follow-up on the project's success or failure.

"The only ones who will be interested in studying what happened will be the parents of these children – who will be derided as 'right-wing fanatics' when they complain about how their children's lives were ruined."

An update on Moreno

In January 2002, the link between sex education and sexual abuse was brought to the attention of the Catholics of Tucson in a shocking way. Bishop Moreno's appalling lack of vigilance and concern with regard to the University of Arizona AIDS study was manifested again when he was forced to admit his own negligence in the case of lawsuits involving pedophile priests that hit the news at the same time as the case involving Fr. John Geoghan in Boston propelled Bernard Cardinal Law into the headlines.

In late January, 2002, the Diocese of Tucson announced a settlement with 16 plaintiffs in 11 lawsuits for an estimated $10-15 million involving four diocesan priests, two of whom are now deceased, which Bishop Manuel D. Moreno predicted will have "very painful consequences to our diocese and its finances."

In addition to offering a public apology to the victims and more than 350,000 Catholics in the diocese, the fifth largest in area in the country, the bishop pledged a new zero-tolerance policy for priests accused of sexual molestation.

What makes this case slightly different from the proliferating number of news stories pertaining to clerical crimes were local press reports that Bishop Moreno asserted in his deposition involving defendant Monsignor Robert Trupia that he was blackmailed by Trupia, who threatened to reveal sexual affairs involving other "high-ranking Church officials."

While the diocese successfully obtained a court order sealing records, the *Arizona Republic's* Nena Baker reported February 10 that Moreno's deposition, which was not sealed, "describes how diocese officials failed to act on information in what amounts to a secret code of the collar.

The deposition and other records show that diocese officials protected one another, lied to a victim's family, failed to counsel victims, destroyed statements, did not notify child protective authorities and were uncooperative with police.

The cover-up began under the previous bishop of the Tucson Diocese [Francis J. Green] but continued under the current bishop, Moreno, who was installed in 1982…

Two of the priests identified in the cases, the Revs. Pedro Luke and William Byrne, have died. Two others, Monsignor Robert Trupia and the Rev. Michael Teta, have been suspended from duties but continue to receive monthly salaries and health insurance benefits paid by the diocese.

Plaintiffs' lawyers filed documents alleging the diocese didn't begin an official investigation of Trupia, the judicial vicar, until 1992, about 17 years after the diocese first heard that Trupia was abusing boys.

The plaintiffs claim that during those years, Trupia's behavior was so notorious he was known as a 'chicken hawk' among other priests. Nevertheless, Trupia was promoted to increasingly powerful positions that gave him ready access to boys…

In a deposition given in August, Moreno testified that Trupia admitted to him in 1992 that he had sexually molested boys and 'was a man unfit for public ministry.' Moreno went on to say he could not explain why he had not been truthful about Trupia's statements in a letter he subsequently wrote to a victim's family and in a secret canonical affidavit to the Vatican, reported Baker.

Furthermore, he could not explain why he waited until 1995 to execute another canonical affidavit alleging that Trupia, during his meeting with the bishop in 1992, threatened to reveal personal sexual relationships with high Church officials if he was not allowed to retire.

At the time of the 1992 meeting, Trupia was appealing his suspension to the Vatican. Moreno said in the deposition he did not immediately inform his superiors of Trupia's blackmail threat because he did not intend to give in to it…

In 1991, Trupia, Tucson's judicial vicar, was studying canon law at the Catholic University of America in Washington, D.C., when Moreno suspended him. Trupia appealed the suspension; but subsequent to his appeal, he demanded that Moreno "retire" him, threatening to disclose information he had about the previous bishop of Phoenix, James Rausch, the second general secretary of the National Conference of Catholic Bishops and a close friend of the late Joseph Cardinal Bernardin.

Trupia is currently living in Silver Spring, Maryland, and has been suspended from duty, though he still draws a stipend from the diocese. Teta is in the process of being laicized.

The Diocese of Tucson's co-defendants, along with the four priests, are the Archdiocese of Los Angeles and the Diocese of Phoenix.

A sick priest

Among the charges one of the plaintiffs made against Trupia is that he was sexually abused by the priest at St. John's Seminary in Camarillo, California.

One of the court documents obtained by *The Wanderer* described a trip in which Trupia took two young teenage boys to California, during which they stayed for two days at the seminary. One of the boys recalled waking up and finding Trupia sitting on his bed, smiling.

Court records indicate that Trupia was an obsessive and compulsive abuser, committing sexual acts in his rectory, office and even his church.

Among the most disturbing charges against Trupia, who was ordained in 1973, is testimony from altar boys he "molested" on a weekly basis for over two years. Plaintiffs claimed that after celebrating Mass, Trupia would commit oral sodomy on them, followed by anal sodomy.

One court document states: "...Fr. Trupia was, upon information and belief, motivated in part by a belief that this sexual contact serve[d] some purpose in the altar boys' service and thus in furtherance of his employer's business."

Trupia began abusing 11- and 12-year-old altar boys during his first parish assignment, at St. Francis of Assisi Church in Yuma, and diocesan officials first learned he was abusing young boys in 1976, after former police officer Ted Oswald, now a priest in California, took statements from boys who were claiming that Trupia was "queer."

The diocese removed Trupia from the parish, and told families he was being sent away for treatment; instead, he was simply transferred to Our Mother of Sorrows in Tucson, where he taught sex education and initiated a program to introduce high school boys to the priesthood.

In a statement on the four priests accused of sexual abuse, Bishop Moreno informed Catholics in Tucson that:

"Four priests are named as defendants in the suits: Fr. William Byrne; Fr. Pedro Luke; Fr. Michael Teta; and Msgr. Robert Trupia. Fr. Byrne died in 1991. The Diocese believes that Fr. Luke was actually Fr. Lucien Meunier de la Pierre, a priest from Canada. The Diocese relieved him of ministerial duties and suspended his priestly faculties in 1975 following his arrest on child abuse charges. Fr. de la Pierre was convicted of child abuse charges, and is believed to have died while serving a prison sentence.

"The Diocese relieved Fr. Teta and Msgr. Trupia of ministerial duties in 1990 and 1991, respectively, in accord with its policies governing allegations of child abuse or sexual misconduct.

"Also, through canon law (the law of the Church), the Diocese suspended the priestly faculties of Fr. Teta and Msgr. Trupia. The Diocese has pursued through its Tribunal the canonical process that could result in the removal from the priesthood of Fr. Teta and is awaiting final action from the Holy See in that process.

"The Diocese also is awaiting action from the Holy See to its response in the process of a canonical appeal by Msgr. Trupia of the suspension of his priestly faculties.

"Just as in the legal system of secular law, canon law provides the right of due process. In respect of that right and in fulfillment of the canonical obligation of a bishop to provide sustenance to a priest who is not able to give ministerial service, the Diocese is providing sustenance equivalent to a priest's monthly salary and health insurance to Msgr. Trupia and Fr. Teta. The equivalent monthly salary and monthly health insurance premium costs amount to approximately $1,475 for Msgr. Trupia and $900 for Fr. Teta…"

Among the charges set forth against the Diocese of Tucson and Msgr. Trupia is that diocese failed to follow its own procedures regarding allegations of sexual abuse.

A time line

Interestingly, a time line on how the Church in the United States has responded to its sexual abuse crisis, available on the Diocese of Tucson's web site, reveals:

1982. NCCB/USCC staff assist personnel from two dioceses in appreciating the civil liability risks involved in child molestation cases. Occasional inquiries about specific complaints follow over the next eighteen months.

1984. Misconduct of Fr. Gilbert Gauthe of Lafayette, Louisiana, focuses public attention. NCCB/USCC staff have limited discussions with diocesan administrative and legal personnel about concerns presented by resulting claims. Additional claimants in other dioceses come forward. NCCB/USCC staff act as resource to Bishops and their staffs who have ultimate responsibility for responding to claims.

Several state legislatures change child abuse reporting statutes. NCCB/USCC legal staff survey and provide summary of statutes to dioceses.

1985. Several state Catholic conferences and individual dioceses begin developing personnel policies governing abuse allegations using their own expert and legal personnel along with consultation with NCCB/USCC staff. Based on operating experiences of dioceses, NCCB/USCC staff begin to make more uniform suggestions to individual dioceses which are: 1) remove the alleged offender from assignment; 2) refer the alleged offender for professional medical evaluation, 3) deal promptly with the victim and his or her family to offer the solace and support of the Church, 4) make efforts to protect the confidential nature of the claim, and 5) comply with the obligations of the civil law and make appropriate notifications.

June, 1985. Sexual abuse claims are discussed in private meeting of diocesan attorneys and in an executive session of the National Conference of Catholic Bishops. The latter, held in Collegeville, Minnesota, includes presentations by a psychiatrist, a lawyer, and a Bishop on aspects of the problem. The Reverend Michael Peterson, president of the St. Luke Institute, the Reverend Thomas Doyle, canon lawyer on the staff of the Apostolic Nunciature, and Atty. Raymond Mouton, lawyer for Fr. Gauthe, draft a resource paper entitled 'The Problem of Sexual

Molestation by Roman Catholic Clergy: Meeting the Problem in a Comprehensive and Responsible Manner.' This offers the authors' opinions of potential size of the situation facing the Church in the United States and suggestions on how to deal with it. Fr. Peterson eventually sends diocesan Bishops copies of text of the entire report as an appendix to a document prepared by the St. Luke Institute with a note requesting recipients to 'treat the contents of this document as confidential' and saying that it contains 'my professional and personal remarks and should not be construed as a national plan' for the Bishops' Conference. An NCCB/USCC staff review finds that, with few exceptions, issues identified in Report have already been analyzed for the Bishops by NCCB/USCC staff and other experts, especially at the Collegeville meeting.

Major difference: the Report's suggestion of a national intervention team (a doctor, a canonist, and a lawyer) to respond to complaints in individual dioceses. Dioceses prefer to respond through their own expert personnel, rather than a national team, due to factual and legal uniqueness of each accusation. Media characterizations of the Report as a proposal either ignored or summarily rejected by the Conference are inaccurate.

1986-1988. NCCB/USCC staff continue to assist dioceses and develop more uniform advice for them. Other actions are: in order to aid diocesan attorneys, General Counsel catalogues liability theories and defenses raised in litigation; diocesan training programs are encouraged; updates are offered to diocesan educators, Catholic Charities personnel and administrators. NCCB Committee on Priestly Life and Ministry begins to work with vicars for priests to help develop training programs. Dioceses develop more definitive personnel policies to respond to claims and training programs for policy implementation.

November, 1987. At the Bishops' General Meeting, certain aspects of molestation cases are reviewed, largely from the perspective of canon law. By end of 1987, NCCB/USCC General Counsel is asked to prepare a public statement acknowledging scope and extent of crisis and expressing perspective of the Conference.

February, 1988. At direction of the General Secretary, General Counsel issues statement.

1988-1990. Several important changes mark the situation confronting dioceses and, therefore, the NCCB/USCC: 1) the number of new cases, i.e., cases involving current problems, begins to diminish and be replaced by cases involving misconduct occurring ten or more years before. (Even with claims beyond the period of legal remedy, NCCB/USCC staff continue to advise the priority of pastoral care and that dioceses ascertain that there is no ongoing threat to any person), 2) priests returning to dioceses from treatment programs cause diocesan officials to ask whether these priests should or could be reassigned to ministry or what could be done to laicize them. This raises significant theological, pastoral, canonical, liability, and medical questions.

November, 1989. The Administrative Committee issues a brief statement on child molestation claims. General Counsel is asked to convene, in conjunction with NCCB Committee on Priestly Life and Ministry, a staff-level study group on questions of reassignment. Representatives of a variety of disciplines meet over a period of a year and a half for several consultations on various dimensions of the problem.

Late 1989. With regard to canonical remedies to deal with priests who would not return to ministry, NCCB/USCC officers and key staff begin discussing alternative approaches to existing provisions of the Code of Canon Law with representatives of the Roman Curia, especially the Code's statute of limitations and its treatment of culpability. Discussions focus on ways to streamline the penal provisions of the Code and the possibility of an administrative process to remove a priest from the clerical state...

As the time line continues documenting steps the bishops took throughout the 1990s as they allegedly confronted the problem, one item indicates that the NCCB's Committee on Priestly Formation and the National Catholic Educational Association (Seminary Dept.), "in 1994 undertook a survey of theologates and college seminaries on psychological screening and formation in sexuality issues.

"As for the theologates, the survey had a response from 29 of 36 institutions for diocesan seminarians. All respondents indicated that psychological testing was required and 26 of the 29 responding seminaries indicated that the pre-acceptance interview includes specific inquiry about sexual history and experience with relationships. Responses also showed that growth in sexual maturity and questions of relationships are specifically identified and dealt with as formation issues. Every seminary is doing something in this regard, some in a more organized way than others.

"As for the college seminaries, 11 of 14 free-standing ones, and 13 out of 28 collaborative college seminary programs responded. As for pre-acceptance interviews, there was considerable variation across the board. However, every responding seminary indicated that growth in sexual maturity and experiences with relationships were specifically identified as formation issues…"

Dysfunction

Despite this "objective" time line, since the U.S. bishops claimed they were responding to the sexual abuse crisis in the priesthood, there have been a number of indications they have yet to address the problem, which we will see in subsequent chapters. One indication is the deliberate programming of the Catholic people to accept homosexuality.

Another indication was the arrest of Fr. Carl A. Schipper, the academic dean at St. Patrick's Seminary in Menlo Park, the Archdiocese of San Francisco's seminary, who was arrested in March 2000 for soliciting a minor male over the Internet, for which he later pled guilty the following August.

His activities, said Santa Clara Deputy District Attorney James Sibley, "shows a compulsion, it's consistent with what we see as online predator activity."

Another indication was the late 1990s seminary experience of Paul Sinsigalli, who graduated from the Archdiocese of Boston's St. John's Seminary in 1999 – though he was advised he would never be allowed to serve as a priest anywhere in the country because he held an unprogressive view about homosexual acting out at the seminary. After his story appeared in *The Wanderer,* archdiocesan officials denied his allegations and lashed out at *The Wanderer.*

Some time later, *Catholic World Report* published a report by Cincinnati journalist and publisher Michael Rose on the ongoing problems in U.S. seminaries, to which Sinsigalli, a former Air Force officer, responded in the April 2001 edition, in an even more blunt fashion than his *Wanderer* interview:

"I was studying at St. John's Seminary in Boston and was told that I did not have the qualities required to be a priest. They said that I lacked leadership, intellectual ability, and emotional maturity, among other things. When I asked them to explain where these traits were exhibited they merely repeated the oft heard mantra: 'It's the consensus of the faculty,' and then would not defend or cite examples of said behavior. They had decided that I did not fit into their mold of what a priest should be.

"What were my crimes, you may ask? I stood up for what the Church teaches every time there was a question about it. I stood against the homosexual atmosphere which pervaded the college at that time and had the temerity to suggest that homosexuality is a disorder. I also did not engage in their pro-masturbation conversations which were commonplace in the halls and the dinner table. I was the target of a homosexual classmate who is known to have a violent history and required a restraining order to be taken out against him by another student..."

The problems in diocesan seminaries, however, may pale beside those in some religious orders. The February 2002 issue of *San Francisco Faith* reproduced a photograph from the California Jesuit web site showing two prospective Jesuits, identified as "Pretty Boy and Jabba the Slut," among a number of photographs of novices frolicking in the surf, in drag costumes, etc., "in order to provide you with a better idea of novitiate life and what it is we do here."

CHAPTER FOUR

Bishop Matthew Clark
& Gay Activism

In September 1996, one day after the United States Senate passed the Defense of Marriage Act sponsored by Oklahoma Senator Don Nickles, a Catholic, the Roman Catholic Bishop of Rochester, New York, Matthew C. Clark, was quoted in his local newspaper hoping the Church might some day find a way to bless long-term homosexual relationships.

Matthew Clark, appointed Bishop of Rochester in April 1979, a priest of the Diocese of Albany, a graduate of the North American College in Rome, where he was spiritual director, and one of the last appointees of Apostolic Delegate Jean Jadot, is one of the most notorious and dangerous of that clique of "fair-haired, boy-bishops" – along with his close friends Bishop Howard Hubbard of Albany, Archbishop Rembert Weakland, Archbishop John Quinn, et al., – who seem to find perverse satisfaction in the sexual scandals that outrage the faithful in their sees.

In an interview published in the Gannett-owned Rochester *Democrat & Chronicle* on September 10, Clark intimated he would like to see changes in Church teaching, suggesting the Church "has found ways to bless many good and beautiful things including relationships among people."

This public act was just a teasing preview of an agenda Clark had long supported but would launch with a new aggressiveness six months later in Pittsburgh at a gathering of this country's leading "Catholic" homosexual agit-prop organization, New Ways Ministry, and thrust into the national spotlight six months later when he helped the National Conference of Catholic Bishops produce a "gay-friendly" pastoral called *Always Our Children*.

One week after his bizarre response to Sen. Nickles legislation, Clark announced his diocese had established a new "collaborative relationship" with Catholic Gay and Lesbian Family Ministry (CG&LFM), which is operated by homosexual lifestyle apologists and advocates Casey and Mary Ellen Lopata – the latter of whom is now (2002) president of the Oakland (California) based National Association of Catholic Diocesan Lesbian & Gay Ministries (NACDLGM), and a booster of Parents and Friends of Lesbians and Gays (PFLAG).

The first formal "collaboration" announced was an event co-sponsored by the diocese and CG&LFM, a "Day of Recollection for Catholic Parents of Gay & Lesbian Sons & Daughters" on October 26, 1996 at the Sisters of St. Joseph Motherhouse.

Clark's September 10 comments appeared in the context of a large feature article by *Democrat & Chronicle* staff writer Doug Mandelaro, "A Question of Faith: Gays and Lesbians Seek Acceptance While Churches Struggle to Define Their Views on Homosexuality."

Mandelaro noted that some Catholic churches in Rochester, notably St. Mary's downtown and Corpus Christi, already had special ministries and support programs for gay and lesbians. In addition, St. Thomas More Church in affluent East Rochester holds an annual "blessing" ceremony for homosexual couples.

For the preceding two years, though Mandelaro did not report this for Catholic readers in Rochester, *The Wanderer* had been reporting extensively on the diocesan-sponsored "homosexual roadshows" presented by the staff of the diocese's theologate, St. Bernard's Institute.

Clark told Mandelaro he's happy parishes are doing more to include gays and lesbians in parish life. "I'm anxious that we continue to explore possibilities for life and peace and contentment for all people, and certainly gay and lesbian people, in their faith tradition. And I think we have a long road to travel to make our communities more welcoming."

Clark also said he is working on a special program for gays and lesbians which he hopes to have in place by year's end, and explained:

"Our community genuinely and truly wants to be open to gay and lesbian people. There are some issues we are going to disagree on. We hope we can do that with respectful dialog, without clashing and arguing."

According to Mandelaro, Clark is convinced the issue of blessing homosexual relationships by the Church will not go away, and change will not happen quickly.

"The Church is going to be extremely slow in putting at risk or to the possibility of misunderstanding that which we hold sacred about the marital union," Clark said, adding: "I support the teaching about marriage and share the concern that we redefine marriage in a way that's foreign to our tradition. Having said that, the Church has found ways to bless many good and beautiful things including relationships among people. It's a very, very tender issue right now."

Also quoted in the story was Mary Ellen Lopata, who runs Bishop Clark's Catholic Gay and Lesbian Family Ministry in Rochester. She, too, acknowledged that it will be a long time before the Catholic Church blesses homosexual relationships, explaining the problem: "It's a societal thing, a religious thing, a sexual thing." But she encouraged gays and lesbians to persevere. "As long as gays and lesbians have the courage to be who they are and let people know them, there will eventually come more acceptance. But there's always going to be conflict."

The CG&LFM seminar

Among the facilitators at the October 26, 1996 "Day of Recollection" was Fr. Robert Kennedy, assistant professor of Liturgical Studies and Coordinator of Student Formation at St. Bernard's Institute, who, at the time, "has been in ministry with gay and lesbian Catholics for 15 years."

At a talk he gave earlier in March that year, reported extensively in *The Wanderer* of April 18, 1996, Fr. Kennedy taught not only that the Bible does not condemn homosexuality – he said the Church has no teaching on pedophilia.

Scriptural passages which "fundamentalists" interpret as condemning homosexual acts, he said, must be re-interpreted in terms of the cultural beliefs of the time, and are no more binding than ritual prescriptions which bar the eating of shellfish or the wearing of clothing made of two or more different fabrics.

At the end of his talk, during the question and answer period, one of the audience asked Kennedy if pedophilia were a sin, and Kennedy responded that he didn't know of any Church teaching on the subject.

Another speaker was Casey Lopata, who earned a Masters of Divinity from St. Bernard's and is the father of a homosexual son. He taught participants at the same March 11 seminar that "sex outside of marriage is not necessarily a sin," and advised sexually active homosexuals to receive the sacraments, just as do heterosexual Catholics do who are practicing contraception or committing adultery.

Lopata praised the work of Detroit auxiliary bishop Thomas Gumbleton on behalf of homosexuals, and also the letter of the French bishops which approved of the use of condoms to prevent the spread of AIDS because it represented an attack on the Vatican's position.

"If we can say 'yes' to condoms to prevent AIDS, then why not condoms for birth control, then why not physical intimacy between same-sex couples?" he asked.

Also speaking at the diocese's first major gay agit-prop event, to which all parishes in the diocese were advised to send representatives, were:

- Sister Kay Heverin, SSJ, an honoree of Interfaith Advocates for Gay, Lesbian and Bisexual People, and the "pastoral associate" at Bishop Matthew Clark's Sacred Heart Cathedral.

- Cheryl Lee, an educator and "conflict resolution trainer/facilitator," who has worked with homosexuals and lesbian Catholics for 15 years.

- Sister Dorothy Loeb, RSM, who "pioneered work with gay and lesbian Catholics in Montgomery, Alabama, New Orleans and Rochester" over the past 21 years.

- Fr. Gary Tyman, Newman Community chaplain at the University of Rochester, at the time pursuing his doctorate at Colgate Rochester Divinity School, where he was writing a dissertation on the "faith of gay and lesbian Catholics."

Speeding up the process

For three days in March 1997, in Pittsburgh, New Ways Ministry, founded by Sister Jeannine Gramick, SSND and Fr. Bob Nugent, SDS, held a big anniversary celebration, where the most prominent agit-prop artists in the Amchurch establishment surveyed the achievements of the homosexual apparat in the Church, and outlined the progress yet to be made.

Among the speakers, some of whom had traveled from Europe and all points across North America to be present, were Bishops Matthew Clark and Detroit Auxiliary Bishop Thomas Gumbleton.

In his address, Clark told the 655 participants – mostly priests, nuns, brothers and other Church employees – that the most pressing need in the

Church today is a broad-based, grass-roots consultation by Catholic Church leaders with "God's holy people" – his term for lesbians and gays and others who reject Catholic sexual morality – on contemporary sexual issues.

In a remarkably candid talk – couched in the standard modernist pettifoggery of convoluted phrases – Clark advised his gay and lesbian audience to ignore the teachings of the Church in the futile expectation that doctrinal change can be stimulated by those who reject infallible Church teaching.

"I do think with growing conviction," said the maverick bishop who delights in his role as a "change agent" in the Church, "based on my own pastoral experience that the Church really needs to engage in an intentional, corporate and systematic reflection on human sexuality.

"It is my opinion that we have lacked that kind of reflection, that is, the Church gathered to reflect on the kind of faith experience – not that every experience sets the norm – and that we can trust the Holy Spirit to lead us to better places than the ones in which we find ourselves now."

Clark, dressed in a tweed sport coat and striped shirt, said there were six areas of Church teaching that he would like to have more dialogue on, and change in: the ordination of women, married clergy, celibacy, abortion and gay and lesbian rights.

"In my opinion, (because) we have not had that broad consultation in the Church about the issues, our answers leave good, faithful people searching for the kind of 'it makes sense' reaction that we'd like all our teaching to find in the hearts of the people of God."

Over and over again, Clark indicated his agreement with Christian "ethicist," *Humanae Vitae* dissenter and radical feminist Sister Margaret Farley, RSM, of Yale University that "we need…to reflect on the faith experience of God's holy people."

He blamed the Holy See for not accepting demands for a change in the Church's moral teaching on homosexuality, and urged more agitation from the "holy people" in front of him, saying at one point:

"It's very easy for us as a religious body with a long history and a complex present reality that is so diverse, it's easy to fall into the trap of just repeating what was passed on to us in the language in which it was passed on rather than making the committed corporate effort to look at the new questions, to look at the new research and read it in the light of our living tradition and to adapt or adjust or nuance the tradition as we're led to do so under the guidance of the spirit.

"Otherwise, what can happen then is it's much too easy to take up a document or quotation and apply it immediately to individual lives and even beyond that to conscience decisions that's almost a litmus test. Without the mediation of the community reflecting together on such issues can get us, I think, into some pretty deep trouble or at least to places that are not very pastorally helpful." After delivering his formal presentation, Bishop Clark took questions from the floor. One question was: "If a homosexual couple came to you and said, 'We want to make a public commitment. We want you to publicly bless our union,' how would you counsel? What would you do in that situation?"

After the whistling, laughter and applause ended, Clark responded in a fashion that should have prompted his superiors in the Church to immediately disqualify him from exercising any episcopal functions ever:

"That is a very tough question. Let me try briefly at least to touch the themes that such things give in my mind. And that has been a very good question with us locally about what to do in that incidence [sic]. One of our parishes has been doing that, and I asked them to cease doing that..

"When we struggle with this, and indeed I think we are all struggling to find freer more loving ways to be together as a Christian family and specifically as gay and lesbian folks struggle to do that, and as the Church wants to do it, I think it will be better as time goes by.

"There have been strong efforts, I think, to honor the reality, the conscious decisions amongst the people. And people have come, I think, in ways that are public and known, to those decisions and lived them out and enjoyed comfort and solace of their faith community. Not in wide numbers, but in a growing number I think, people are more at home and accepted in those physical, stable relationships than they were before. At least I speak about.. and I rejoice in them.

"My concern with the practice is not so much a concern with the practice, but the practice as it communicates to the wider community, that that issue is settled, that it is in exactly the same place as the Sacrament of Marriage is in the faith and understanding of the people at large. And I simply ask that any practice of blessing or validation, whatever it is called, and I know it's called different things in different places, my concern is that it's carried out in such a fashion that there is a visible equation made to the Sacrament of Marriage in the sense that I just described, as that is understood and commonly held by the Christian assembly."

Then, referring to an initiative under way by his Office of Worship to develop prayers for same-sex blessing ceremonies, Clark continued: "I have asked at the same time precisely to honor loving relationships, that we look for ways in which we can do that without opening up other issues and concerns that we don't need in the Church right now. My contention is that the Church over centuries, and once again this usually happens with a time line that can be frustrating, has learned to bless all kinds of beautiful things eventually that in earlier times it couldn't bless. It didn't know how to. My best fallible pastoral judgment at this time is that in most places we are not there yet, but I hope one day we will be…"

Come out, Come out, wherever you are

If Clark was "nuanced," Bishop Gumbleton could not have been more direct in his call for gay priests and bishops to announce their homosexuality. The long-time gay activist told his audience:

"I can't tell you the number of letters I have received from priests who say they are gay, but who are afraid to come out," he said. "What a loss that is to our Church. If they were willing to stand up on Sunday morning in front of the community and say who they really are, our Church would much more fully and effectively appreciate the gifts that homosexuals can bring to the whole community of our Church and our society as well…

"I encourage this because I hope that within our Church every gay person, every lesbian person, every bisexual person and every transgendered person will come out. Because that is how our Church is going to truly change, when everyone from this homosexual community is courageous enough…to come out…

"I can honestly tell you that as more and more people come, more families are changed, more churches are changed, parishes are changed and our whole Church is changed, and so I appeal to you publicly to create a community where this can happen…Please come out, come forward! Share your gifts with the Church!"

Later, in a question and answer session, in the context of a confession, Gumbleton revealed his total immersion in the homosexual world-view and all of the clap-trap psycho-babble that has been constructed as a palisade around that bizarre and vile position. Completely ignoring the moral dimension of homosexuality and its naturally disastrous consequences, Gumbleton said:

"I am not homosexual but that does not give me or any other heterosexual person the right to be morally superior to any gay, lesbian, bisexual or transgendered person. None of us chose our sexual orientation... But I know that I, along with other heterosexuals still harbor homophobic tendencies in my heart and soul...Frankly, I do not know why there is so much fear and loathing of homosexuality and gays and lesbians, especially in the Church, unless it is fear and loathing of one's own self for the latent homosexual tendencies that are part of the heterosexual's own human make-up...

"I especially do not understand why so many gays and lesbians themselves, gay clergy included, allow themselves to become part of anti-gay and anti-lesbian initiatives, unless it is their subconscious way of denying their own homosexuality and it is a way for them to distance themselves from this 'demon force' within them.

"There is no biblical evidence that I am aware of that Jesus had a problem with gays and lesbians. Neither is there any historical evidence of which the Catholic Church was so pre-occupied or concerned with the existence gays and lesbians in the Church as in our own time when gays and lesbians are coming out of the closet...

"It seems to me that homophobia, being the loathing and fear of gays and lesbians, is at least as much an ethical problem for the Church as the homosexual behavior we presume to judge and condemn."

To better appreciate the enormity of the violence these two "Successors of the Apostles" inflicted on the Church, consider the milieu they were in and the other speakers they applauded over the four-day conference.

Among the star-studded cast joining Clark and Gumbleton at the gathering was Joseph Selling, chair of the moral theology department at the Catholic University of Louvain (where many U.S. bishops, including Clark and Howard Hubbard of Albany send their seminarians for advanced studies) who assailed Pope Paul VI's encyclical *Humanae Vitae* for "short-circuiting" the evolution of Catholic sexual morality, and who predicted that Church acceptance of same-sex sexual relations is "inevitable."

Also present was Patricia Beattie Jung, a moral theologian at Loyola University in Chicago, who spoke on the "sin of heterosexism" and provided her audience with a key for "deconstructing" the heterosexual "paradigm" of society.

The conference opened with an address by Dr. Richard Isay, who is Jewish, and the only non-Catholic among the keynote speakers, who spoke of the importance of introducing adolescents who think they are homosexual into the gay lifestyle.

Homosexuality is neither pathological nor reversible, he said, but a biological and genetic trait, often inheritable. But because of society's homophobia and religious strictures that describe homosexual acts as sinful or sick, many homosexuals grow up with low self-esteem. Thus, he stressed the importance of "coming out" for homosexual youth and outlined the reasons gay youth are entitled to "sexual experimentation" and "affectionate relationships" with adult men.

Though it might seem bizarre that a professional would deliver such an opinion to Catholic clergy and religious at a time when clerical pedophilia was both a legal and financial problem for the Church in the United States, Isay insisted such sexual activity is the only way gay youth can integrate their sexuality into a positive self-image.

Dr. Isay, a clinical professor of psychiatry at the Cornell Medical College and a faculty member of the Columbia University Center for Psychoanalytical Training and Research, briefly surveyed the history of the acceptance of homosexuality by the psychiatric community, but focused primarily on the "homosexualization" of gay youth and their need for parental acceptance and adult mentors.

The most terrible threat to the homosexual youth's self-image, he warned his audience, is attempts by some in the psychiatric community – he mentioned Catholic psychiatrist Dr. Joseph Nicolosi by name – to counsel homosexuals into heterosexuality. He described such attempts as "insidious," and said they lead the client to destructive behavior.

Isay's address was enthusiastically received by his audience, and the priest sitting next to this reporter at the table directly in front of the podium – a

Chicago-based provincial of his religious order – remarked, "Dr. Isay is so wonderful. I've read all his books."

Conference participants were 51 percent lay, 27 percent religious sisters, 18 percent priests, and four percent religious brothers. Of the 655 present, 50 percent were involved in pastoral ministry, 16 percent were diocesan or congregation leaders, nine percent were in religious formation or education, six percent were students or seminarians, and four percent were parents of gays or lesbians.

The second day of the three-day conference began with a presentation by Sr. Margaret Farley, RSM, of Yale University.

Farley, a prolific author and the recipient of the Catholic Theological Society of America's John Courtney Murray Award for Excellence in Theology in 1992, talked about the origins of Catholic moral teaching on sexual issues in the late Hellenistic period, the influence of Protestant Reformation theologians in reformulating Christian sexual ethics, and the revolution in Catholic sexual ethics in the 20th century, driven, she said, by new scientific discoveries, the changing relationships between men and women and the technological control over human reproduction.

As long as the Christian sexual ethic was focused on procreation and the control of sexual desire, she told her audience, "there was no room for a positive evaluation of homosexuality."

But in recent decades, under the pressure of new discoveries in the social sciences and scientific fields, traditional Catholic sexual morality is crumbling. Now, she said, "the procreative norm is gone," the "view of sex as a disorder is gone," the "rigid stereotypes of male/female complementarity are gone" and the time is ripe for a positive evaluation of homosexuality and same-sex sexual relations.

There is also, she said, "a cosmic struggle" on this issue of sexual ethics being fought between theologians and Church leaders.

While Church leaders remain constricted by traditional views of male/female complementarity, theologians are asking questions, such as, "how do we know if heterosexuality is good?" and "how do we know heterosexist assumptions are accurate?" This is the nun-theologian Bishop Clark praised in his address!

Dr. Patricia Beatty Jung defined heterosexism as a "cognitive system of differential behaviors and practices developed in response to sexual orientation which results in preferential treatment for heterosexual people and prejudicial treatment of all others," and scored heterosexuality for creating a society of sexual predators.

She said Church leaders are currently divided about the seriousness of the sin of heterosexism, but acknowledged that some Church leaders do recognize that "dismantling" heterosexism is a fundamental work of justice in the effort to make a better community.

Part of the work of dismantling or deconstructing heterosexism, she added, includes pointing out its own internal weaknesses and contradictions, the facts that it does not provide a credible view of procreation and gender complementarity, is based on a false understanding of the Bible, does not take into account human sexual physiology, and "does not square with people's experiences of good sex."

In the question and answer session after Farley's talk, Fr. Bruce Williams, O.P. who had flown in from Rome where he teaches at the Angelicum, asked Farley, "Have we or have we not come to the point where we must say that traditional Church teaching is not just wrong but is evil, because it is part and parcel of a package that is oppressive?"

Farley answered: "I agree with you. It is evil because it harms people, but subjectively it may not be evil on the part of the people saying it because they may not know better."

Another speaker was militant lesbian Virginia Apuzzo, the first executive director of the Gay and Lesbian Task Force, a top aide to New York Governor Mario Cuomo, then working as an assistant deputy secretary at Bill Clinton's U.S. Department of Labor.

Apuzzo was introduced by Fr. Paul Thomas, archivist for the Archdiocese of Baltimore, who informed his audience that when a "national Catholic conservative newspaper" – *The Wanderer* – first announced this conference, it described Apuzzo as a "militant lesbian – as if that was somehow derogatory!" He told her how he met her – she was wearing blue and he was wearing pink, a color he still wears, at a time when she was completely "out" and he was just starting to "poke my head through the closet door."

Another speaker was Fr. James Schexnayder of Oakland, a long-time militant gay activist and founder of the National Association of Catholic Diocesan Lesbian and Gay Ministries.

In his address, he highlighted St. Frances Cabrini Church in the Archdiocese of St. Paul-Minneapolis for its progressiveness and openness to gays and lesbians, and suggested all Catholic parishes should strive to imitate it: "...that has become a welcoming and reconciling parish by vote of the congregation. They went through a process like some Protestant congregations have gone through and, you know, studied the issue, came to a consensus."

Schexnayder praised the parish's statement on outreach to the gay and lesbian community, which he quoted at length: "To reach out to the gay and lesbian community, encouraging them to join the parish. Regularly publish our welcome in the gay press. Promise to educate ourselves about gay and lesbian issues and work to overcome stereotypes. Include a gay/lesbian perspective in catechesis at all levels, including elementary school age. Support lesbian and gay men in ways that support stable, healthy relationships. Stand willing to accept qualified, openly-gay and lesbian priests and lay ministers. Zealously work for and guard the civil rights of lesbians and gay men, knowing that all of our civil rights are compromised when theirs are. Pray for greater understanding and acceptance of gay and lesbian people in official Church teaching and encourage other parishes to become publically reconciled with gay, lesbian, transgendered and bisexual community...One of the things on here they committed to but are not implementing at this time is to publicly bless the relationships of a same-sex couple after the couple completes a process of discernment similar to what heterosexuals would do. The primary reason they are not implementing that is the archbishop did not welcome that statement as being compatible with Church teaching...It takes a lot of education to move a parish community into that kind of awareness."

He also boasted of his success in establishing student and peer-mentoring groups for gay activists: "It's interesting that, on the Catholic high school level, besides my meeting with principals, I'm currently arranging to talk with school campus ministers and student activities people to broaden it out – especially to push peer support, trying to train students – youth to support other youth – not just gay youth with gay youth – but straight youth who could understand and support other youth in a climate helps them. One of the Catholic high schools in our diocese that has a support group is for gay, lesbian and bisexual and straight students who care. And I've been part of the development of that group and it's just wonderful to see heterosexual students who care about the environment of that school and who will challenge homophobic kind of behavior. And that really requires peer support. So, student activities and campus ministers would be the context for that, whereas faculty would look at curriculum issues and how you integrate this – librarians, policy-makers – kind of make it a broad reality."

CHAPTER FIVE

Always Our Children:
Bishops Acting Up

Just ten days before National Coming Out Day on October 11, 1997, when homosexuals publicly proclaim their perversity, the Administrative Committee of the National Conference of Catholic Bishops released *Always Our Children*, a "pastoral" letter affirming their belief in the unscientific notion of homosexual "orientation" and advising parents of homosexual sons and daughters to accept them as they are – even if it means accepting their homosexual lifestyle at the cost of remaining silent on Church doctrine.

Here was a prime instance of homosexual agit-prop at work: for the document took nearly every Catholic by surprise, even many bishops, who had no idea the document would be released without some preliminary discussion, or even a chance to review it privately!

To Dr. Richard Fitzgibbons, a Philadelphia-area psychiatrist whose specialty is reparative therapy for those who suffer from same-sex attractions, whom *The Wanderer* had just interviewed two weeks earlier in the wake of the Kos verdict, this was a "dangerous document."

The pastoral, he said in a follow-up interview, "reflects a lack of compassion for both parents and children."

"This document is very misleading," said Fitzgibbons, who was not consulted despite his international stature as an expert on the causes and treatment of homosexuality. "It expresses pessimism, lack of hope and lack of compassion. There are so many troubling statements one hardly knows where to start...

"To begin with, homosexuality is an attraction and not an orientation.

"The first step for a parent to take is understanding, not 'accepting' their homosexual child. The parents must understand that there are significant emotional conflicts in the child that give rise to same-sex attractions or behavior, and understanding this gives hope to both the parent and the child.

73

"Rather than being understanding or compassionate, the document is based on the false notion that there is such a thing as a 'homosexual orientation.' Its thrust is that homosexuality is unchangeable, and therefore this pastoral takes away hope." The truth that the bishops should be preaching, he added, is that "same sex attraction is preventable and treatable. Christians should proclaim this good news with joy from the roof tops…

"Some men and women who experience same-sex attraction may be discouraged or afraid. They may have tried and failed. They need prayer, support from same-sex friends, and a place where they can be honest about their struggle. Unfortunately, they have not always found this in the Church. We must be very careful about labeling men and women who experience a constellation of emotional, behavioral and cognitive conflicts of which same-sex attraction is only one aspect as homosexuals or homosexual persons. Such labeling can lead people to believe that these persons constitute a separate category of human beings.

"But these men and women are like all other human beings created in the image and likeness of God either male or female, there are no other categories. They have a right to claim their proper manhood or womanhood. In some ways homosexuality represents a false identity – a failure to develop that proper masculinity or femininity which God desires. Homosexuality is therefore considered to be an objective disorder.

"The document's pervasive lack of hope for prevention and change are not its only flaws. One statement, in particular, could be easily misunderstood and misused: 'it seems appropriate to understand sexual orientation (heterosexual or homosexual) as a fundamental dimension of one's personality and to recognize its relative stability in a person.'

"Sexual desire is healthy and proper only when it is directed toward the opposite sex. It is important, therefore, to distinguish between the proper opposite sex orientation and a misdirected same-sex orientation. Misdirected orientations cannot be considered the 'fundamental dimension of one's personality.'

"Chronic illness and health are not equivalent and while both may persist, the goal must be if at all possible to move the chronically ill toward a state of health. To imply that a misdirected 'orientation' is a stable and fundamental dimension of one's personality cuts off the reasonable hope of change and freedom and is not consistent with Catholic teaching."

A milestone
or a millstone

Always Our Children was a milestone for the sexual revolutionaries in the U.S. hierarchy and their efficient operatives in the bureaucracy, the culmination of their decades-long campaign to promote homosexuality and change Catholic attitudes towards perversion, an agenda that opened with the "new catechetics" in the very early 1960s, when unsuspecting Catholic school children would be groomed to be participants in a sexual revolution few knew was coming.

As this reporter showed in a series of articles, "Retrospect on a Revolution," published in *The Wanderer* from June-August, 2001 on the "new catechetics" produced in the early 1960s, Catholic children were manipulated into accepting the concepts of sexual libertinism, androgyny, homosexuality, "free-love," contraception, abortion and divorce as marks of evolutionary progress. The first productions of "Vatican II" catechisms, such as Regnery's *To Live Is Christ*, cleverly manipulated students into accepting all the premises of the about-to-arrive sexual revolution – even though most Americans had no idea at the time such a revolution was on the horizon.

So *Always Our Children* must be understood in terms of an agenda set 30 years earlier; but to better appreciate the context in which a clique of progressivist, pro-homosexual bishops and their "consultants" prepared this pastoral, consider some of the major stories appearing on the front page of *The Wanderer* that spring and summer, the same time as the Kos court case was underway.

- Bishop Matthew Clark of Rochester hosted a special, highly-publicized Mass for "gays, lesbians and bisexuals" at Sacred Heart Cathedral. During his homily, he not only affirmed the "lifestyles" of gays and lesbians, saying they had much to teach the wider Church, but he delivered a stinging rebuke to faithful Catholics and admonished them to "update" themselves on contemporary biblical scholarship. ("Bishop Emerges As Spokesman For Homosexual Party Line," March 13, 1997)

- The Archdiocese of Baltimore's annual Social Ministry Convocation, jointly sponsored by the archdiocesan Campaign for Human Development, Catholic Charities, the St. Vincent de Paul Society and the archdiocesan Peace and Justice office was fixated on the subject of homosexual rights, and showed how powerfully the banned Dignity and the dissident New Ways Ministry organizations control "social justice" in the archdiocese. ("At Workshop, Speakers 'Chip Away' At Church Teaching on Homosexuality," March 13, 1997)

- When Catholics in the Diocese of Palm Beach wrote to Bishop J. Keith Symons objecting to a workshop offered in Catholic facilities by homosexual agit-prop artists Sr. Jeannine Gramick, SSND and Fr. Bob Nugent, SDS, whose New Ways Ministry had been "under investigation" by the Holy See for more than a decade, Symons shot back telling them *their* organization was "not approved" in his diocese, that their letter was "neither respectful nor totally factual," and that he had "carefully investigated" the pair, who assured them they were completely faithful to Church teaching. ("Florida Bishop Gives Imprimatur to Homosexual Agitprop Team," May 22, 1997)

Symons would later resign, one of five bishops who resigned in the 1990s in a cloud of allegations that they were pedophiles.

- Bishop Matthew Clark, stung by public criticism from the local chapter of the Catholic Physicians Guild that he dissented from Church teaching on homosexuality, disciplined the association of laymen by prohibiting them from distributing "any teaching material of any sort of a theological or moral issue" without his "explicit permission."

The crime of the Physicians' Guild: the officers had mailed to all physicians and priests in the diocese a statement of the Society of Catholic Social Scientists on the advance of the homosexual agenda in society. ("Rochester Bishop Tightens Screws on Physicians' Guild," June 5, 1997)

- Homosexual fashion designer Gianni Versace, who attained fame by introducing homoerotic and sadomasochistic themes into his fashions and advertising, was buried out of St. Patrick's Church in Miami Beach, after he was murdered by homosexual gigolo and former altar boy Andrew Cunanan. For his eulogy, Fr. Patrick O'Neill canonized Versace, proclaiming God "has put him in charge of redecorating heaven and dressing everyone in Versace-orchestrated colors." ("Slain Homosexual Designer Honored at Funeral Mass," July 31, 1997)

- On July 24, 1997, a jury in Dallas sent a $120 million message to the Diocese of Dallas in the form of a negligence judgment, bringing to an end the 11-week trial. The sum would later be reduced by the plaintiffs and their attorneys to $24 million – a figure they seemed more likely to be awarded by the financially distressed diocese. Among the highlights of the case: Kos' brothers revealed in court they had been sexually abused by him; Kos' wife revealed he had never consummated their marriage because he was fixated on young boys; one plaintiff said he had been abused more than 500 times by Kos; in 1986, Kos' superior at St. Luke's Church in Irving, Fr. Daniel Clayton, testified he had warned the top two officials in the diocese of Kos' proclivities, but was ignored; another victim testified that Kos called him from a pedophile treatment center in Arizona; Judge Anne Ashby threatened to hold Monsignor Robert Rehkemper, the number two man in the diocese, in contempt of court for refusing to directly answer questions about his supervision of Fr. Kos ("Dallas In The Wake Of The Kos Trial," August 28, 1997).

- On September 4, 1997, Roger Cardinal Mahony of Los Angeles welcomed 170 Catholic homosexual activists to a conference in Long Beach hosted by the three-year-old National Association of Catholic Diocesan Lesbian and Gay Ministries, the high point of which was a burlesque performed by Fr. Peter Liuzzi, O.Carm, his top "minister" to the lesbian and gay community. Liuzzi pretended to bless attendees with puppy urine, and then simulated a strip show, tossing his clerical collar into the crowd ("Diocesan Gay Ministries Group Moves Into The Mainstream," by Teresa Cepeda, Sept. 18, 1997).

- One month before National Coming Out Day, Karen Rinefierd, Bishop Matthew Clark's liaison to Catholic Gay and Lesbian Family Ministry, sent a letter to all pastors and chaplains in the diocese requesting they participate in "Solidarity Sunday," Oct. 4-5, in order to show their solidarity with their lesbian, gay, transgendered and bisexual "brothers and sisters."

The purpose of Solidarity Sunday, she explained, is to "raise awareness of discrimination against gay, lesbian, bisexual and transgendered people. It asks people to pray for an end to discrimination and violence, to pledge to work to stop verbal and physical gay bashing, and to wear a rainbow ribbon in solidarity with our gay, lesbian, bisexual and transgendered brothers and sisters who, with us, are God's beloved children.

"The Solidarity Sunday project was started by Dignity/USA in 1995. The project's sole purpose is to end discrimination and violence against gay, lesbian, bisexual and transgendered persons. Last year, over 100,000 persons participated in the project. In one local parish over 340 parishioners took ribbons and cards proclaiming their caring and desire for justice.

"To participate in Solidarity Sunday, all you need to do is run a brief article explaining the project in your bulletin the week before and then make the ribbons and cards available. It's nice but not essential for a few people to volunteer to hand out the ribbons and cards and perhaps offer a word or two of encouragement…"

In addition to the prayer cards, the diocese provided pastors with an information sheet advising them where they could purchase rainbow ribbon with the six colors of the official red, orange, yellow, green, blue and purple colors, which are unavailable in the Rochester area at major fabric stores.

Because Clark's "Solidarity Sunday" coincides with National Coming Out Day, explained one layman, he's encouraging his homosexuals "to publicly proclaim themselves as perverts. He's saying: 'perversion is good; perverts are better than other people. Maybe the next item on his agenda will be youth rallies for Catholics who are coming out. Maybe he'll make 'coming out' part of his confirmation ceremonies. You can never predict what Clark will do next." ("Rochester Diocese Pushes Homosexualist Agenda In Parishes," August 28, 1997)

Time line of a pastoral

Always Our Children was prepared by the National Conference of Catholic Bishops' Committee on Marriage and Family Life, chaired by Dolores Leckey, a long-time dissenter from *Humanae Vitae*, and headed by Bishop Thomas J. O'Brien of Phoenix, a diocese long-plagued by serious problems of clerical pedophilia. The origin of the pastoral, Detroit Auxiliary Bishop Tom Gumbleton told the *Washington Blade* just after its release, went back to 1993, when 15 bishops wrote a letter to the late Joseph Cardinal Bernardin asking for "help" they could offer the parents of gay children.

Though the NCCB, as is standard policy, would not disclose the authors of the pastoral letter, Fr. Robert Nugent, a founder of New Ways Ministry, revealed – before the release of the document – at a September 10 retreat held at the Sisters of St. Joseph of Orange Mother House in Orange, California, that he was a consultor for the pastoral, along with Fr. Peter Liuzzi and Fr. James Schexnayder, director of AIDS services for Catholic Charities in the Diocese of Oakland and a long-time militant west coast gay activist.

The pastoral had been in the process of preparation for at least two years, but unlike the bishops' famed "women's pastoral" there was no opportunity for public input and almost no information disseminated about it to the public prior to its release.

The first indication that *Always Our Children*, "approved" by the Administrative Committee of the NCCB on September 30, 1997, was a "work in progress" appeared in an item buried in the "Agenda Report" prepared for bishops for their November 1996 plenary meeting in Washington, on page 43 in the report by the Committee on Marriage and Family.

Following is what the committee report says on this:

"1. MINISTRY TO FAMILIES IN DIFFICULT SITUATIONS: HOMOSEXUALITY

"The Committee has drafted *Always Our Children: A Pastoral Message to Parents of Homosexual Children and Suggestions to Pastoral Ministers*, after two years of study and consultation. The document is an attempt to reach out to parents who are trying to cope with the discovery of homosexuality in an adult child, and to urge them to recognize that the Church offers enormous spiritual resources to strengthen and support them. After reviewing the draft in September [1996], the Administrative Committee [of NCCB] asked for certain revisions, including a 'preamble' stating that the message is not intended to endorse (however implicitly) a homosexual lifestyle. The Administrative Committee asked that the document be placed on its November agenda."

Significantly, and underscoring the secrecy behind the project, it was not listed explicitly under the "priorities & plans" section of the Agenda Report, which usually summarizes proposed projects, allocates funding, etc.

The bishop-members of the Committee on Marriage and Family in 1996 were Bishops Joseph Charron, Chairman, from Des Moines; Carlos A. Sevilla, SJ, Yakima; Thomas J. O'Brien, Phoenix; Joseph Imesch (of Joliet, former head of Women's Committee, and a long-time public dissenter from *Humanae Vitae*); John McRaith, (Owensboro); and Bernard Schmitt (Wheeling-Charlestown).

In 1997, member-bishops were: Thomas O'Brien (Phoenix, chairman, also member of Priestly Formation); John Kinney (St. Cloud, the chairman of the bishops' Sexual Abuse subcommittee and a member of Priestly Life & Ministry); Archbishop Elden Curtiss (Omaha); Cincinnati Auxiliary Bishop Carl Moeddel, who at a future homosexual agit-prop conference in California explained how he tried to mandate pro-homosexual educational programs in Cincinnati's Catholic schools); Richard Sklba (auxiliary bishop from Milwaukee, also a member of the bishops' Doctrine Committee and Review of Scripture Translations); John M. Smith (co-adjutor bishop of Trenton); and John Yanta (Amarillo).

Cardinal Bernardin, a former chairman of the committee, served as a "consultant."

Curiously, while the public was left completely in the dark about this forthcoming document, so too were most bishops: this document was not on the agenda for discussion and/or vote either at the November 1996 plenary assembly or at the bishops' June 1997 summer meeting; nor was there any indication it would be discussed at the November 1997 meeting.

Meet the Source

With Fr. Nugent's revelation that Fr. James Schexnayder was among the consultants that produced *Always Our Children*, it is now time to look at one of the most influential homosexual propagandists working in Amchurch, the founder of the National Association of Catholic Diocesan Lesbian and Gay Ministries (NACDLGM).

The January 1, 1998 issue of *The Wanderer* featured a report from a California correspondent, based on published news reports and her own extensive investigation into public records, headlined: "Amchurch's Homosexual Leader Displays His Lifestyle and Attitude."

Among the facts presented in the report:

- Schexnayder, head of the Gay Task Force for Catholic Charities of the East Bay, in the Diocese of Oakland, created the NACDLGM in the aftermath of the Holy See's Congregation for the Doctrine of the Faith's 1986 letter on the pastoral care of homosexuals, in which the bishops of North America were asked to cut their ties with homosexual organizations, such as Dignity and New Ways Ministry, that claim to be Catholic while agitating for a change in Church teaching and subverting it with every means at their disposal.

While Schexnayder, a long time Dignity chaplain in San Francisco, denied having any ties to Dignity, *The Wanderer* revealed that he and his roommate, Mario Torrigino, co-owned a $283,000 house in Oakland. Torrigino was, at the time, co-chairman of Dignity/San Francisco.

(Schexnayder's denial that he had anything to do with Dignity was similar to that made by Fr. Robert Nugent, who denied to this reporter that he had anything to do with New Ways Ministry, even though his roommate, Fr. Paul Thomas, is on New Ways Ministry's board of directors.)

- While Schexnayder denied his new organization had any connection to Dignity, Dignity/San Diego's head, Pat McArron noted his approval of the NACDLGM position expressed at the September conference, in an article in *Dignity Dimensions*, "The Bigger Picture," posted on the group's web site:

"As a member of both Dignity and the NACDLGM, I observed an emerging relationship between the two groups that is encouraging," McArron wrote, and expressed his belief that diocesan groups are adopting the Dignity position that "sex is a legitimate expression of love for lesbians and gays. In so doing, we [Dignity] have set ourselves apart by saying publically [*sic*] what virtually everyone else believes and practices privately."

Furthermore, the article discussed the need for Dignity, because of its long experience with gay and lesbian "ministry," to become involved with and guide the newly-emerging diocesan groups, such as those affiliated with the sympathetic group NACDLGM.

- As director of the Diocese of Oakland's Task Force for Outreach to Gay and Lesbian Communities and Their Families (operated out of

81

Catholic Charities), Fr. Schexnayder has worked closely with his secular counterparts in the public schools to create pro-homosexual programs for school children – and, indeed, his work in Catholic schools has been praised as a model by gay activists in the public schools.

- Other documents connecting Schexnayder and Dignity included an October Dignity/San Francisco events calendar, revealing that on October 19, 1996, Schexnayder conducted a retreat for Dignity San Francisco, "Engaging Our Gifts: A Journey Toward Action." He also wrote an article in the December 1992/January 1993 edition of the Dignity SF newsletter, *Bridges*, discussing the "pastoral plan for our chapter."

- The September, 1997 Long Beach NACDLGM conference further illustrated unity of goals and beliefs between Dignity and Schexnayder's group. The Dignity philosophy was promoted by conference speakers. Dignity pamphlets and rainbow pins were distributed. Approximately a quarter of the attendees at the conference Mass wore their Dignity t-shirts as a sign of protest, but were nonetheless given Communion by L.A.'s Roger Cardinal Mahony.

  At this event, Fr. Ken Waibel of Richmond, Kentucky (Diocese of Lexington) presented a workshop on "Gay and Lesbian Spirituality," saying that "the only authentic spirituality is gay spirituality... Heterosexual men cannot fall in love with Jesus Christ because of their own homophobia. Jesus wants us to be erotically in love with him." Waibel also revealed that the rituals he performs to marry heterosexual couples emphasize disunity, in contrast to the same-sex "union blessings" he has performed. (Fr. Waibel was forced to resign his pastorship when members of his parish learned of his statements at the NACDLGM conference.)

- Schexnayder has credited his success to the support he receives from his Ordinary, Bishop John Cummins, and from the Superintendent of Catholic Schools, he told a New Ways Ministry conference, but he worried about what would happen in a few years when Bishop Cummins retires. "We want to make sure they are institutionalized in the parishes so we can't be marginalized by a new bishop," he remarked.

The Diocese of Oakland's Task Force, headed by Fr. Schexnayder, does not even pretend to respect Church teaching on sexuality. A January, 1996 flyer sent to participants described an upcoming series of talks for the group, titled, "Making Love for the Whole World to See," by Joseph Kramer (an ex-Jesuit), described in the flyer as a "body-based theologian and massage therapist...Director of EroSpirit Research Institute – a network of lesbian and gay ecstatics exploring erotic spiritualities." The two workshops included talks by Kramer and "body meditations."

Promotional materials from EroSpirit, downloaded from the Internet, reveal that Kramer's new "ministry" involves teaching people how to masturbate and selling pornographic videos. His productions include how-to videos on masturbation and "self-anal massage for men."

- A flyer describing the Diocese of Oakland's Task Force – again, chaired by Schexnayder – distributed in parishes, schools and other locations, refers readers to the Pacific Center for Human Growth. An Internet search reveals that the group's web page includes links to radical gay groups (proudly self-described as "queer") and political groups. A list of the center's counseling groups is included on the web site. People referred to the Pacific Center by Fr. Schexnayder can attend such groups as the Married Bisexual group on Wednesdays or the Ethical Nonmonogamy support group the second Saturday of each month. On the third Sunday of each month, they can visit the group for "children of lesbians, gays, bisexuals and transgendered people." Sundays, they can attend the Pagan Recovery Support Group.

The same flyer recommends such books as *Coming Out to Your Parents* published by Parents and Friends of Lesbians and Gays, and *A Challenge to Love* by Fr. Robert Nugent. Citing long-discarded Kinsey statistics, the flyer claims "ten percent of the human population is lesbian and gay." No mention is made of the immorality of homosexual activity or of the possibility of psychological treatment.

- Local Catholic activists who attended the conference of the Bay Area Network of Gay and Lesbian Educators (BANGLE) held at Holy Names College in 1995 reported that Fr. Schexnayder was involved in organizing that event. A workshop at the conference about how to make Catholic schools gay-friendly held up the program at Bishop O'Dowd High School in Oakland as a model.

In honor of the event, the Holy Names College library set up a display of gay and lesbian erotic books, located in a glass case next to a statue of the Virgin Mary. In his workshop at the conference, Schexnayder joked, "There are six or seven scripture passages referring to same-sex sexual activity and there's over 600 referring to heterosexual activity. And this doesn't mean that God does not love heterosexuals; it's just that they need more supervision."

- The December, 1996 issue of the *National Monitor of Education* covered the October 26, 1996 second annual BANGLE conference and described the award given by the group to the Diocese of Oakland, represented by Fr. Schexnayder. Said the award presenter, "I think the Diocese of Oakland exemplifies how people should carry out the work of the Gospel...In the Diocesan schools you might be aware there are two of them that have already established Gay-Straight alliances to support their students. All teachers in the secondary school level have been trained in the needs of gay/lesbian, bisexual, transgendered (g/l/b/t) youth, and the system has appointed Rev. Jim Schexnayder who has the responsibility to see that those schools are welcoming to their youth. This is true leadership and true ministry."

- The pamphlet for the Diocese of Oakland's High School Youth Project is titled with one of Schexnayder's characteristically long names, *High Schools as Welcoming Communities for Gay and Lesbian Youth and Their Families*. The pamphlet claims: "Many gay men and lesbians sensed something 'different' about themselves as early as age four or five. The age at which most acknowledge their homosexuality is between 14 and 16 years for males and between 16 and 19 years for females."

According to the pamphlet, the project is funded by a grant from Horizons Foundation (a Lambda Youth Project affiliate) and the Pacific Gas & Electric Fund for Lesbian and Gay Youth and Education, "in collaboration with the Diocese of Oakland Schools Department" and provides faculty and staff in-service education, education for students and families, resources for classrooms and libraries, policy making, community services, as well as individual and group counseling for gay students. A January 15, 1996 article in the *Catholic Voice* newspaper for the Diocese of Oakland, touted the Catholic schools' gay support groups. The article accepts the premise that homosexuality is a God-given orientation which must be accepted and affirmed by society. The life of Nellie Taillac, a former Carondelet

High School student who returned to the school to talk about lesbian issues at a teachers' in-service, is chronicled as an example. The article describes Taillac's difficulties growing up as being caused by lack of acceptance of her lesbianism and the fact that the parents of a girl with whom Taillac had a two-year relationship separated the girls when they discovered the nature of the girls' relationship, "nearly breaking Taillac's heart," the article says.

The article mentions the gay support groups at Moreau High School in Hayward and Bishop O'Dowd High School in Oakland, started in 1994 and 1995, respectively. The O'Dowd group, known as Gay and Lesbian Education and Affirmation (GLEA), is moderated by Fr. John Malo, a religion teacher, who also teaches the "Living and Dying" and "Christian Sexuality" classes at the school.

This, of course, is just the beginning of Schexnayder's résumé. What was interesting was his response to *The Wanderer's* exposé. He threatened legal action if the "defamation" did not stop.

Some Catholics may wonder: Where is Schexnayder's bishop? How does he allow one of his priests to do such things? The answer is that his bishop, John Cummins, ordained in 1953 for the San Francisco archdiocese and appointed bishop of Oakland in May 1977, is himself an advocate of what Schexnayder preaches.

As Mike Arata reported in *The Wanderer* (June 23, 1999), Bishop Cummins boasted of how he and the other California bishops "worked behind the scenes" to pass the "consenting adults" legislation known as AB 489 in 1975 at a meeting coordinated by Fr. Schexnayder's homosexual outreach ministry at Our Lady of Lourdes parish on June 5.

AB 489 legalized adulterous cohabitation, oral sex, and sodomy between consenting adults, and Cummins was the head of the California Catholic Conference at the time!

At the time Cummins made his boast, his own diocese – a cesspool of New Age, sexual libertinism, and liturgical abuses – was reeling from a number of high profile sex scandals: In April, the head track coach at De La Salle Catholic High School, Rico Joseph Balatti of Concord, was jailed in Martinez on charges of oral copulation and sodomy with a minor. (Contra Costa *Times*, April 23, 1999). In July, the Dignity/San Francisco chaplain, Fr. William S. Green, was sentenced to a two-year prison term after pleading guilty to oral copulation with a minor and sending pornographic material over the Internet with the intention of seducing a minor. Another priest in Oakland, Fr. Padraig Greene, of Christ the King parish in Pleasant Hill, was caught soliciting sex at a public place from an undercover cop.

Views from the gallery

In his comments to his hometown newspaper, the Rochester *Democrat & Chronicle*, Clark said *Always Our Children* reflected the desire of the bishops "to reach out to gays and lesbians and their families with love and healing in a time of pain and struggle. It is hard for me to imagine how this particular document will do anything but bring people together."

Clark's co-director of the diocesan Catholic Gay and Lesbian Family Ministry office, Mary Ellen Lopata added, "I think the biggest message (from the bishops' letter) is that it tells parents they don't have to choose between their children and the Church, and some parents feel that way."

That, too, was the message the *Associated Press'* David Briggs found in the document. His report on the pastoral opened with the line: "U.S. Catholic bishops are advising parents of gay children to put love and support of sons and daughters before Church doctrine that condemns homosexual activity."

Not all bishops agreed with Clark and his supporters. One bishop who subsequently banned the use of the document in his diocese, speaking anonymously to *The Wanderer*, commented:

"I can't imagine a more impolitic time for this document to come out, especially after the Dallas trial and so many reports about pedophile clergy…As a bishop, I'm also shocked by its release, since it comes less than a month and a half before our national meeting. Why should there be such urgency in releasing it before our entire body has a chance to discuss it? I can only conclude that the Administrative Committee was frightened by the idea of discussing this in the open, and so they pushed it out the door.

"That's disgusting – a typical example of the criminal activity they engage in."

Outrage aside, the bishop identified some of the very serious problems in the pastoral, starting with the fact that the document "is not cognizant of changes in the new Catechism" which stated that the "homosexual inclination" is "intrinsically disordered."

The most important reaction to *Always Our Children* came from Fr. John Harvey, OSFS, one of the most prominent Catholic authorities on homosexuality and the founder of Courage, a support group for men who suffer from strong same-sex attractions.

He blasted the pastoral during an October 8 interview with Mother Angelica on her EWTN cable television network, and said it did not represent Catholic teaching because it made no mention of sin and did not counsel against getting involved in same-sex relationships.

Harvey also said that he had spoken with 38 bishops who objected to the document and had promised him they would raise the issue of the pastoral at the upcoming November meeting of the U.S. bishops and ask that it be withdrawn.

Fr. Harvey, author of several books on homosexuality, including *The Homosexual Person* (Ignatius), one of the most important works on the pastoral care of homosexuals, was not consulted by the NCCB's family life office during the preparation of the pastoral.

Fr. Robert Nugent, telling Washington's premier homosexual newspaper *The Blade* that he had "reviewed" drafts of the document for the bishops prior to its publication, said he was impressed by the bishops' document because "In the face of reparative therapies and some Catholic ministers in church who deny there is homosexual orientation, the bishops are affirming this reality and asking parents to accept the reality in their children."

Other prominent activists were also pleased with the bishops' pastoral. Sister Jeannine Gramick, SSND, (who has since left her order for the Sisters of Loretto after defying the Holy See's request that she stop promoting homosexuality) described it as "very pastoral, very compassionate…It will be of great value in helping the Catholic community become more welcoming and sensitive."

Bob Miailovich, president of Dignity/USA, which agitates for Church acceptance of same-sex genital relationships, told the *National Catholic*

Reporter the pastoral was "tremendously positive" and a sign "some of our message is being heard."

Nancy Mascotte, who works for L.A. Roger Cardinal Mahony's gay and lesbian ministry office, and who is the mother of a 34-year-old gay son, told the *National Catholic Reporter*: "For the bishops to say we don't need to be ashamed, that this can even be a blessing, is a great step forward...I want my son to be able to love someone, to be loved, without the Church suggesting it's wrong. I wish the bishops would finally get their act together on that point."

In Rochester, New York, Casey and Mary Ellen Lopata, in a nearly full-page feature article on them and their bishop, Matthew Clark, in the *Democrat and Chronicle* in the Sunday feature section just days after the pastoral was released, praised the document for moving the homosexual agenda along.

Mr. Lopata observed: "The message [of the pastoral] is that love for your child is most important and don't let Church doctrine get in the way of that...The first step is to break the silence, to talk about gay and lesbian people not as 'they' but as 'we' – as people in the pews."

CHAPTER SIX

Brainstorming In Rochester:
Pushing The Gay Agenda In Schools & Parishes

One year after the 1997 meeting in Long Beach, the National Association of Catholic Diocesan Lesbian and Gay Ministries convened in Rochester, with some 250 homosexual advocates "brainstorming" to devise strategies to promote homosexuality in Church structures.

The many "interactive" seminars and workshops were revealing on several levels. Not only did they provide chancery apparats such as Sister Kay Ryan, family life director for the Diocese of Albany or Karen Rienfierd, head of adult education for the Diocese of Rochester (now in charge of "pastoral planning"), to both educate and learn from participants, but these seminars were forums where Church ministers candidly and forthrightly boasted of their dissent and dissatisfaction with Church teaching and leadership.

Speakers and listeners alike tossed out hundreds of ideas and techniques for promoting homosexuality in Church structures, from how to win approval from reluctant bishops for promoting the U.S. bishops' statement *Always Our Children*, to sensitizing parishioners to the "gay ideology" during Sunday homilies, to brainwashing "right-wing, fundamentalist" Catholics who believe sodomy is condemned in the Bible.

One of the funniest – albeit serious – ideas came from conference speaker Carl Archaki, a lay minister from the Diocese of Richmond.

He suggested plying the bishop with a couple of bourbons and then "hitting him with the agenda."

That's how he won approval from his bishop, Walter Sullivan, for a special Mass for homosexuals in his diocese.

Here's how Archaki explained the technique before his audience:

"…Because in one of our dialogues, Bishop Sullivan – he's sitting there with a little bourbon and ice to loosen him up. That always helps. 'Have a second, bishop' – and then the agenda and we hit him. And we're talking about the success of Bishop Clark's Mass and he says" – and here Archaki mocks Sullivan slurring his words as if severely drunk – "'If Matt Clark can do it, I think I'm capable of that.' (Much giggling from Archaki and laughter from the audience.)

"What a revealing! Our second Mass is for Halloween. I've already told him to prepare himself for anything." (More laughter.)

In his workshop, Archaki spoke about his efforts in the Diocese of Richmond's official gay and lesbian commission to promote the homosexual agenda in parish-based religious education programs for children, in the RCIA, in Catholic schools, in youth and campus ministry, at the Catholic teachers' biennial education congress and in the state legislature. "We have become an integral part of the diocese," he gloated.

Richmond, he said, has had great success in advancing homosexuality because the diocese is "blessed" by the leadership of Bishop Walter Sullivan over the past 28 years.

There has been controversy, however. He mentioned that when his commission distributes pro-homosexual videos, books and pamphlets at the diocesan Catholic teachers' conference, "whether the teachers like it or not," he sneered, some teachers ask, "Why are you here?"

"Why not?" Archaki blasts back.

He boasted of the Richmond diocese's gay and lesbian commission's leadership in advancing a legislative initiative to pass so-called "hate crimes" laws in Virginia.

Though Archaki regretted the proposed legislation is still in committee, the diocese's Office of Justice and Peace has embraced the legislation and made its passage a part of its broader social justice agenda during lobbying days in the capital. Even more, the diocese's Justice and Peace Office is now officially working with the state's premier gay rights lobby, Virginians for Justice.

"That's been a real success," said Archaki.

He closed his talk by quoting Fr. Peter Liuzzi, who runs Los Angeles Roger Cardinal Mahony's gay and lesbian office:

"As Peter Liuzzi says, 'We've won the war; we just haven't realized it yet.'"

Confidence

Archaki's boastfulness may not be too far off the mark.

With representatives from 58 dioceses, including 50 priests, six deacons, 19 women religious and nearly 200 other church employees – chancery bureaucrats, teachers and parish-based lay ministers – present, NACDLGM speakers spoke with confidence of their determination to change Church teaching during the 1998 meeting.

As well they should, for many of the speakers at this NACDLGM conference hold national positions. Sister Kay Ryan, family life director for the Diocese of Albany, who admitted at the conference she told her bishop, Howard Hubbard, that she doesn't accept Church teaching, is president of the National Association of Catholic Family Life Ministers. Deacon Steve Graff, who led a workshop on ways to introduce gay themes in Sunday homilies, is a member of a team writing guidelines on the diaconate for the National Conference of Catholic Bishops. And, as *The Wanderer* revealed a week prior to the NACDLGM meeting, ex-priest Marv Mich, a moral theologian on sabbatical from Rochester's St. Bernard's Institute, travels the country advising Catholic Charities staffs to allow same-sex couples to adopt children.

And despite the presence of Los Angeles Auxiliary Bishop Gabino Zavala, NACDLGM's episcopal moderator and liaison to the NCCB at the Rochester conference, none of the speakers seemed inhibited from venting their rage and anger at the "hierarchical, patriarchal" Church and real or "fundamentalist" Catholics.

Zavala, indeed, expressed his gratitude to the NACDLGM participants and approval of its agenda, telling his audience: "Look what you've done to the Church… I am full of gratitude."

In his address, Zavala – as did most speakers during this conference – paid tribute to homosexual propagandist Fr. Richard Peddicord, OP, for showing how the Catholic Church's social justice tradition and teaching opens the way for full acceptance of homosexuality by Catholics.

According to Zavala, NACDLGM members need especially to work on the conversion of those Catholics who still object to homosexuality.

"Both social justice and pastoral practice demand constancy and discipline for the followers of Jesus," he said. "Members of the Christian community need to be informed, open, generous, compassionate persons, willing to grow and be stretched. We know what happens when this is not true. We have people who have been standing outside with signs" – a reference to the protesters. "How informed are they? We know what happens if that is not the case – and this is why we need our pastoral ministers. They have to be liberated persons – those without borders who are committed to tearing down these barriers which diminish the human person and inhibit the development of the community. The disciple must be creative, interactive, and have energy for the mission and stamina for the long-haul…

"Inclusion must be taken seriously…The skill, talent, giftedness, insight and grace of gay and lesbian members of the faith community is to be called forth, welcomed, and allowed expression. And this receptivity promotes the full development of the human person, enhances the life of the community, and serves to reveal the true face of God."

Gay activists in the Church must also take the lead in special rights legislation for homosexuals, Zavala said, employing the vocabulary of the homosexual rights movement.

Into the schools

Among the most noxious speakers at the conference was Bill Kummer, from the Archdiocese of St. Paul-Minneapolis, who explained how easy it has been for him, over the past 20 years, to manipulate a Catholic archbishop, "contaminate" – his word – Catholic schools and frustrate the parents of Catholic school students.

Kummer, a self-described activist in gay, lesbian, bisexual and transgendered causes, publicly disclosed his step-by-step plan that transformed nine of the eleven Catholic high schools in the Archdiocese of St. Paul-Minneapolis into gay-friendly schools.

He's been so successful, he proudly boasted that some Catholic high schools in his archdiocese have gay student clubs, survey students on their "homophobia," publish queer newspapers, have queer literature in their libraries and even permit same-sex couples to dance at their high school proms.

In just three years under his direction, Kummer gloated, Catholic high schools have adjusted their curricula to include gay, lesbian, bisexual and transgendered ideology in most classes, including history, literature, science, religion and even math.

And if any parents of Catholic school students dare object to what he's doing, well – there's always an affirming letter from Archbishop Harry Flynn to put them in their place, he revealed.

To start, Kummer explained that the late Joseph Cardinal Bernardin's "seamless garment approach" is the best shield for advancing the homosexual agenda in Church structures and overcoming opposition from "fringe parent elements."

Kummer, who is co-founder and general coordinator of Family and Friends of Gay, Lesbian, Bisexual and Transgendered Persons in Catholic Education, which works with the archdiocese's office of Catholic Education and Formation in Ministry (as well as the pro-life office and the office for separated and divorced Catholics), conceded to his audience that opposition to the homosexualization of Catholic schools is growing, but it's still easy for school administrators to bludgeon parents who object.

And in a most revealing moment, Kummer – who serves on the Catholic Committee on Sexual Minorities and who has taught and held administrative posts in Catholic elementary and secondary schools – illustrated how he's been able to use Archbishop Flynn as a stooge for his cause.

Responding to a questioner who asked why Flynn would exempt two Catholic high schools from participating in the archdiocese's "safe staff" program – which trains administrators, faculty and staff to be gay-friendly and supportive of homosexual students – Kummer explained that "we're trying to be respectful, trying not to push too hard" lest "we be perceived as too political."

But he quickly added that "as we move along in the process with other schools, some of this will rub off [on the non-participating schools] and be kind of – in a good sense – a contaminating effect…

"If people aren't ready to embark on this, there's no sense in spinning your wheels, trying to get them to do something they're not prepared to do."

Giggling throughout his presentation, Kummer was suddenly afflicted with continuous hebephrenic laughter as he spoke of how he manipulated Archbishop Flynn and used his office to dispel parental opposition to his queer agenda for the schools:

"We don't have any real official statement at this point from the archbishop on this – other than what he told school presidents and so forth. But the way we get it – especially as we face opposition from parents – especially white, heterosexual, upper-class – you know, that whole thing – they always have to have their way at any cost – but – and the way we've tried to work with that is to get schools that are engaged in the process, for example, to write to the archbishop – and it's a kindofa way to touch base and kindof say this is what we've been doing over the past year or two, this has been a blessing for our school, yielded these benefits, these fruits and so forth and so on – and he's happy to write back and say all kinds of wonderful things in personal correspondence.

"The value of that in this stage of the process is that it's a letter that can be used appropriately. Okay?

"So, if an administrator, and often this is the case, has some parent – a delegation of parents – that come in and say, 'I just found out after this has been going on for a whole year and I'm just sick to death to hear this and I want it stopped immediately and blah, blah, blah and we're going to pull our funding' – and so forth and so on – and appropriately, that school president might take that letter out and say, 'Well, you know, the archbishop is behind this and here's a letter he just sorta wrote to me.'

"Now, some people might say that's a little backhanded kind of backwards way to do it but you've got to be creative about this and you gotta sorta use what works and anything that works use it, as long as its ethical and so forth and moral and doesn't get you caught in a corner."

This tactic – of using a contrived "personal" letter from the bishop as if it were an official document to bamboozle or demoralize any parents who might have the knowledge and courage to oppose what Kummer is doing – is a masterpiece of Alinskyite manipulation: to identify, divide, isolate and demoralize the opposition.

Another tactic Kummer suggested is to have a chancery official at school meetings where the gay agenda will be introduced.

One of the "pivotal" and "controversial" events Kummer described was held in November 1997, at which members of all the high school boards were present, in the midst of rising parental ire at the intrusion of the homosexual agenda in their schools, along with vicar general Fr. Kevin McDonough.

"The archbishop was not there," Kummer related. "I don't know where he was that night. But the vicar general was there, and the vicar general, I might tell you, is generally very supportive of what we are doing in our archdiocese, but all he managed to try to get out that night was celibacy. That's all he kept talking about, was celibacy," – and here, mocking the vicar general in an inebriated voice, laughing uncontrollably, Kummer spit out: "It's very important to maintain celibacy."

Pleased with himself and bursting with laughter, Kummer continued:

"And so, you know, people kept questioning that through the evening – 'Well, but I thought the point of this was' – not so much – I mean, we all agree that sexual abstinence, particularly for adolescents – is a very, very good thing for obvious, for obvious reasons.

"So we were kinda looking past that and saying but isn't the point of this safe schools? Isn't that really the point that we're trying to really promote here, a climate, or an environment that fosters not only safe schools – safe schools for everybody, but also the kinda climate that can be affirming, inclusive and so forth regardless of anybody's sexual orientation or sexual identity.

"But it didn't really matter: the reason I share this with you is because the long and short of it is that it didn't matter what the vicar general said: the very fact he was there people took as permission to go ahead. That's the lesson of that particular event."

What "going ahead" means

Of all the presentations at the Rochester NACDLGM conference, Kummer's was, far and away, the most explicit in detail on how gay activists employ dirty tricks and subterfuge to achieve their goals.

Kummer's project began three years earlier, he explained, when Catholic schools in the archdiocese were suddenly faced with a large number of adolescents announcing their "coming out."

"A lot of people threw up their hands. There were no policies, no procedures. Presidents were getting alarmed. In one school 23 kids presented themselves [as gay]. The presidents met with the archbishop who decided there needed to be some sort of official response," Kummer said, as he detailed, how, with the assistance of Sr. Mary Gevelinger, OP, director of personnel and placement for archdiocesan schools, he managed to manipulate and take over the first "study group" of school presidents, and then push his gay agenda.

He revealed how the first group was composed of "impassioned straight persons" and "impassioned GLBT persons," who could not work together, necessitating the need for a "community based resource" to help members work together. Kummer then seized control over the crisis, and began implementing his gay schools agenda.

1. "Present the accurate and full teaching of the Catholic Church because many people reduce that to three paragraphs in the Catechism and we all know there's much more than that."

2. "Provide a respectful and faithful position that unites the archdiocese through the Archbishop, the Catholic Education and Formation in Ministry office and community groups," i.e. homosexual activist groups.

3. Develop a "strategy to respond to express needs, i.e. kids presenting themselves."

Kummer then told how his organization, the Family and Friends of Gay, Lesbian, Bisexual, Transgendered Persons in Catholic Education, was accepted as a full partner with the school personnel and the archdiocese.

The study group then declared its agenda: full faculty in-service programs to sensitize teachers to homosexual issues.

Immediately, some faculty objected because they sensed the materials they were instructed with contradicted Church teaching. Other teachers wanted to know why they had to receive this instruction.

"The response we were tempted to make," Kummer said, "was 'the archbishop said so,' though we didn't like to because sometimes an appeal to authority can backfire." In some schools, he continued, where as many as one-third of the teachers are evangelical, a lot of teachers wanted to opt out because they didn't want to get involved.

For faculty and staff who attended the meetings, Kummer's job was "to bring people up to speed on Church teaching. A lot of people have a time-warp on this issue – the Church of the '50s – that's where they left off and so that's what they brought to the table – what it said in the Baltimore Catechism – or 'I always thought this was a choice' – so there was a slow and painstaking process of providing training opportunities."

Payback

Kummer's commitment paid off, and his first great achievement was developing and implementing an "inclusive curriculum."

"That means we take the gay, lesbian, bisexual and transgendered experience and find ways to write that into the curriculum," he explained. In this project, "we don't write the curriculum and say 'do it.' We are part of a process and offer it as part of a program for literature, art, religion and history…It gets really interesting when you get to the basics. Math teachers have told me how they've included it in math programs…"

An example he cited is: If a certain city has such-and-such a population, and x percent is gay and x percent is lesbian and x percent is bisexual and x percent is transgendered, what is the total percentage of people who are GLBT?

The next step was to form a core group of teachers who would sign up for ten hours of training to be "safe school staff." The course was titled GLBT 101 and had a 250-page training manual with "lots and lots of handouts" designed to help teachers understand and learn "coming out strategies" for GLBT youth, family issues, family dynamics, cultural and professional issues and "pastoral practices."

Next, the study group defined its "operating principles":

First, it must provide "story-telling" opportunities for gay and lesbian students in Catholic schools and provide a safe and affirming environment for such students.

Second: it must respect the "culture and climate" of each school. "What you can get away with in one school isn't what you can get away with in another school," Kummer said. For example, in some schools it is accepted that gay students can attend the prom together, but in others it would not go over well.

Third: "empower families and students to be advocates for themselves."

Fourth: "The process must involve the entire school community," and the benefit here is that it "relieves general tensions that exist around the issue of sexuality and reduces the level of homophobia; it frees a lot of our students to think much more broadly about such things as gender role stereotyping – that's something that effects a lot of straight people, too."

Since his project began, there have been many successes, including: a student-written publication, "The Rainbow Journey" which focuses on gay and lesbian student issues; "liturgies celebrating diversity," commissioning rituals for safe-staff; "lots and lots of articles and op-ed pieces in school newspapers," one of which, "Is God Homophobic?" was "a real barn-burner…a lightning rod for discussion in the parishes"; "protocols for restorative justice," i.e. a "process that tries to bring offender and victim together"; a zero tolerance or anti-slur policy which mandates that any student who makes an anti-gay remark will be severely disciplined; a support group for GLBT students; student diversity committees in schools, some of which conduct surveys on homophobic attitudes; teen retreats for GLBT students; anti-discrimination policies that allow same-sex couples to attend school proms; the formation of GLBT alumni groups to come into the schools to talk about their coming out experiences; and the influx of gay reading material into school libraries and media centers.

Kummer concluded his talk by explaining that parents will often become irate if they are told such programs are planned for the school, so it is always important to put them in place before informing parents.

For exposing Kummer's talk and his connections in the Archdiocese of St. Paul/Minneapolis, *The Wanderer* was denounced for conducting a "reign of terror against anyone who disagrees with their understanding of Catholic doctrine" in the archdiocesan newspaper, *The Spirit.*

Since that exposé, however, the archdiocese's Catholic Pastoral Committee on Sexual Minorities has continued in community lobbying for "gays, lesbians, bisexuals and transgendered persons," expanded its work to rural communities such as St. Cloud, Duluth, New Ulm, Rochester, Little Falls, Marshall, and River Falls, bonded with Catholic Charities to promote homosexuality and in May 1999, in recognition of its leadership role in the state, the Sisters of St. Joseph of Carondelet, St. Paul Province, made an unrestricted gift of $100,000.00 to CPCSM in support of its ministry.

Round-up of other talks

Even though there were no ground-breaking, creative or original thoughts expressed at this NACDLGM conference, this Rochester meeting was highly significant in several respects:

- It showed that "queer theology" has reached its completion as a composite of psycho-babble and pseudo-theology, cemented by the language of dissent.

- It showed the anti-apostolic spirit of homosexual activists who, despite their aged, enervated, debilitated and often sick appearance, are determined to be missionaries for a "queer church" – and have the support of at least 58 bishops.

- It provided irrefutable evidence of how the pontificate of John Paul II has been rejected by Bishop Matthew Clark and his top theologians, starkly illustrated by Rochester priest Robert Kennedy's lament the Church needs to develop a "biblical theology of creation…about what our sexuality means" – apparently unaware Pope John Paul II began his pontificate with a most comprehensive commentary on Genesis and the theology of the body and the meaning of sexuality.

- It demonstrated that Clark's chancery apparat – his top officials – are determined to deceive Catholics about Church teaching, exemplified by the "pastoral" advice Sister Kay Heverin, SSJ, "pastoral associate" at St. Mary's Church gave one conference participant: "To be faithful to your conscience, you need to break the [Church's] law."

- It illustrated the consequences of 20 years of institutionalized dissent, and the nasty intolerance for authoritative Church teaching by some of Rochester's most prominent priests, religious and laity.

- It proved homosexual activists working in Church structures are rabid in their determination to impose their ideology on parishes and schools, as Rochester Catholic Libby Ford – a partnered-lesbian and artificially-inseminated mother – showed when she exhorted her peers with children in Catholic schools or religion programs to insist children receive "no negative messages" about homosexuality – in effect, making children shills for the gay rights movement in the Church.

Despite Rochester Bishop Matthew Clark's fierce public declarations that all speakers at NACDLGM's conference were good Catholics and NACDLGM "is a legitimate group, loyal to magisterial teaching, with an official liaison to the National Conference of Catholic Bishops," each of the major presenters delivered addresses that repudiated and ridiculed Church teaching.

Marching behind Christa

And when the conference closed with a Mass presided over by Bishop Matthew Clark (his master of ceremonies was Joan Workmaster, who directs his Office of Worship and assisted him at the altar), Clark thanked all the participants "for a most significant conference."

The Mass opened with Bishop Clark processing behind a cross bearing the figure of Christa, a partially-draped female Jesus, accompanied by dancers festooned in ribbons, two females and a male.

"It is a joy to celebrate our liturgy at St. Mary's Church," Clark told the congregation of 600 in his homily.

"In this most privileged moment of this most significant conference, we come here to pray for vision, for wisdom, for courage and commitment for ourselves and the whole Church in our work for inclusion and pastoral care for our gay and lesbian sisters and brothers as an integral part and cherished part of our life.

"It is good for us this night to keep what we're doing in perspective. Not too many years ago, such an event as this was unheard of. No such groups as gay and lesbian family ministries existed in dioceses around the country, much less was there a…NACDLGM, too long ago. And something like *Always our Children* and earlier documents in support of that were a far-off dream.

"I cannot tell you how happy I am that the utter silence of my youth – and most of yours – about this issue, has been broken. Tonight we need to thank all those who have gone before us who have patiently and courageously planted the seeds that have yielded such growth – theologians, biblical scholars, experts in the human sciences who have studied and shared their findings with us, gay and lesbian persons, their parents and all of their loved ones who have had the courage to speak their experiences and share their pain and hopes with us, pastoral ministers who have stood by both and done their very best, sometimes at great personal cost to mediate and encourage the absorption of these findings, these experiences into the heart of the Church's life. All of these and many more we cannot name tonight have done us tremendous service. We should remember and celebrate them as we gather tonight.

"Much of what I've mentioned, and a whole lot more, were summarized and or catalyzed by Vatican Council II. That Council renewed our vision of who we are as a people, how we are to treat, and relate to one another, how we can and should deal with complex – even volatile – issues in our community of faith. The Council is the recent seminal event without which our gathering tonight would be inconceivable."

While acknowledging how far the Church has come, as evidenced by the NACDLGM conference, a sign of how much work remains, Clark said, was the presence of some 100-plus protesters outside St. Mary's, demonstrating against his NACDLGM Mass.

"The presence of protesters outside our Church, the questions of good people for whom this is still very, very new – all from our same faith family – keeps in perspective how far we have yet to go."

The speakers Clark praised

Keynote speaker Fr. Richard Peddicord, O.P., prior and professor of moral theology at the Aquinas Institute in St. Louis, was introduced by Fr. Peter Liuzzi, O.Carm, director of the Archdiocese of Los Angeles' ministry to gay and lesbians and their families, who remarked that both he and Peddicord belong to religious orders which were founded at a time when the Church "couldn't deal with people on the fringe."

Peddicord delivered the identical speech he gave in March 1997 at the New Ways Ministry conference in Pittsburgh, a fact which he acknowledged when he mentioned that "much of what you'll hear you've heard before. I'm preaching to the choir...but preaching to the choir is not a bad thing."

Not only did he preach the same message, he preached it to the same New Ways Ministry/Dignity/P-FLAG/NACDLGM audience that gathered in Pittsburgh – though two-thirds smaller.

His talk was on the "studied ambiguity" of the U.S. hierarchy on the issue of legislation conferring special rights for homosexuals, along with a frontal attack on the 1986 and 1992 statements on homosexuality issued by the Congregation for the Doctrine of the Faith.

After acknowledging the intellectual debts he owed to his late mentor, the queer propagandist Fr. Andre Guindon of St. Paul University, Ottawa (who was ordered by the Vatican to retract the statements he published in his book *The Sexual Creators*, and who died suddenly after refusing), and to Sister Jeannine Gramick, SSND and Fr. Robert Nugent, SDS, for their inspiration, he tore into Church teaching.

His major thrust was an attack on the Catholic position that discrimination against homosexuals in housing or certain employment positions is morally licit, and he supported his assertions with reference to Vatican II's *Declaration on Religious Liberty*:

"If, for instance, as Vatican II will teach, one accepts the right of people to follow their conscience, on such an important matter of their religious affiliation and practice, it follows very, very powerfully, it seems to me, one should be free from social or governmental interference in terms of a conscientious decision to enter into an intimate relationship with a member of the same sex.

"In other words, if the Church teaches authoritatively that the adherents of all of the world's religions ought not to face discrimination because of their beliefs or practices, by what logic are gays and lesbians subject to discrimination?

"The Decree on Religious Liberty accepts the proposition that – all things being equal – one should not lose one's job for denying the divinity of Christ, and that one ought not lose one's lease for failing to keep the Sabbath holy. Does it not follow that people ought not to face penalties for denying, theoretically, or in practice, that the sharing of sexual intimacy is only licit between a man and a woman in marriage?

"From the vantage of the Church's teaching on human dignity, human rights and the dignity of the human conscience, Gregory Baum [a former Augustinian priest who served as an "expert" at the Second Vatican Council for Archbishop Philip Pocock of Toronto] writes: 'Even if Catholics are convinced that homosexual love is unethical, justice demands that they defend the human and civil rights of gay people.'"

The first question after the Dominican's talk came from Frank DiBernardo, executive director of New Ways Ministry, who asked if Peddicord could agree with Fr. Gerald Coleman, rector of St. Patrick Seminary in the Archdiocese of San Francisco, who believes that the Church could support domestic partnerships.

"Fr. Coleman's instinct is one I would share," he answered, explaining: "In terms of a pluralistic society, we've decided – as a Church – that there is not a hierarchy of principles that are important to uphold…We don't insist everything in Catholic tradition be codified and we would be fools if we thought we could or should…"

Exemplifying the bravado some participants have in mocking "straight" society and their ordinaries, Sister Barbara Regan of the Archdiocese of New York reflected: "I have lesbian friends who when they embrace say, 'Oh! We've just wrecked a marriage in Kansas!'"

After the laughter died, she asked Peddicord if there were anything in Catholic moral theology "that I missed in Divinity School" to explain why the late John Cardinal O'Connor of New York would oppose homosexual rights legislation in New York City.

Peddicord, who looks like the devil without a tail, smirked and said: "psychological fear." But, he said, that has nothing to do with moral theology, rather it is the fear that "sexual orientation is so fluid and changeable" that "everybody will jump on the bandwagon. This is a question for sociologists and psychologists."

An observation was offered by Sister Jeannine Gramick, SSND, who accurately observed many more bishops have supported homosexual legislation than have opposed, citing, as examples, the bishops of California, Minnesota and Florida; but their support is not as well-known as Cardinal O'Connor's opposition because he knows how to generate publicity.

The final question pertained to the respect a Catholic should give the Holy See's Congregation for the Doctrine of the Faith's statements.

"We have to *not* rely on them as mature Christians," Peddicord answered emphatically.

Celebrating queer relationships

Deacon Jim Campbell, from the Diocese of Oakland's Task Force for Outreach to Gay & Lesbian Communities & Their Families (and Director of Religious Education, K-12, for his parish) spoke about the beauty, honesty and superiority of same-sex relationships, how much he has learned from gays in unions, and why it is important for the Church to bless them.

Deacon Campbell, who recently had, in his words, his "wrists slapped" by his bishop, John Cummins, because his blessing of same-sex unions became a public scandal, believes that God exists in a special way in the gay community, "especially if gays are in relationship."

In his view, neither Scripture nor Tradition are "definitive" when trying to understand same-sex relationships, and Campbell assured his listeners that the Church will inevitably find a way to bless such unions. Even though such unions are unprecedented in the Church, he said, that is no reason why God cannot work "outside His own precedents" to make them happen.

"We need to get the word out that God's activity for the whole Church is being given prophetic voice in the gay community," he said, adding that this voice is leading to new "discussions" and understandings about sanctification, holiness and grace.

"It's clear the Church cannot say 'yes' to what Paul in 1 Corinthians 7 refers to as sexual immorality," he said. "The Church can only say 'yes' to that which builds up the Church and its members. The question then is: Is it possible for a covenantal gay friendship to demonstrate sanctification? I claim that it is."

The bulk of Campbell's address was a description of the same-sex blessings he performs as a deacon in Oakland, and how those who favor blessing homosexual unions can "push the envelope."

He advised those who might bless same-sex unions to avoid "sloppy talk" so people are not alarmed, but he also advised: "The word 'blessing' puts us on thin ice…but not to be on thin ice is to play it so safe as to be meaningless to the couple and the potential meaning for the People of God in their community and so we did take the risk…"

Even though the Bishop Cummins has asked that priests and deacons not "bless" homosexual relationships, Campbell revealed, "some pastors are continuing to do blessings in private homes with a small number of witnesses...This also raises issues: Let's get into this, let's tell the truth to each other...Okay, this was a dumb thing to do. What could we have done that provides, as heterosexual marriage does, sign value to the community, is of value to the couple, and sanctifies the Church?

"I am absolutely convinced that there is a way to do that publicly but we need to really prepare ourselves and the community before we push again – at least in our area."

Clark's in-house wrecking crew

Among the line-up of speakers at this NACDLGM conference were three men who exemplify and epitomize the advance of the homosexual agenda in the Diocese of Rochester: Ex-priest Marvin Mich, on sabbatical from his position as professor of moral theology at St. Bernard's Institute (Clark's theologate); Fr. Robert J. Kennedy, professor of liturgy at St. Bernard's Institute, and Monroe County Family Court Judge Anthony Sciolino.

Though not "plenary" speakers, Mich, Sciolino and Kennedy are three of Clark's biggest guns in blasting away at both Church teaching and ordinary Catholic family life in the Diocese of Rochester.

Mich, who has degrees from the Archdiocese of Milwaukee's St. Francis Seminary and the Alphonsianum (Lateran University) in Rome, is a nationally-known pioneer working in Catholic circles to facilitate the adoption of children by homosexual couples.

He spoke of the work he has done for Catholic Charities, in both Rochester and nationally, in persuading Catholic Charities staff to understand the importance of following state non-discrimination laws, rather than Church teaching, in the placement of adoptees in the homes of same-sex couples.

His presentation consisted of a critique of the 1992 *Some Considerations* letter on homosexuality produced by the Congregation for the Doctrine of the Faith (CDF), and sent to all the bishops of North America, and which called on the bishops to oppose special rights legislation for homosexuals, then making progress in most state legislatures.

105

Mich repeatedly dismissed this letter as a "memo" and an "internal memo" that "was never meant to go public," and said it was a statement which "concluded that discrimination is justified because it would endanger the heterosexual family…

"I have some criticisms of this document. If you don't buy mine, there's others," he cracked, mentioning Fr. Richard Peddicord's and Gramick's and Nugent's.

His main objections to the document, he said, were: "the people who put the memo together have not followed thoroughly our Roman Catholic moral tradition," "have not used resources adequately," and are "kind of stepping around the inside of our moral tradition to defend the sexual ethic as they understand it…

"That's a pretty strong indictment," Mich continued. The CDF document, he maintained, "uses natural law in a fixed way. It views sexuality in terms of the animal world, pro-creation…When we look at peace and economics, we look at natural law in a different way. We stress more the order of reason, that humanity has the gift of reason. And we trust more in human experience and reason.

"As a moral theologian, I step back and say: Why do we have two systems? Why are there two different yardsticks. This is understandable from a medieval perspective…but the order of reason should predominate."

Judge Sciolino, who was just recently ordained a deacon by Bishop Matthew Clark, is a former Mich student and the first Family Court Judge in New York State to grant adoption rights to an artificially-inseminated lesbian (Libby Ford) and her partner.

He explained both the legal status of homosexuals' adoption rights in New York, why homosexual couples are often preferable to heterosexual couples (they are more loving, caring, stable, etc.) and how much he learned from Mich.

He mentioned that he went "through the process of evaluating the '92 [CDF] letter" with Mich, who helped him conclude that a "well-formed conscience would justly demur the need to discriminate."

Since his ground-breaking judicial decision on homosexual adoption, Sciolino said, "we've gone from something heroic to a ho-hummer. It's accepted. That's how it goes in Church and society." The progress has been so rapid, he gloated, that in November [1998], Rochester would host a conference on adoption, with one presentation on "Lesbian Perspectives" in adoptions.

"Same sex adoption is now routine in New York," he said, "so routine that one judge says there is no need to treat homosexual couples and heterosexuals separately; that there is no need to do anything out of the ordinary."

After detailing why the courts accept the reality – if not the preference – of homosexual adoption, Sciolino said he learned from Mich that "a well-formed conscience could dissent from the CDF statement," and he parted with a shot at the Church for *not* being counter-cultural enough to accept same-sex adoptions.

In the question and answer session, the aunt of Libby Ford wondered why the Church allows the baptism of children in same-sex unions in practice but not in teaching (Libby Ford was the Mich-Sciolino seminar facilitator and the artificially-inseminated lesbian mother in Judge Sciolino's ground-breaking case).

How is it, the aunt asked, the Church "says one thing and lives another?"

Moral theologian Mich answered: "It takes time for Church teaching to evolve. We have to be patient with an institution when it is inconsistent," and he noted gleefully a number of bishops "completely disagree with the Vatican...There are cracks in the wall," and the "natural process of the Church learning from the people" is underway.

"On moral questions," Sciolino offered, "when you study with Marv [Mich] you learn there is a process for checking...Checking out Scripture, checking out the Magisterium, checking out lived experience, checking out social sciences...

"You can come to an informed decision that it is okay to dissent from this particular [1992 CDF] document – that it's okay to discriminate against gays and lesbians. So for me it was a good exercise because I was able to reaffirm what I did as a judge and I was able to do it as a good Catholic...

"Thank God I'm in the Diocese of Rochester."

Fr. Robert J. Kennedy, associate professor of liturgy at St. Bernard's, co-ordinator of student formation, editor of "Reconciling Embrace:

Foundations for the Future of Sacramental Reconciliation" (Liturgy Training Publications), and a team member of the Re-Membering Church Institute sponsored by the North American Forum on the Catechumenate, spoke on "Finding Ways to Reconciliation."

Many in his audience were St. Bernard's students, so Kennedy's talk was filled with self-deprecating and self-revealing humor, as when he elaborated on "healthy human development...

"I am trying to figure out who am I and what makes me tick. People help us do what healthy people do, keep on growing, maturing...Here I am in mid-life. I wonder when I will get to mature adulthood."

Then he mused: "Is the Church on the side of healthy, human integration? Do we promote in all of our efforts – religious education, liturgical celebrations, pastoral ministry in all its forms – Do we promote the healthy development of the human person?

"Certainly our social teachings – before you quickly say no, look at how dysfunctional we all are – um – the um – certainly look at our teaching but always take a deeper look – always not just a knee-jerk kind of thing – and I'm not letting the Church off the hook because there's a lot of dysfunctionality to be found even when you take a different look..."

Throughout nearly an hour of this kind of pseudo-psycho/pseudo-theological babble, Kennedy tried to discern five phases in a "conversion process" which, in secular parlance, translated into five steps for "coming out" or accepting homosexuality as a legitimate lifestyle.

In Phase 3, "Deciding to live into the new life," Kennedy explained the importance of imagination. "We need imagination to live in new life...Our imagination needs to have stories of Scripture...the way they speak to the heart and the heart of the community...

"Throwing at people a Catechism, throwing at people Church doctrine, throwing at people Canon Law – that's not imaginative literature. I've tried reading that Catechism, and I keep doing it – okay? And I'm not saying all that literature is not important. It has its place in our life – okay? But when we are dealing right at the core of peoples' beings it has to be a much more imaginative, poetic kind of literature...

"The great story of how God is walking among a beloved people...What if we simply developed a biblical theology of creation and then thought about what our sexuality means? By that I don't mean procreation, but just that God made us and formed us and found us very good, by the way, but made us sexual beings?

"Unfortunately, a great deal of the Western Christian tradition has taken a very negative read on that and not been faithful to the biblical tradition of creation…I could do a whole course on that."

He continued by explaining how rich the 2000 year tradition of Christianity is, but complained that some people limit it to just what the Magisterium says in the 20th century. "It's like having a cupboard full of food and you only offer the saltines."

CHAPTER SEVEN

The Depth Of The Crisis:
Looking North

One thing that became increasingly clear as the 1990s drew to a close was the depth of the problem of clerical sexual abuse. While the American bishops and their bureaucrats accelerated their educational initiatives, and more and more cases of clerical pedophilia came to light, at the same time, gay activists accelerated their legislative agenda for special rights – such as domestic partnership benefits, adoption rights, etc., and found little or no opposition from the Catholic Church.

What was happening in the United States was almost a mirror-image of what happened in Canada years earlier, and to understand the depth and scope of the problem in the United States, one must look at what happened in Canada in April 1996 – at the same time as Canada's Catholic bishops went limp before an onslaught of special rights legislation for homosexuals went through both houses of Parliament.

Through the 1980s and 1990s, the Canadian Church was rocked by one large-scale sexual abuse scandal after another, but the largest by far was the "Alfred case" named after St. Joseph's Training School in Alfred, Ontario, in the Archdiocese of Ottawa, which erupted into public view during the plenary assembly of the Canadian Conference of Catholic Bishops in August 1990.

The *dramatis personae* and the bizarre twists and tragic turns in this case would defy the imagination of the most creative novelist, proving once again that the truth is far stranger, and often more crushingly disappointing, than fiction.

Alfred recap

Briefly, the "Alfred case" involved more than 500 men who claimed they were physically and sexually abused in two Ontario reform schools run by the Brothers of the Christian Schools (an order separate from the Christian Brothers who ran the Mt. Cashel orphanage in Newfoundland, where similar problems erupted a decade earlier). By 1992, some 300 of these men formed "Helpline," demanding compensation from the Ottawa branch of the Brothers, the Government of Ontario, and the Archdioceses of Toronto and Ottawa. Between 1990 and 1992, nearly 200 charges, ranging from buggery to assault, were laid against 29 members and former members of the Brothers of the Christian Schools. In August 1992, Catholic leaders and the government proposed a $16-million compensation package demanding that ex-students sign a waiver promising never to sue, and end the investigation. The victims refused to sign.

Among those eventually convicted by a jury was "Fr. Joseph," Lucien Dagenais, 67, known as "The Hook," of 15 counts of physical and sexual assault of students at the school. During the 5-week trial, Albert Daigneault, then 50, testified that in April 1954, he was beaten by a goon squad, handcuffed, stripped naked, held in solitary confinement and sexually assaulted almost daily.

The case came to the attention of the public through the efforts of one David McCann, a former resident at Alfred, sent there in 1956 after committing six "break and enters" in a week-and-a-half. Subsequent testimony by McCann and others revealed that McCann has great difficulty separating truth from fiction, and he suffers from an inability to tell the truth.

But in August 1990, two years before the public heard the story, McCann appeared at the Weston Hotel in Ottawa where the bishops were holding their plenary session, and charged up and down the hallways singing a little ditty implicating one of Canada's cardinals in a pedophilia scandal. McCann spoke freely about what he knew to any reporter who would listen, and apparently he was granted great credence by the bishops, who agreed to meet with him promptly.

After meeting with three bishops, McCann was told he would be welcome to participate on a committee investigating sexual abuse in the Catholic Church.

His revelations about sexual abuse at St. Joseph's in Alfred led to an investigation covering a period from the 1930s to the 1970s, when the Brothers ran the training center as an agent for the government.

It quickly led to further revelations and investigations, and the formation of a victims' association, Helpline, with McCann as chairman.

To manage the "reconciliation process" and in an apparent effort to prevent civil lawsuits, the archbishops of Ottawa and Toronto and the Christian Brothers hired Douglas Roche, one of Canada's pre-eminent Catholic laymen and the ultimate insider in the Church, the Federal Government, the United Nations, UNICEF, and various other international bodies such as the World Conference on Religion and Peace, Parliamentarians for World Order, and the North-South Roundtable and Society for International Development, to chair the Reconciliation Process Implementation Committee.

Roche, then 66, diplomat, ambassador for disarmament and member of Parliament, began his career as a journalist in Ottawa in 1949. After various newspaper jobs in Montreal and Toronto, he went into the Catholic press as a reporter and columnist for the Diocese of Cleveland's *Catholic Universe Bulletin*. He was editor of the now defunct *Sign* magazine from 1958-65, and then became founding editor of the *Western Catholic Reporter*, where he served as Canada's mouthpiece for the IDOC-Consilium liberal/modernist faction in the Church.

The author of several books, such as *The Catholic Revolution* (1968) and *In the Eye of the Catholic Storm*, written with prominent dissenters such as Sister Mary Jo Leddy and Bishop Remi de Roo, Roche is one of Canada's foremost critics of Catholic teaching on contraception and homosexuality.

He is also Canada's most prominent disciple of Teilhard de Chardin and a close personal friend of former U.N. assistant Secretary-General, Robert Muller, the world's leading proponent of global education and a new "global religion" based on Buddhist respect for the earth.

Roche's job was to negotiate the compensation for the victims, and almost exactly two years after the Alfred case exploded into public view, he announced the "settlement," prepared with the help of Helpline's attorney, Roger Tucker, on August 14, 1992.

Tucker, incidentally, was Roche's son-in-law when he was appointed to craft the agreement, though today he is now Roche's ex-son-in-law.

The $16 million settlement called for the Province of Ontario to give $6 million, since it had received allegations of physical and sexual abuse beginning in the early '60s; $5.9 million from the Christian Brothers in Ottawa; and $290,000 from the Archdiocese of Toronto and $250,000 from the Archdiocese of Ottawa.

The "Helpline Reconciliation Model Agreement" also stipulated the Christian Brothers in Toronto would kick in $3 million, but the Toronto brothers never signed the agreement, charging it was unfair since the bulk of the abuse took place in Ottawa, and they didn't trust David McCann.

The average settlement was supposed to be approximately $10,000 to each abuse victim, which would be distributed by a "special committee" composed of members of the government and Church groups. In addition, the Christian Brothers were to "top off" the award, essentially doubling it to $20,000.

Also, the "agreement" set up an "opportunity fund" to provide medical and dental coverage, job training, literacy and other educational services. A special counseling service was also established, and a special "recorder" was provided, at $93,000 per year, to record the history of the scandal in lieu of a public inquiry.

For the nearly 500 victims, the award was peanuts.

But Roche worked a miracle for the Church. Included in the agreement – in addition to the legal provision of benefits for non-family members of the victims (i.e., "domestic partners") – was a provision that no names of alleged abusers would be made public, "unless they have publicly confessed or have been convicted" and the Church got off by paying a mere pittance.

Then, nearly four years later, in April 1996, CBC-TV investigative reporter Simon Gardiner revealed on a nationally-broadcast program that claims have still not yet been paid to many of the victims, though Roche's lawyer/son-in-law and his firm received $750,000 for their legal work.

Roche would not divulge his salary for heading the reconciliation committee. But Gardiner's exposé focused primarily on the incredible gauntlet the victims were run through. Since the settlement "agreement" was announced four years earlier, at least 30 of the sexual abuse victims had committed suicide, with one of the suicides known to have been committed out of desperation because the agreement was not being expeditiously settled.

In the subsequent years, other sexual abuse victims were left to deal with their overwhelming psychological and emotional problems on their own. One of the major complaints victims made against Roche was that, not only was he inaccessible, but that he cut the victims' contact with higher level officials.

From his first day on the job, the report makes clear, Roche's job was to minimize the cost to the dioceses, prevent full disclosure of the extent of the crimes, and hang the victims "out to dry."

The Preying Liturgists

On April 2, 2000, the *Ottawa Citizen* informed the general public that one of Canada's most prominent liturgists, a priest who had taught in Canadian seminaries for nearly 40 years and was presently teaching at St. Paul University in Ottawa, was being sued for sexually abusing altar boys.

"The Rev. Barry Glendinning, a retired Catholic priest who lives in Toronto and teaches a summer course in liturgy at Saint Paul," reported *The Citizen*, "is the target of a civil law suit based on alleged incidents of sexual abuse between 1968 and 1974 in London, Ont... ."

Two months earlier, *The Wanderer* raised the issue of Glendinning's assignment at St. Paul's, based on a tremendous amount of investigative work by Ottawa resident Sylvia MacEachern, editor of *The Orator*, an independent Catholic newsletter.

MacEachern, perhaps the most competent and determined Canadian writer probing the extent of pedophilia in the Canadian Church, spoke with Glendinning's victims and, unlike others, began a meticulous search for those names connected to Glendinning's in the liturgical establishment.

On February 17, 2000, *The Wanderer* published "Canadian Journalist Charges: Liturgical Renewal Has Been Run By Sexual Liberationists," one of the first among a number of subsequent reports which would clarify the role of homosexuals and pedophiles in the deconstruction of the Catholic Mass.

Certainly there had been prior indications this was the case: In "Requiem for A Liturgist: Endgame Dissent At Notre Dame," E. Michael Jones (*Fidelity*, January 1988), reported on the suicide of one of Notre Dame's top liturgists, Fr. Neils K. Rasmussen, O.P., who was found by South Bend police, dressed in his leathers, with a bullet through his chest. The 53-year-old Danish Dominican, was, wrote Jones, a "world-class liturgist," having picked up his doctorate at the Institut Catholique in Paris in 1978. His suicide note indicated there was to be no Catholic funeral Mass. Rasmussen, Jones discovered, had been living in a sadomasochistic fantasy world.

Six years later, on January 6, 1994, *The Wanderer* disclosed, on the eve of his appearance at Roger Cardinal Mahony's annual religious education congress, that Buffalo priest Fr. John Aurelio, the nation's foremost promoter of "children's liturgies," was a pedophile.

Aurelio, a star on the religious education circuit who had received the Catholic Press Association's top honor for his work on children's fairy tales, who was famous for wearing his "Raggedy Ann" vestments at Masses, who was the subject of a 1978 CBS television special, admitted that he and his best friend, Fr. Bernard Mach, had sodomized 12-14 year-old boys after plying them with alcohol and drugs. At the time he made his confession, Aurelio was spiritual director of seminarians at the Diocese of Buffalo's Christ the King Seminary.

Another prominent liturgist is Fr. Gerald Shirilla, a.k.a. "Shirilla the Gorilla" when he ruled as director of the Archdiocese of Detroit Worship Department. Known as a strong enforcer of progressive liturgical norms, he once told a reporter that as far as the traditionalists who wanted the Latin Mass go, "You have to fight them every inch of the way." He gave frequent talks in parishes and his star shined brightly when he planned the papal Mass for 90,000 worshipers at the Silverdome when Pope John Paul II visited Michigan.

But Shirilla was abruptly fired – actually given "administrative leave" – from both his worship department post and his teaching job at Sacred Heart Seminary when a lawsuit was filed against him for sexual abuse in 1993. His victims included two brothers, one a seminarian, from a family of twelve children in a devout Catholic family.

According to press accounts at the time, Shirilla was a pedophile who called altar boys out of their classrooms in the 1970s at Our Lady of Loretto parish, where he was an associate pastor. Complaints were lodged against him for sexual involvement with seminary students in 1973 and again in 1980.

No criminal charges were filed against him and the civil lawsuit was thrown out of court in 1999 due to Michigan's statute of limitations.

Shirilla's whereabouts were unknown to the public until the Detroit Free Press reported on March 2, 2002 that he had been transferred to another parish in another diocese. He is, as this is written, pastor of St. Anne Church in Alpena, Michigan.

And the suspicion that the liturgy has become a plaything for homosexuals and pedophiles was buttressed, yet again, just last year, when it was revealed by the Baltimore *Sun* (June 27, 2001) that the U.S. bishops' associate director of the Committee on the Liturgy, Fr. Kenneth Martin, 55, was arrested and charged on June 26 with molesting students while he was a lay teacher at the Jesuits' prestigious Loyola Blakefield high school in Towson, Maryland. The incidents of abuse dated back to the 1970s.

Police charged him with child abuse, third and fourth degree sex offenses, and perverted practices. After teaching at the Jesuits' high school, he studied for the priesthood and was ordained a priest for the Diocese of Wilmington, Delaware.

The *Sun's* reporter Tim Craig wrote:

"Before he became a priest, Martin was a language teacher at Loyola Blakefield, a Catholic high school in Towson, from 1970 to 1986. Martin was arrested after one of his former students, now 38, said he was abused from 1977, when he was in 10th grade, until his senior year.

"'He started helping me, as my father was not there for me in my life. He started playing with my head,' the former student told police, according to the charging document. 'The first time anything happened, I was at his house. He was tutoring me [in] Spanish.'"

Another revelation came in September 2001, at the trial of Fr. Paul Lapierre, in Cornwall, Ontario, who described himself on the stand as one of the most prominent leaders of the Vatican II "liturgical renewal" in Canada, the United States, and Europe in the 1960s and 1970s. Lapierre stunned the court and trial observers – especially his own defense attorneys and the Ontario Provincial Police's lead investigator, Detective Inspector Pat Hall – by stating that he knew priests who abused the man who had accused him, but denied committing the abuse himself.

Fr. Lapierre's accuser, now a prominent Montreal attorney, claimed he was 12 years old when he was sexually abused and passed on like a "used toy" from predator to predator, including Lapierre, who allegedly abused him repeatedly over a four-year period.

Fr. Lapierre, at 72 still a very imposing figure, was ordained in 1959 at St. Felix Cathedral in Alexandria. Three years later he was asked by Bishop Rosario Brodeur to become the director of a "retreat house" in Alexandria which, he explained with great pride, was designed to train Canadian priests and religious on how to implement Vatican II decrees.

He said the Church introduced so many changes that people had to "go back to school" and that he was the one selected to do the schooling, both at the retreat house, and, between 1969 and 1971, on local and CBC radio and television where he hosted shows focusing on the value of good liturgical celebrations, informing people about the renewal, and answering questions regarding the Church and the renewal.

Lapierre was charged by Project Truth in May 1999 with three counts of indecent assault and two counts of gross indecency in connection with alleged sexual assaults on a boy between 1964 and 1968, at the same time he was implementing the liturgical renewal in Canada. He pleaded not guilty, and still maintains his innocence. He was acquitted at trial, but the Ontario Crown Attorney, as this is written, is appealing the judge's verdict.

At one point in his cross-examination, Crown Attorney Alain Godin called Fr. Lapierre "one of the rising stars of the Catholic Church," at the time to which Lapierre responded, "My modesty and humility would advise me not to agree with you – but if you like…"

It is of more than passing interest that Fr. Lapierre's brother, Laurier Lapierre, is one of Canada's most distinguished TV journalists, and for years hosted the popular CBC program, "This Hour Has Seven Days." Now Senator Laurier Lapierre, a partnered gay man, he made news on March 6, 2002 with a speech in Ottawa in which he excoriated the Catholic Church and compared its doctrine on marriage to Nazi persecution of Jews and homosexuals.

In the March 6 speech, mocking his peer, Senator Anne Cool, co-sponsor of legislation that would define and defend the traditional understanding of marriage in Canada, a "Bill to Remove Certain Doubts Regarding the Meaning of Marriage," S.9, Lapierre thundered:

"The stubborn refusal by some heterosexuals who are determined at all costs to exclude some Canadians from the right and status and recognition they themselves enjoy unless their fiat is accepted – a fiat originating in the far, far away antiquity of time – is disheartening and bodes badly for the harmony that must exist between the different groups of a modern and democratic society."

After lashing out at Catholic leaders, he added:

"The Taliban, who also wear skirts, were only following the dictates of tradition. It is obvious to me that to achieve the end of the subjugation of women it was necessary for the promulgators of marriage to launch a horrible campaign of discrimination against homosexuality – a campaign that coincided, oddly enough, with what became the compelling obsession of most religions: anti-Semitism…"

The drivers of renewal

In her block-buster exposé on Glendinning, MacEachern showed beyond a reasonable doubt that for more than 30 years, the Catholic liturgical "renewal" was – and remains – driven in a significant measure by homosexual and pedophile clerics to change Catholics' understanding of the nature of the Church, and to express their vision of a new church: one that is "tolerant," "compassionate," and "loving"; not "rigid," "formalistic," and "legalistic."

Her 100-page research project named the homosexual clerics, the convicted pedophile priests, the radical feminists, Marxists, and other assorted fifth columnists who "renewed" the Catholic liturgy in Canada and engineered one of the greatest debacles in the history of Church: the nearly total destruction of the Church in Canada.

Most Catholics in the United States and Canada who still attend Mass, of course, are not aware of how their psyches are manipulated in the "process" of liturgical "renewal", and are blissfully ignorant of the fact that the liturgical revolution will remain in full swing until, as Fr. Richard Fragomeni of the Catholic Theological Union in Chicago remarked in Los Angeles at a national social justice confab in 1999, "it becomes as attractive as sex" (see *The Wanderer*, August 5, 1999).

But Fragomeni isn't the only liturgist who believes "we haven't yet begun the renewal."

As MacEachern showed, Fragomeni's line is the mantra of the liturgical renewal establishment in North America; and the "renewal" underway, which has deformed the Roman Rite of the Mass in ways never imagined by a majority of the council fathers at Vatican II, is linked to advancing gender dysphoria, narcissistic psychotherapy, and the entertainment obsession which are all components of the sexual revolution.

With meticulous and depressing detail, MacEachern showed how, just as Cranmer's liturgical revolution at the time of the Reformation was engineered to liberate England from the political and economic controls of Rome, so the liturgical "renewal" imposed upon unsuspecting Catholics after Vatican II was designed and implemented to effectuate a permanent moral revolution against the papacy and the universality of the Catholic faith.

Among the many reminders she offered her readers to make her point is this: At precisely the same time that the Canadian bishops, at the prompting of the Canadian Conference of Catholic Bishops' English Office of Liturgy – headed by bishop, later cardinal, G. Emmett Carter – decreed the vernacular, turned the altars around, instructed their people to receive Communion standing, in the hand – all of this years before Pope Paul VI decreed the Novus Ordo – the bishops sent a letter to Canadian Justice Minister and future Prime Minister Pierre Elliott Trudeau supporting his proposals for the decriminalization of abortion, divorce, contraception, and homosexuality.

The year was 1966.

That same year appeared the Canadian Catechism, which said nothing about the Ten Commandments, the precepts of the Church, original sin, the divinity of Christ, the Real Presence, the Sacrifice of the Mass, the Immaculate Conception, the Virgin Birth, the sacraments, the infallibility of the Pope; but it did say a lot about the "spirit of Vatican II."

Not coincidentally, 1966 is also the year the Canadian bishops made the sex education of children a priority in their Catholic schools.

Sylvia MacEachern's research into Canada's liturgical establishment began in early 1999 when a lawsuit alleging sexual abuse was filed against prominent Canadian liturgist Fr. Barry Glendinning, a priest of the Diocese of London, Ontario.

"I started interviewing Glendinning's victims and their families," she told *The Wanderer*, "and others who knew him, and when I saw these allegations go back decades, I started reading his material. What struck me was his great aversion to the Real Presence, and I was reminded of an old article from the *Dublin Review* which observed that Queen Elizabeth refused to stay at Mass if the Host were elevated.

"The more I read about what happened in Cranmer's England and meditated on what we've been going through here for the past 35 years, I realized we were reliving the Reformation, but that ours was driven by a sexual agenda," she added.

The more she delved into Glendinning's professional past as a liturgist, and looked at his connections to other liturgists, bishops, and seminaries, she realized that he could serve as a profile and model for the modern liturgical deconstructionist.

Her investigation, titled "The Painted Preying Liturgist," opened with several horrific descriptions of Glendinning's sexual abuse and torture of children in his apartment at St. Peter's Seminary in London, at a cottage he owned and in area parks in the late 1960s and early 1970s, while G. Emmett Carter was bishop of London.

Her accounts were based on her personal, face-to-face interviews with five of Glendinning's victims, the mothers of two of the victims, one victim's sister, numerous private investigators, police officers, and detectives, as well as court documents and newspaper reports.

At the same time Glendinning was teaching at the seminary, and serving as the vice chairman of the London Liturgical Commission, a number of other future bishops and archbishops, as well as prominent liturgists, were either students or professors at St. Peter's, including Marcel Gervais, the future archbishop of Ottawa; Eugene LaRocque, the bishop of Alexandria-Cornwall; and Bishop James Doyle of Peterborough.

In May 1974, Glendinning, then 40, pled guilty to six counts of gross indecency involving six children, ages 11-16, was placed on probation for three years, and sent to Southdown, a rehabilitation center outside of Toronto. Sadly, however, his careers as a pedophile and liturgist did not end then. Rather, his careers took off, under the tutelage of the future cardinal archbishop of Toronto, G. Emmett Carter, who would eventually serve as a president of the Canadian Conference of Catholic Bishops, president

(1971-1973) of ICEL, the International Commission on English in the Liturgy, a member of the Concilium under Archbishop Annibale Bugnini, and a member of the Congregation for Divine Worship.

Glendinning, after ordination in 1964, was sent to Sant'Anselmo in Rome to pursue advanced studies in liturgy, and upon his return was appointed professor of liturgy at St. Peter's in London. He helped Bishop Carter prepare the Canadian conference's first post-Vatican II hymnal (which established the precedent for the "I worship me" genre of church music), and after working in London, took assignments as a liturgy professor in Edmonton at both the Newman Theological College and St. Joseph's Seminary. He also served on the Archdiocese of Edmonton's Liturgical Commission. While in Edmonton, Glendinning continued sexually abusing young men – altar boys – though no charges were filed against him. In 1983, with Carter now in Toronto, Glendinning was invited to work in parishes in the Toronto suburbs. Ironically, the pastors he was assigned under were also accused of "misconduct."

Cardinal Carter appointed Glendinning to chair the Liturgical Commission of the Archdiocese of Toronto. Subsequently, in 1987, Glendinning was invited to teach liturgy courses at St. Paul's Seminary in the Archdiocese of Ottawa, which works closely with the National Liturgical Office of the CCCB and awards a "Certificate in Pastoral Liturgy," a degree coveted by would-be liturgists in both the United States and Canada.

At the time the London newspapers reported the lawsuits against Glendinning the previous summer, he was still teaching at St. Paul's and speaking on the North American liturgical circuit.

Glendinning's invitation to teach seminarians and liturgists in Ottawa, MacEachern discovered, came from the "guru" of the Canadian liturgical scene, Fr. William Marravee, professor of sacramental theology at St. Paul's, and a member of the *Societas Liturgica*, the Catholic Theological Society of America, the Canadian Theological Society, and the North American Academy of Ecumenists.

As MacEachern documented thoroughly by footnoting sources and quotes, Marravee does not believe in God; nor does he believe in the Real Presence or the Holy Sacrifice of the Mass. He thinks the idea of an ordained priesthood obstructs the development of the community and speaks and writes in favor of lay homilists and female presiders.

Joining Glendinning in teaching at Canada's most prestigious Summer Institute for liturgists are these major personalities (just a few of the many MacEachern identifies) pushing liturgical "renewal" across North America:

- J. Frank Henderson, adjunct professor at St. Stephen's College (Edmonton), a longtime member of ICEL, who believes: "Liturgies that are just and in which true freedom is experienced are inclusive; they include and unite persons in the local community, persons all around the world, and ourselves and all creation…" Henderson worked on ICEL's "inclusive language" project from 1977-1987 and, as Helen Hull Hitchcock pointed out in her work *The Politics of Prayer* (Ignatius), revealed that ICEL's advisory committee considered producing a feminist liturgy a priority.

- Dr. Mary Schaefer of Nova Scotia, a Notre Dame Liturgical Studies graduate who now teaches at the Atlantic School of Theology in Halifax. As MacEachern wrote: "Schaefer contributes a particularly feminist perspective with her notion that probably in the early Church 'householders served as liturgical presidents' but in later years 'Catholic tradition has excluded persons otherwise apt on the basis of race, marital status, or gender'." She hopes that someday bishops will "authorize laity, including 'lay' religious, to preside at the parish [E]ucharist."

- Caryl Green, a CCCB staffer with the National Office of Religious Education, who believes that a major obstacle to ecumenism is "the inhumanity of theological positions."

- Fr. Eugene King, another Notre Dame Ph.D. with a licentiate in biblical studies from the Pontifical Biblical Institute, who is rector of St. Paul's Seminary and director of the university's Institute for Pastoral Studies. He regrets that most people attending Mass today do not appreciate "the liturgy of the word [is] the spiritual meal of the week," and says Mass should be understood as "partying."

MacEachern's list of St. Paul's liturgy staff (and their credentials) made a number of powerful points, perhaps the most essential of which is the importance of the Notre Dame University Center for Pastoral Liturgy in maintaining the liturgical revolution. Almost all of Canada's most influential liturgists acquired their degrees there – perhaps under the influence of Fr. Rasmussen – and even the most casual glance at their subsequent writings and speeches reveals their disconnectedness to Catholic Tradition and their commitment to the deconstruction of the Latin liturgy.

In this milieu of Marxists, radical feminists, pro-homosexualists, and New Agers at St. Paul's, Glendinning, no doubt, felt comfortable.

As this work is underway, Spring 2002, Glendinning is awaiting trial in London on the charges brought two years ago, with the legal wrangling taking a bizarre twist: the plaintiffs (i.e., his victims) were countersued.

Due to the touchy libel situation in Canada, it is difficult – and becoming nearly impossible – for Canadian and American newspapers to report on clerical sexual abuse when it occurs in the Catholic Church. But just a glimpse of the headlines from the London *Free Press* in the Glendinning lawsuit give the reader a sense of the development of the case:

- "Brothers' Suit Over Priest Getting A Lot Of Attention," March 23, 2000.

- "Church Uncomfortable About Publicity," March 25, 2000.

- "Shedding Light On Abuse: To Remain Anonymous Insinuates That We Have Something To Hide," about victim John Swales, March 25, 2000.

- "Priest In Lawsuit Quits Teaching," June 6, 2000.

- "Catholic Church Can't Be Sued, Lawyer Argues", June 20, 2000.

- "Catholic Chancellor Faces Sex Charges," July 13, 2000.

- "Brothers' Sex Abuse Suit Against Church Rejected," July 19, 2000.

- "Diocese Suing Abused Brother Counterclaim in $11.6M Suit," September 2, 2001.

According to this London *Free Press* report by Jane Sims, "The counterclaim, which contains allegations that have not been proven in court, says John Swales sexually, physically and emotionally abused his siblings and deliberately induced his brother into illicit behaviors such as illegal drug abuse and male prostitution…The Church contends if it is found responsible for any damage, that John Swales is partially or wholly responsible because of the abuse of his siblings.

"But Swales said any sexual behavior with his brothers was initially under Glendinning's direction.

"'None of us ever engaged in this behavior prior to meeting Glendinning and it became acceptable and permissible to engage in this behavior at his direction'…

"One local sexual assault victim's advocate called the countersuit 'evil' and added the diocese 'ought to be ashamed'…"

On the other side of the lake

When two women from Oswego, New York contacted me in August 1999 to inquire whether I would be interested in hearing their story about a clerical pedophile ring that operated in that small Lake Ontario city north of Syracuse for decades, I told them I'd visit them and see their documentation.

For nearly three hours, I sat wide-eyed and stunned. Despite all that I had read and heard, nothing has affected me as deeply before or after as to hear the mother of two sexually abused sons and the counselor of many other abused boys and girls describe how their down-and-out city had become a "nest of vipers." In fact, the box of documentation they gave me sat in a corner of my office for nearly six months, uninspected after the initial talk-through; and it was not until the mothers called and requested I return their documentation that I decided to go forward with their story.

After the story appeared, the most disturbing and troubling thing was the total lack of response from the community and the Diocese of Syracuse after an initial flurry of publicity from the local press, and even a New York City television station.

That report, appearing in *The Wanderer* (April 6, 2000), as *"A Nest of Vipers...Clerical Pedophile Ring Operated Freely for Decades"* began with this basic fact:

> On March 9, 1999, the plaintiff in a sexual abuse lawsuit against the Diocese of Syracuse and Monsignor Francis J. Furfaro was settled out of court, with the victim agreeing to "release" Furfaro and the diocese from "any and all claims, actions, lawsuits, injuries, demands, obligations, actual legal fees and expenses, losses, costs, losses of services, expenses, attachments, garnishments, liens and compensations of any nature

whatsoever, whether direct or derivative, under federal or state statutory or common law."

It continued:

> A short time later, Furfaro, 80, one of the most prominent priests in this old shipping city on Lake Ontario, disappeared. His absence was unexplained, even in the parish bulletin, and it was widely rumored by people close to him that he was sent away for treatment of a nervous disorder and depression.
>
> Thus ended Furfaro's (at least) 40-year career as a child molester in Oswego, according to two women now writing a book on what they call a "pedophile-protection racket" involving priests, the police, a former district attorney, judges, a probation officer, teachers, a former mayor, a 'Big Brother' at the YMCA and others.
>
> For the last ten years, these two women, one in her 40s, the other in her 50s – the latter the mother of sexually-abused sons – have conducted an intensive investigation, including interviews with victims, and assembled a picture so horrifying that Catholics in this heavily-Catholic city insist on ignoring it – just as local, state and national law enforcement agencies are.
>
> Before Furfaro was sent away by the diocese, these two women, Marianne Barone-Trent and Susan Sweet, prepared a dossier of statements from Furfaro's victims – some young men, many now older. These statements claim Furfaro – who once served as president of the Oswego Public School Board and contemplated running for mayor – was the sadistic leader of a pedophile ring, that included several other priests and prominent citizens with connections to organized crime and the pornography racket.
>
> Through the schools, the probation system, and several volunteer agencies, these pedophiles had unrestricted access to young males for their sexual torture sessions, many of whom were threatened that they would be 'thrown away' if they ever told, and that all legal loopholes were covered.
>
> Other victims died in car accidents or committed suicide; others now suffer from depression, drug and alcohol addiction and sexual dysfunction and sexual identity problems.

> For the past 45 years, Furfaro, a clinical psychologist by profession (reputedly a very competent hypnotherapist) and a member of the board of the State University of New York at Oswego, was pastor of St. Joseph's Church…

In researching Furfaro's background, one of the first disturbing facts to surface concerned the drowning of a young boy under his supervision at a picnic for altar boys from Our Lady of Pompey Church in Syracuse in the 1950s.

Another was a news clipping from the *Palladium-Times* of May 8, 1961. Two young men, 18 and 19, were killed in a terrible car wreck. The car belonged to Furfaro, described as a "close friend" of the 18-year-old driver. No autopsies were ordered or performed, and the boys were buried two days later.

In subsequent years, the women told *The Wanderer*, fatalities occurred in two other cars owned by Furfaro, which he had lent to his young boy friends.

In developing her case against Furfaro, Mrs. Barone-Trent interviewed dozens of local citizens, including former parish employees, parents, siblings and relatives of victims, tradesmen employed at Furfaro's parish from time to time, therapists and police. In addition, she retained one private investigator and worked with special investigators in state and local law enforcement.

One therapist told Barone-Trent that he estimated Furfaro must have abused "at least 100 boys" based on the number of adult males coming to him for treatment.

"One of Furfaro's 'ins' with parents," Sue Sweet told *The Wanderer*, "was the fact that he was a psychologist, and he could go to parents with troubled boys and say, 'Let me help.'"

Sweet is a native of Oswego, and Barone-Trent arrived in Oswego as a teen, having lived in both Rochester and Syracuse, where she was raised and lived as a devout Catholic. Barone-Trent's relationship with Furfaro goes back a long way.

He was her religious education teacher in 1963, and spent much of his time in the "family life" course talking about sex, including telling dirty jokes to his mixed audience of young teens. Barone-Trent's father, a professor at

Oswego College, was aware of a "relationship" Furfaro had with the wife of a faculty member.

In May 1972, when Barone was teaching in Connecticut, her 16-year-old brother was raped by former Oswego Mayor Vince Corsall, on his 16th birthday. Her brother called the Oswego County Sheriff, who immediately went to his home. The police asked if the family would press charges, they replied in the affirmative. After Corsall was arrested and jailed, Furfaro came to their door, pleading with them not to press charges on his friend, the former mayor.

Mrs. Barone ordered Furfaro out of the house; and at that time, the Barone family switched to another parish.

The family retained an attorney for the case, and on advice of counsel, agreed to drop charges to save their son the trauma of a grilling by the prosecution. In return, Corsall was to resign his teaching position at Oswego High School, and leave the city for good. Corsall landed a job teaching at a Catholic boys' school in the Diocese of Rochester – the Jesuits' prestigious McQuaid High.

In the early 1980s, Mrs. Barone-Trent returned to the Oswego area with her four sons. Over and over again, she heard talk about Furfaro, whose reputation was known all over Oswego; and yet Catholics never blinked when they saw him leading groups of young boys on nature walks through area parks. It was something, she said, that people just joked about.

Mrs. Sweet said Furfaro's sexual proclivities were common knowledge among Oswego's 20,000-plus citizens.

"Most parents knew from their youth what he was doing, because they either went to his parties or they knew people who hung out at the rectory. Some parents warned their children to stay away from him; others didn't. But Furfaro was always very clever about the people he targeted. He always chose kids from broken homes, or kids whose parents had an alcohol or drug problem. The police have always known what he's been up to, because they hung out with him when they were younger."

In many cases, Furfaro had been very generous to his boys, even going so far as to buy them expensive clothes and new cars; in some cases, he even paid for their college educations. Some boys have even claimed that Furfaro had left them in his will.

The first step Furfaro took when he arrived in Oswego in the 1950s, Sweet said, was arranging for his appointment as chaplain to the city police force.

And from the time he arrived in Oswego, he was embraced by his parishioners. "He was loved immediately," Sweet said. "He is very charismatic, and very handsome, and he loved to sing. From the first, he became involved in every aspect of the community."

Furfaro's church, with its new Monsignor Furfaro Parish Center, is directly across the street from the city's police headquarters.

Repeat

In 1987, while Barone-Trent was teaching art at St. Paul's Academy, her two older sons, then 10 and 11, were sexually abused by Fr. Dan Casey in a pool shower at Oswego College, and also sexually assaulted in the college gym.

In 1992, Barone-Trent and her sons filed suit against St. Paul's Academy, Fr. Casey and the Diocese of Syracuse. The case dragged on through the stages of discovery and depositions, and several attempts to go to trial.

"The diocese always found reasons to postpone the trial," Mrs. Barone-Trent said. "One time it was, 'Fr. Casey is in Israel.' Another time it was 'our lawyer has a bad leg.' There were so many excuses."

In July 1998, settlement talks collapsed because the plaintiffs refused to agree that the diocese was not at fault in any way, shape or form – in a formula similar to that quoted in the first paragraph of this story.

Finally, however, one month later, the case was closed when Mrs. Barone-Trent accepted a one-sentence apology from the diocese and a settlement of $150,000 for her sons and lawyers.

Learning through the years

In the eleven years between her sons' abuse and the settlement, Mrs. Barone-Trent received an education in criminal politics, starting at the chancery in Syracuse. Along for the experience came Mrs. Sweet, a commissioned lay youth minister for the diocese who works for the Oswego County Clerk's office, who contacted Barone-Trent after the publicity about her sons' lawsuit.

In her work as a youth minister, Mrs. Sweet had heard countless stories of sexual abuse, including violent pedophile orgies involving women and men, teenage boys, and even younger girls and boys at Furfaro's rectory.

More than a dozen confessions by individuals abused at these orgies were gathered by Barone-Trent and Sweet, and they describe – in the victims' own words – Furfaro's skill at "hypnotizing" his sexual prey; of his ferocious sexual energy; of a group of priests who took Polaroids of the orgies, etc.; of Furfaro's trips with his boys to New York City to make pornographic movies; of complaints lodged by victims to police, who always replied there was not enough evidence to investigate.

In 1993, Barone-Trent received a call from a traumatized young man who said he had been repeatedly molested by Furfaro. They spoke for three hours, and then the two scheduled a meeting, but "David," after pouring his heart out with details of Furfaro's violent orgies, decided not to meet, telling Barone-Trent that "they were watching," and he'd be a "throw-away" if they met.

In 1997, Mrs. Sweet was contacted by another of Furfaro's boys, who came to her house to report a "house full of pornographic videos" Furfaro had. Sweet immediately went to the District Attorney with "David's" statement, and the report about Furfaro's video collection. The D.A. called back, asking Sweet for the address of the house.

The next day, the house burned to the ground. Ironically, Sweet's husband, Ron, was the fire captain called to the blaze, eventually ruled an arson.

Revealing depositions

As the second trial date in July '98 approached, Barone-Trent and Sweet by now knew the names of at least seven active pedophile priests operating in the Oswego-Syracuse area, many of whom had parish schools.

Mrs. Sweet had just been deposed, and related three separate conversations she had with Syracuse Auxiliary Bishop Thomas J. Costello in which she informed him that Fr. Casey and other priests in Oswego were sexually abusing young people.

In one of those conversations, Sweet said in her deposition, Costello told her that he had tried to help Casey for 15 years. In another conversation with Costello, Sweet told *The Wanderer*, the auxiliary bishop admitted he was aware of Furfaro's proclivities, and wondered aloud to her, "Do you think Satanism might be involved?"

Bishop Costello had given his deposition two months earlier, on May 22, 1998.

He said he was ordained in 1954, served as associate pastor for four years before being appointed to the diocese's Marriage Tribunal. From 1960 to 1975, he was diocesan superintendent of schools, and many Catholics in the Syracuse Diocese recall bitterly his obsession with pushing sex education for Catholic schools in the early 1960s, before other dioceses in the state; in 1978, he was named an auxiliary bishop.

At the time Costello gave his deposition, he was, incidentally, chairman of the Communications Committee for the United States Catholic Conference. Under oath, Costello was testy and unhelpful, answering "I don't know," or "I refuse to answer."

But he did explain how the chain of command in the diocese worked, and that Monsignor Furfaro, as regional vicar, would have had responsibility for informing the bishop directly of any charges pertaining to clerical misconduct, such as Fr. Casey's, in his region.

On most matters, Costello was tight-lipped.

Barone-Trent's lawyers raised the issue that Casey was known to have had a sexual fixation on children even as a seminarian. After he was ordained, like many pedophile priests, he moved from parish to parish, region to region around the diocese, shifted whenever problems arose.

At the time he was in Oswego, when he abused Barone-Trent's sons, Casey was one of three pedophile priests working among the city's seven parishes.

If Costello knew Casey had a problem, he wasn't telling anyone – neither law enforcement nor his superiors, as this exchange from the deposition shows:

"Q: Do you recall telling anyone that the Church had been aware of problems with Fr. Casey's sexual abuse for years?"

"A: I don't recall broadcasting that to anyone, no, or even shortcasting it to anyone."

"Q: Is that the same as saying that you never said it to anyone?"

"A: I never said it to anyone."

Later in his deposition, Costello denied ever speaking to Sweet about Casey. All he could remember from their three meetings was that "she was concerned about some children who she thought had been abused."

Asked, "Did she tell you who had abused the children," Costello snapped back, "She made an accusation."

"Who did she tell you abused those children?"

"I refuse to answer that," Costello exhaled, claiming clerical privilege.

Can't break that cover-up

After having read Costello's deposition, Sue Sweet was livid.

On July 19, 1998, she called the Syracuse chancery office and spoke with Bishop James Moynihan's secretary, Fr. Joseph Zaresky, seeking an appointment with her ordinary. On July 20, 1998, Zaresky called back and told her that she should continue meeting with Costello. Sweet told Zaresky she needed to meet with Moynihan, to disclose to him personally the extent of the pedophilia among clergy in Oswego. On July 23, Zaresky told Sweet that the bishop could not meet with her.

In the fall of 1999, Sweet again tried to set up a meeting with Bishop Moynihan. "I told Zaresky in no uncertain terms that I needed to tell the bishop about a pedophile ring operating here and about the abuse of children. I told him that if the bishop would not meet with me I would go national with this story, and I asked him to give me a specific time when he would call back and give me the time of a meeting.

"On the next day, a Wednesday, Zaresky called me back and said the bishop would meet me on Monday. But that Friday, at 3 p.m., Zaresky called and informed me the bishop could not meet with me. My response was: 'Really? You've got to be kidding.' 'Are you lying?'"

The women's efforts to bring law enforcement to bear on the problem met with similar results.

Neither the local police, the State Police, the County Sheriff, former New York State Attorney General Dennis Vacco, not even the FBI, has shown any interest in pursuing an investigation into the ring, though individuals working in various agencies have all reviewed the material, and some remain interested on a personal basis.

One local television reporter has been pursuing an investigation into the ring of pedophile clergy, based on the information gathered by Barone-Trent and Sweet. *The Wanderer* has seen a copy of a proposed transcript for broadcast, in which the reporter names seven other pedophile priests (excluding Furfaro and Casey) working in the Syracuse Diocese, many of whom worked in Oswego.

Strange death

In January 2000, Fr. Casey, 52, allegedly died in Israel; allegedly, of a massive heart attack.

Purportedly, his body was returned to a funeral home in Syracuse, and twin services were held in Syracuse and Rochester, where Casey had studied for the priesthood at St. Bernard's Seminary.

Curiously, even though Casey was a priest for more than 20 years, none of the obituaries published in either Syracuse or Rochester newspapers identified him as a priest; only as a "scripture scholar."

Just before leaving for Israel at Christmas time, Casey gave a talk on Scripture at a Rochester-area Catholic church. One local Catholic, concerned that this known pedophile was speaking to Catholic audiences in Bishop Matthew Clark's diocese, attended the talk. Afterwards, he was so distraught at what he heard, he wrote a letter to Bishop Clark. (Clark never responded). At that lecture, Casey mentioned that he was leaving for Israel, where he had received a special assignment from the Holy Father to work in Jerusalem.

After reports of Casey's death reached Rochester and Syracuse, Mrs. Barone-Trent wrote a "private and personal" letter to Bishop Matthew Clark, informing him that she had read an obituary for a Mr. Daniel W. Casey, and wanted to know if this was the same Casey who had abused her two sons, because she felt she needed to continually monitor his whereabouts.

Clark did not answer her letter. Instead, the moderator of the curia, Fr. Joseph Hart, replied:

"While Bishop Clark is away, please permit me to respond to your inquiry of Feb. 10, 2000. Mr. Daniel W. Casey, formerly a priest of the Diocese of Syracuse, was found dead of natural causes on January 9, 2000 in Jerusalem. Mr. Casey had just bid goodbye to one of his pilgrimage tour groups and was expecting another in a week. He had eaten lunch with some friends, and had gone to his room for a nap. When he did not appear at supper, someone went to see if he was okay and found him dead. An autopsy revealed he had died of a heart attack.

"May God have mercy on his soul!

"Sincerely yours,

"Joseph A. Hart, V.G."

Barone-Trent wrote a similar letter of inquiry, marked "private and personal" to Bishop Moynihan in Syracuse. She received a nearly identical letter from Fr. Michael Minehan, chancellor, explaining that he must answer because the bishop was on vacation. Minehan did, however, assure Barone-Trent that Casey was not on an assignment from the Holy Father as Casey had stated at his public appearance in Rochester.

Meanwhile, Furfaro has returned to Syracuse from the undisclosed treatment center, and is living in a private home, but is seen from time to time in Oswego. As this report was being prepared, he was seen with Bishop Costello at a Syracuse hospital where they had been visiting a patient. People who saw him said the octogenarian "looked just great. You'd never think he was over 60."

Keeping faith

Despite the evil in Oswego, both women keep faith. Mrs. Sweet assists at daily Mass, and explains:

"This community," she says, "and the entire diocese have been blessed with good priests, regardless of what we know of the bad ones."

Mrs. Sweet, in addition to being a commissioned youth minister for the diocese, has also served as a member of the diocesan pastoral council, the regional pastoral council, a religious education teacher since her sophomore year of high school, in addition to her ongoing work as a youth minister.

"The whole reason for my pursuit," she said, "is a result of my strong belief in the vocation of motherhood, and I could not consciously turn my back on these children, because then I would be committing the sin of omission. Throughout all of this ordeal, my faith has increased immensely, because I kept focused on prayer, and reading Scripture, always meditating on the words Jesus spoke, especially those regarding scandal and the corruption of the innocent."

Mrs. Barone-Trent was once asked by a television reporter during the media reports on her refusal to sign a gag order with the Diocese of Syracuse, "why are you stirring the water?" She replied, "when water is stagnant it gets murky and stinks. We have to keep the water moving."

CHAPTER EIGHT

Bishops In Trouble

On June 2, 1998, Bishop J. Keith Symons of Palm Beach resigned after confessing he had sexually molested five altar boys early in his priestly career, just five weeks after one of his former victims disclosed the abuse.

He was one of five bishops to resign in the wake of sexual abuse scandals in the decade of the 1990s, following Archbishops Robert F. Sanchez of Santa Fe and Eugene Marino of Atlanta, and preceding those of Bishop Daniel Ryan of Springfield, Illinois and G. Patrick Ziemann of Santa Rosa.

Symons, then 65, was ordained in 1958; he was appointed an auxiliary bishop of St. Petersburg in January 1981, appointed second bishop of Pensacola in September 1983, and in June 1990, was appointed second bishop of Palm Beach. As he told Catholic laity more than once, he considered himself a close friend of the late Joseph Bernardin and inferred that he owed a debt to Bernardin for making him a bishop.

Symons was the first bishop to resign for molesting young boys. Bishop Joseph Ferrario submitted his resignation to the Vatican for "health reasons" more than five years after he was publicly accused of sexually abusing a young man who subsequently died of AIDS. Two archbishops, Eugene Marino of Atlanta and Robert Sanchez of Santa Fe, also submitted early resignations after their affairs with women were exposed. The Holy See's quick acceptance of Symons' resignation, Monsignor Francis Maniscalco, a spokesman for the U.S. bishops, explained to the press, is indicative of a new approach to such allegations. Though the resignation was "locally determined and locally done," he said, the Vatican is now prepared to act "with immediacy."

Symons' victims are all presumed to have been altar boys, and the 42-year-old man who leveled the accusations against Symons said he was abused over a two-year period, more than two decades earlier.

St. Petersburg Bishop Robert Lynch was appointed by the Vatican to oversee the transition process in Palm Beach. At a press conference at St. Ignatius Cathedral in Palm Beach, which Symons did not attend, Bishop Lynch said he wanted to believe Symons' claim that he had not sexually abused anyone in the past 25 years, "but I don't know for sure. Sometimes (pedophiles) are in such deep denial they don't remember what they did."

Symons' admission that he had sexually molested altar boys raised the issue of clerical pedophilia to a new level, but one that the public should have expected, especially with the bombshell allegation several years earlier by a former seminarian that Joseph Cardinal Bernardin, the "bishop maker" in the American Church was, himself, a molester.

This allegation clearly indicated that the systematic sexual abuse of minor males by priests in the United States – often followed by the recruitment of these victims into the priesthood – has been an ongoing problem for at least 50 years, perhaps 80.

The Bernardin Legacy

The nurturing of a homosexual/pedophile network in the Catholic Church in modern times, which parallels similar networks in government, business and education circles, may, some suggest, date back to the late 1920s and early '30s when the "Cambridge Apostles," that elite clique of homosexual Marxists under the direction of Anthony Blunt (and including such notorious spies as Kim Philby), determined to seize control of the major institutions, especially the churches, newspapers, cinema and radio (and, later, television), universities, museums and government cultural agencies.

If this strikes the reader as difficult to believe, all I can plead is that there is a tremendous amount of information that supports the theory. The late John Costello's masterful biography of Anthony Blunt, *Mask of Treachery* (William & Morrow, Co., 1988) provides copious documentation on how Blunt placed his friends, both Marxists and homosexuals, in some of the most important cultural agencies in the western world, and even gloated how many were totally unqualified for their positions. In addition, there is the Congressional testimony of former Communists in the United States, such as Manning Johnson and Bella Dodd, who told how they encouraged more than a thousand communists or fellow travelers to enter Catholic seminaries in the 1930s. Bella Dodd testified: "In the 1930s, we put eleven hundred men into the priesthood in order to destroy the Church from within," and the chief tactic devised, once these men came to power, was to label the Church "of the past" as oppressive, authoritarian, full of prejudices, arrogant and closed to the world.

If the problem of a homosexual network in the Church is viewed in this larger perspective, one can understand more fully the remarkable role of Joseph Cardinal Bernardin in creating an "American Church" that has become a trusted ally of all those various social, political and cultural forces promoting sexual libertinism.

Bernardin's legacy to the American Church will be discussed and debated, quite possibly, for centuries. No one disputes his influence: as creator of the National Conference of Catholic Bishops and United States Catholic Conference; as a bishop-maker who, working with former Archbishop Jean Jadot, gave the American hierarchy its pronounced pro-gay orientation; as a subtle provocateur who nudged, consoled and empowered dissenters while professing his loyalty to his Roman superiors; as an architect of proposals to deconstruct the Roman liturgy, Catholic education and the all-important field of catechetics.

Bernardin, it must be recalled, at least briefly, was sponsored, tutored and promoted by a number of dubious characters, not only his clerical godfather and mentor, Archbishop Paul Hallinan of Atlanta, who served as a bishop in Bernardin's hometown, Charleston. Bernardin's other "godfather" was Archbishop (later cardinal) John Dearden, who would be responsible for the appointment of such notorious pro-homosexual bishops as Detroit Auxiliary Tom Gumbleton, Ken Untener of Saginaw, Joseph Imesch, of Joliet, and Springfield's Daniel Ryan.

Bernardin's supporters look at all his accomplishments and call them good. To do so, they have to overlook many things, including his connections to some of the most evil men to ever enter the priesthood.

When Joseph Cardinal Bernardin, Archbishop of Chicago, died November 14, 1996 of pancreatic cancer at age 68, he proved himself an impresario to the end, conducting a public relations/media blitz that crescendoed with calls for his canonization.

Typical of the sycophantry he was so skillful at evoking was that of the *National Catholic Reporter's* Tim Unsworth, who wrote a week after Bernardin died:

"Bernardin's final months were spent just as he planned and predicted: in loving, compassionate and gentle service. He spent much of his time comforting other terminally ill cancer patients. He came to know many of them during his hospitalization at Loyola. 'I felt like a priest again,' he said often…Bernardin's biographer and close friend, Eugene Kennedy, has called him 'the most influential bishop in the history of the American church.'…[A]t the time of his death he was the senior active American prelate among the country's more than 350. But his influence far exceeded his seniority. His writing and speaking on national and even global issues caused him to eclipse megabishops of the past such as Baltimore's James Gibbons (1877-1921), Boston's William O'Connell (1907-1944), Chicago's George Mundelein (1915-1939), New York's Francis Spellman (1939-1967) and Bernardin's own mentor, John Dearden of Detroit (1958-1980)…"

Everything he did, from the well-publicized death-bed visit by his dear friend Ann Landers, to the gay choir that sang at his funeral Mass, the visit by Hillary Clinton and the letter from her husband, Bill, to the Bernardin books and the documentary video produced and released as soon as he was buried, was orchestrated perfectly.

One of his closest friends – one of the original "Bernardin Boys" – Santa Fe Archbishop Michael Sheehan, who served as one of Bernardin's four assistant general secretaries at the beginning of the National Conference of Catholic Bishops, commented that Bernardin "was able to look at death as a friend, rather than as an enemy."

There were many reasons why Bernardin welcomed death, least of which was that his carefully crafted image as the saintly prelate, the good listener, the consensus builder, the faithful son of the Church, was rapidly dissolving.

His closest friend from his South Carolina days, Monsignor Frederick Hopwood, had been accused of abusing hundreds of boys dating back to the early 1950s, when he and Bernardin shared a residence at the Cathedral of St. John the Baptist in Charleston – where some of the alleged abuse took place.

An attorney involved in representing some of Hopwood's victims told Roman Catholic Faithful, "Hopwood was not your ordinary pedophile. He abused hundreds of boys at the rectory – at a time when Bernardin was serving, theoretically, as assistant chancellor – and at Camp St. Mary's in Beaufort."

Coming to the legal defense of Hopwood and the Diocese of Charleston came the Archdiocese of Chicago's powerhouse firm, Mayer, Platt and Brown, which negotiated the cash settlements to Hopwood's victims.

At the time the Hopwood allegations became public in late December 1993, Bernardin was having trouble on another front.

A former seminarian from the Archdiocese of Cincinnati, Steven Cook, filed a $10 million lawsuit against Bernardin and Cincinnati priest Ellis Harsham The suit accused Harsham, when he was a priest at St. Gregory seminary in Cincinnati in the mid-1970s, of numerous coercive sexual acts against him, and then delivering him to Bernardin, then archbishop of Cincinnati, for the same purposes.

Several months later, however, in February 1994, Cook dropped Bernardin from the suit, saying he couldn't trust his memory. Cook never retracted his charges; nor did he say they were inaccurate – contrary to the accepted party line that Bernardin had been exonerated, which persists to this day. Four months later, Cook's suit against Harsham was conveniently – at least for Bernardin – settled out of court. While Bernardin was allowed to remain as Archbishop of Chicago, Harsham was placed immediately on administrative leave when the lawsuit was filed; he left the priesthood a few months later.

While Bernardin went on to have a very public (and filmed) reconciliation with Cook, showing the world what a generous man he was in forgiving a man who had accused him of sexual crimes, Bernardin's lawyers were involved in hushing up another case in which seminarians in Winona, Minnesota, had accused Bernardin and three other bishops of participating in sexual/satanic rituals at the seminary. Among the facts that the plaintiffs in that case marshaled for their suit: Bernardin was frequently accompanied by Steven Cook. The settlement stemming from the lawsuit has been sealed, but details of the settlement have made their way to select individuals, including this reporter, from a bishop who received a copy of the settlement.

In the two years leading up to his death – even as he orchestrated brutal assaults against clerical sexual abuse victims of clerical sexual abuse and their parents in Chicago – one after another of Bernardin's closest clerical friends from his native Diocese of Charleston made the newspapers – all for charges of pedophilia: Fr. Eugene Condon, Fr. Justin Goodwin, Fr. James Robert Owens-Howard, Fr. Paul F.X. Seitz, in addition to continuing allegations against Hopwood.

It is the Hopwood case that, perhaps, raises the most suspicions about Bernardin.

139

Hopwood, ordained in June 1951 in Maryknoll, New York, began working as a priest in the Charleston Diocese in January 1952. He was incardinated into the Charleston Diocese in November 1954, and appointed assistant chancellor. Reputedly, he was Bernardin's best friend and seminary roommate.

Bernardin was ordained April 26, 1952, at St. Joseph's Church in Columbia. In 1954, he was appointed Chancellor of the Diocese by Bishop John Russell, who, himself has been accused of Satanism and sexual abuse by the same woman, "Agnes," who accused Bernardin of sexual abuse and took all her charges to the Vatican – in person. Agnes' story and the ritual she was subjected to, was dramatized in the opening chapter of the late Malachi Martin's frightening novel of ecclesiastical intrigue, *Windswept House*.

According to Marion Lafong, who was sexually abused by Hopwood in the late 1950s, Bernardin and Hopwood (and the other priests named above) "were buddies." In an interview shortly after Bernardin's death, Lafong said that one of his co-plaintiffs in the lawsuit against Hopwood was sodomized in the cathedral rectory by Hopwood and another priest, though that victim didn't know who the perpetrator was because he had been blindfolded.

He also declared that in negotiations with the Archdiocese of Chicago lawyers in the efforts to settle the lawsuits without a trial, "Bernardin's name came up a large number of times," along with charges that Hopwood had presided over satanic rituals involving animals in the woods where some of his victims were abused.

While Hopwood was resident at the cathedral in Charleston, he was also working at Bishop England High School and was chaplain at the Citadel.

Bernardin was named monsignor in 1959, and continued to serve the bishop as chancellor and, after 1966, as an auxiliary bishop in Atlanta, under Archbishop Paul Hallinan, his mentor who was among the most strident and aggressive "Americanists" in the U.S. hierarchy at the time.

Bernardin acquired power rapidly. As his friends back in Charleston continued buggering little boys, Bernardin used his influence, starting in 1968, as General Secretary of the U.S. Catholic Conference, to select bishops (many of whom are still ordinaries) who would, to put it charitably, condone and promote homosexuality as an acceptable lifestyle and tolerate the sexual abuse of children by priests.

In December 1994, another of Bernardin's circle was accused of sexual abuse, Fr. Paul Seitz, then 67, pastor of Prince of Peace parish in Taylor, South Carolina

At the time charges were filed, diocesan spokeswoman Mary Jeffcoat said, the abuse happened while Seitz was stationed in Aiken County 30 years previously, in 1964.

In June 1996, another priest in Bernardin's circle of friends, Fr. Eugene Condon, then 66, retired from active ministry, three weeks after the 9th Circuit solicitor's office informed the diocese it was investigating Condon on charges he had sexually abused minor males and exposed them to pornography and alcohol.

In June 1995, Fr. Justin Goodwin, then 89, was charged with sexual abuse of minor males.

Goodwin had served in the Charleston diocese, which includes all of South Carolina, since 1953. Before that he served in Washington, D.C., New York and North Carolina churches.

Interestingly, he too spent time at the Cathedral of St. John the Baptist in Charleston.

Another aspect of the "Bernardin Legacy" was the notorious Rudy Kos case that ran for nearly four years in the Diocese of Dallas.

As the trial involving Kos evolved, it was revealed that two of "Bernardin's boys" – his closest friends in the episcopacy – Archbishop Thomas C. Kelly, OP, of Louisville and Archbishop Michael Sheehan of Santa Fe – were responsible.

In 1976, Kelly, as assistant general secretary of the National Conference of Catholic Bishops (who moved to the post after serving as a secretary to the papal nuncio in Washington, Jean Jadot), fraudulently approved the annulment of Kos' marriage, so that he could enter the Dallas seminary, then under the direction of Fr. Michael Sheehan, and train for the priesthood.

The annulment Kelly approved, canon lawyer Fr. Thomas Doyle, OP, explained during the trial proceedings, was patently invalid for at least five reasons: Kos lied in the evidence he presented; his ex-wife, who claimed that the marriage was never consummated and that her husband was a

141

pedophile, was never interviewed during the process; Kos' ex-wife was never notified that the annulment process had been initiated; and that the Dallas priest who supervised the annulment process in Dallas acted as both judge and defender of the bond – a conflict of interest.

Sheehan, who had served as Bernardin's "hatchet man" at the NCCB, ordering the resignations of longtime employees when Bernardin was restructuring and reorganizing the conference, accepted Kos into the Dallas seminary, little more than a year after he received his annulment, and less than a year after his predecessor, Monsignor Gerald Hughes, had rejected Kos.

Another Bernardin creation was Bishop Robert N. Lynch, of St. Petersburg, who once revealed how, when he was a young man not knowing what to do with his life, he met Bernardin and was encouraged by him to enter the priesthood.

He took the advice, and enjoyed a great career, moving, from his ordination in May 1978 as a priest of the Archdiocese of Miami, to seminary rector, to general secretary of the NCCB, and bishop of St. Petersburg in 1996.

Other Bernardin creations are Bishop Wilton Gregory of Belleville, a native of Chicago, the current president of the United States Conference of Catholic Bishops; and Archbishop John Vlazny of Portland, former seminary rector in Chicago and former bishop of Winona.

Mention must also be made of the dissenter Archbishop John Quinn of San Francisco, a native of San Diego and close friend and working ally of Bernardin. Bernardin thought so highly of Quinn that when he wanted to move Quinn into a bishopric, Oklahoma City, Quinn was made its first archbishop – so that he could have a rank equal to his talents – not bad for a man whose seminary rector had advised Quinn's bishop in San Diego *not* to ordain him after graduation from the North American College in Rome.

Quinn's reign in San Francisco was marked by numerous scandals involving pedophilia and theft by some of his closest aides.

Quinn's clan

Two of the most notorious of his priests were his close friends and advisers, Fr. Martin Greenlaw and Fr. Patrick Shea, both of whom served in the archdiocese's Society for the Propagation of the Faith, where they were given responsibility for raising funds to support Church missions.

In August 1995, Greenlaw was charged with 22 counts involving theft and embezzlement of Church funds, estimated at more than $600,000, including nine counts of money-laundering, and counts of grand theft, embezzlement, filing false tax returns, etc. Greenlaw's theft came to light after he was found beaten in his residence two years earlier and reported his assailant stole 31 credit cards. Investigators realized that his lifestyle – which included a luxurious home, fast cars, lavish dinners, and a fine arts collection – did not jibe with his $12,000-a-year salary. "Police investigating the Greenlaw beating," reported the San Francisco *Examiner* in August 1995, "said the priest 'admitted to picking up gay men for sexual liaisons.' Police investigators also found 'boxes of gay pornography video films in Greenlaw's house.'"

For two years prior to the charges, parishioners, reported the *Examiner,* had brought their concerns to Church officials; but nothing was ever done.

Greenlaw's frequent dining companion, Fr. Patrick O'Shea, was Greenlaw's predecessor at the Society for the Propagation of the Faith, which he oversaw for 22 years, until Greenlaw replaced him.

On March 15, 2002, eight years after the Archdiocese of San Francisco paid out $2.5 million to 15 men who said they were sexually abused by O'Shea and other priests, O'Shea was back in the news, with a judge's ruling that dismissed 224 counts of sexual molestation against O'Shea, who was then in jail unable to meet his $5 million bond.

The Associated Press' David Kravets reported (March 15, 2002) that a "hypertechnicality" released O'Shea from the charges. "The decision, unless overturned on appeal, means San Francisco County prosecutors cannot try O'Shea on charges of molesting nine boys in the 1960s and 70s…[T]he O'Shea case has zigzagged though the court system since its filing in 1995, a year after the California Legislature approved a law allowing prosecutors to file molestation charges even after the six-year statute of limitations expired.

"Prosecutors did so in this case, but a state appeals court dismissed it in 1997, saying the law did not apply retroactively. State lawmakers then reworked the legislation to make it retroactive and to let prosecutors re-file past charges if they were first filed under the 1994 law.

"But Superior Court Judge David Garcia, citing a January decision from the California Supreme Court on a different sex-abuse case, said prosecutors could not re-file the charges because an appeals court had dismissed them…

"Most of the boys attended San Francisco parochial schools and were altar boys where O'Shea worked…According to grand jury transcripts, O'Shea allegedly gave them alcohol, let them drive his sports cars and gave them other inducements. The men testified that the abuse included sodomy and oral copulation. O'Shea often took them on weekend trips throughout California, according to the transcripts…Prosecutors have also charged O'Shea with embezzling more than $250,000 in donated funds to the church. That case is pending and not affected by Garcia's ruling…"

On August 17, 1995, at the height of the media publicity on the Greenlaw and O'Shea scandals, Archbishop John Quinn announced his early resignation, interpreted by the press as a "power shift" from a "reform-minded" prelate to the "ambitious," "conservative" Levada. Quinn, Loyola University professor Eugene Kennedy told the *Examiner*, "was among a remarkable group of American bishops who looked to the future for healthy and progressive – but not radical – change."

But Levada has changed virtually nothing in San Francisco, and perhaps the low-point of his ecclesiastical career was his "third way" groveling capitulation to Mayor Willie Brown and flamboyantly gay Tom Ammiano (a former comedian and school board chief), chairman of the City County Board of Supervisors, who ruled that all city contractors must provide full domestic partnership benefits to their employees, which the archdiocese accepted, even though the Salvation Army rejected the ordinance.

Archbishops may come and go, but their gay bureaucrats dock-and-dodge their way across the nation, exemplified by Paul Woolley, originally a member of the Alexian Brothers teaching order, who made his way to the Archdiocese of Louisville and occupied top-level positions there, including director of Archbishop Thomas C. Kelly's archdiocesan lay council. From there, he showed up in Bishop John Cummins' Diocese of Oakland, across the bay from San Francisco, as a bureaucrat in East Bay Catholic Charities office, where he worked with Fr. James Schexnayder. While in that role, he was a high-profile gay activist, becoming co-chair of the San Francisco chapter of Dignity, writing extensively in its newsletter. Active in the same chapter was Mario Torrigino, Schexnayder's housemate in Oakland. When an article appeared in the Diocese of Sacramento's newspaper, *The Catholic Herald*, announcing that Woolley had been selected and hired by Bishop

William Weigand to replace radical leftist Georgia Lyga, head of the peace and justice office, local Catholics who knew of Woolley's activities in the Bay Area were shocked. After sending information to Weigand, there was the usual silence from the diocese and the frivolous position remained vacant. Some time later, Woolley showed up at a high level position at the Jesuits' Santa Clara University, in a management position for their foundation.

Sacramento Catholics thought Woolley's background would surely disqualify him for the peace and justice position, because he had boasted in his writings of his efforts to include the sado-masochistic branch of Dignity, the Defenders, to be more active in the Church; and Woolley himself had hosted Dignity meetings in bars that cater to the S/M crowd. Apparently, Weigand thought that Woolley's S/M background would not play well in the press for a man he had appointed as a peace and justice director for Sacramento's Catholics.

Under Bernardin's influence, the national episcopal bureaucracy became honeycombed with homosexuals and radical feminists. (Two deceased friends of Bernardin were the late Fr. John Muthig, a former editor at *St. Anthony Messenger* in Cincinnati [and a former co-worker of this reporter at the National Catholic News Service], to the priesthood, and to posts at the United Nations and the Vatican, where he became the first American editor of *L'Osservatore Romano*. Muthig died at age 42, in January 1991, allegedly of liver cancer; and John Willig, died of AIDS, after he was exposed as the head of Dignity in Washington, D.C.)

Not the only one

If Bernardin was the grand impresario of Amchurch, he certainly wasn't lacking in assistants, and mention must be made of one of his fellow Princes of the Church, James Cardinal Hickey, former Archbishop of Washington.

Born in 1920 in Midland, Michigan, Hickey is, arguably, one of those most responsible for the plague of bad bishops that beset the United States today. Chief among them are Albany's Howard Hubbard and Rochester's Matthew Clark, both of whom he would have known well from their days at the North American College in Rome, where he was rector, until being named an auxiliary bishop of Saginaw, Michigan, in 1967, when Detroit's Joseph Cardinal Dearden was at the height of his power. It was Hickey who appointed Clark "spiritual director" of the seminarians at the North

American, and as one priest told this reporter, "Clark would persecute any seminarian who believed in one Person of the Blessed Trinity, let alone all three."

As a prelate, Hickey showed his poor judgment in the men he ordained on numerous occasions; among some of the most notable are convicted pedophiles Thomas Chleboski, Art O'Brien (mentioned above in the Ferrario chapter) and former Catholic priest George Stallings, who was on the "fast lane" out of the priesthood until he was rescued by Hickey, then rector at the North American.

As *Washington Post* reporters Bill Dedman and Laura Sessions Stepp wrote when Stallings announced his intention to leave the Church ("Years of Defiance: Roots of Stallings Rebellion" April 29, 1990), the "bond" between the prelate and the fiery black preacher broke when Hickey discovered that Stallings had lied to him about where he was living.

"People who know Stallings well," wrote the reporters, "particularly fellow black clerics, said it had been inevitable that Stallings would leave the Church.

"He was a working-class man striving for affluence in a Church that values asceticism, they said, and a homosexual man in a Church that brands homosexuality a sin… 'It was obvious the man had a great deal of promise. He still has,' said a black priest who was Stallings' friend for a dozen years. "They were grooming him, but he missed the boat because of the indiscretions.

"'They were never going to make him a bishop if he was so openly homosexual…'"

Originally intending to be a priest for his native Diocese of Raleigh, Stallings was judged unfit for the priesthood by Bishop Vincent N. Waters after he returned from studies at the North American; so Stallings called Hickey for help, and Hickey had him transferred to the Washington Archdiocese. For at least 12 years, beginning in late 1978, Stallings' parishioners had complained about the wild parties at Stallings' home and the men visiting at all hours. In 1982, a pastoral assistant quit his job at his parish, St. Teresa's, after he walked in on a naked Stallings in the company of a naked boy who looked "about 14." Three years later, as Stallings' notoriety only increased, Hickey asked him to go to Rome for advanced studies.

146

A few years later, Stallings began his own church, and a few more years later, joined the Reverend Moon's Unification Church, and married in one of Moon's mass marriage ceremonies.

Another of Hickey's products was Fr. Paul Murray, who also attended the North American College when Hickey was rector. Murray become a Washington celebrity and an icon in the city's gay community after a well-publicized spat with Hickey after he was ordered to stop his involvement with the gay community. Murray, who came "out" in 1975, the year he was ordained, is now at Bard College in New York where he teaches "Modern Catholicism."

Questions for a cardinal

On June 12, 1998, Los Angeles Roger Cardinal Mahony was grilled for four hours by attorneys representing plaintiffs in a sexual abuse lawsuit against the Diocese of Stockton who wanted to know why he, Mahony, when he was Bishop of Stockton, permitted a known child abuser, Fr. Oliver O'Grady, to continue serving as a parish priest.

In 1994 Fr. Oliver O'Grady, a priest from Ireland working for the Diocese of Stockton, California, was sentenced to 14 years at Mud Creek State Penitentiary in Ione, California for molesting two brothers, Joh and James Howard, ages 19 and 22 when the lawsuit was filed.

The lawsuit sought financial compensation from the diocese for allowing O'Grady to function as a priest, despite his serious pedophilia problems, in some cases acted out on infants. The lawyer suing the diocese was Jeffrey Anderson of Minneapolis, one of the nation's foremost experts in clerical sexual abuse cases.

Mahony defended his actions as attorneys asked the cardinal such questions as:

- How could he claim he was unaware of O'Grady's problem when the parents of one abused child reported the molestation to his closest aide, Monsignor James Cain?

  Mahony answered that "it's difficult for me to speculate what Monsignor Cain would have or should have said at different points."

147

- Why did he appoint O'Grady a pastor at St. Andrew's Church in San Andreas in 1984 when he knew that police had investigated O'Grady for sex molestation?

  Mahony said he thought police dropped the investigation for lack of evidence.

  (A day earlier, former police officer Jerry Cranston testified that the investigation was dropped after the diocesan attorney pledged O'Grady would never work near children again.)

- Why did he advance O'Grady after he had received a psychiatric evaluation indicating O'Grady has a "severe defect in maturation, not only in the matter of sex, but more importantly in the matter of social relationships."

  Mahony responded that the report did not state O'Grady was unfit to be a priest.

  Mahony also testified that he believed pedophiles could be cured by professional counseling.

The Howards' civil lawsuit against the diocese went to trial June 10, with the brothers claiming they had irrefutable documentation and numerous eyewitnesses to prove that three bishops (including Cardinal-to-be Roger Mahony) allowed Fr. O'Grady to prey on children in parishes in Turlock, Lodi, San Andreas and Stockton, California, knowing the priest to be a pedophile.

In 1981, Cardinal Mahony, who was on a first-name basis with O'Grady, awarded him an honorary position as "special delegate serving students at the parochial school" even though the priest had admitted in writing to having molested children.

In 1984, according to the Howards, a year before Mahony ended his five-year stint as bishop of Stockton, Mahony's staff persuaded police to drop child molestation charges against O'Grady, falsely claiming the incident in question was isolated, with no other complaints reported, and saying that O'Grady would never again work with children.

On June 11, the jury heard testimony from Carmen Correia, the mother of a girl who had been molested by O'Grady.

O'Grady had written the family a letter of apology, having been told to do so by his pastor. According to Mrs. Correia, when she told Bishop Merlin Guilfoyle (the bishop before Mahony) about O'Grady's actions, "his attitude was one of patronizing disbelief. So when we produced the letter that Fr. O'Grady had given us, then he got very quiet and very serious...As he read the letter, he was visibly angry."

Guilfoyle told the family he would remove O'Grady from the parish and put him in a position where he would not work with children. However, the following year, O'Grady was appointed associate pastor of Sacred Heart Church in Turlock, where he met the Howard family.

At trial, Nancy Sloan-Ferguson testified that in 1986 she presented Bishop Donald Montrose and Vicar General Monsignor James Cain with a copy of a letter of apology she received from O'Grady after he molested her, also at age 11. Now working as a rape crisis counselor, Sloan-Ferguson warned the bishop and vicar general that O'Grady might be continuing to molest children.

She claimed she asked them if there had been any further complaints about O'Grady since her 1976 case and was told there had not.

Lawyers for the Diocese of Stockton claimed that Church officials did not consider O'Grady to be a continued threat to children because in the 1970s and 1980s mental health professionals did not know much about pedophilia and thought the disorder could be controlled by counseling, which O'Grady was receiving.

In his deposition, Cardinal Mahony allegedly claimed that he did not know Fr. O'Grady and his reported child molestation. Testifying at the trial on June 12, Mahony reiterated that diocesan officials believed they were following the correct course, as advised by mental health experts of the day.

Numerous other people have come forward claiming O'Grady molested them as children, many having had their lawsuits thrown out of court (as happened with another Howard brother and one of their sisters), because they waited too long to report the abuse.

Since O'Grady's 1994 criminal trial, the diocese claimed it held several workshops for local priests, bringing in lawyers and psychologists to address questions of appropriate behavior toward parishioners, laws concerning reporting suspected child abuse and other issues.

Did Cardinal Mahony learn anything from this experience? Perhaps nothing except that he would never, if he could prevent it, appear on the stand in a courtroom again.

As Dallas attorney Sylvia Demarest told me after the summer 2001 sexual abuse case involving Monsignor Michael Harris: "I can tell you as a fact that [Roger] Cardinal Mahony paid out $5.2 million last summer in the case of Monsignor Harris because he didn't want to be subpoenaed and he didn't want all the documents on Bishop [G. Patrick] Ziemann and the perversion in his seminary to come out."

Pieces of the puzzle

The year 1999 saw two bishops resign their posts, Ziemann and Ryan, but another major piece of the puzzle of clerical pedophilia fell into place when *The Wanderer* received information in June 1999 that refuted denials made by Bishop Joseph Fiorenza, president of the National Conference of Catholic Bishops, that he never allowed known clerical pedophiles to function in the Diocese of San Angelo while he was ordinary there.

After a lawsuit involving Fr. Dennis Peterson was filed against Bishop Fiorenza and the Diocese of Galveston-Houston, which said Fiorenza had a history of assigning known pedophiles, the diocese issued a statement describing the charge as "false and defamatory."

In a June 16, 1999, news release issued by the Diocese of Houston, Bishop Fiorenza "says he knew of no sexual record and that there were no allegations against the priest [Fr. David Holley] while he served in San Angelo."

According to published news reports, court documents and letters written to and from Bishop Fiorenza obtained by *The Wanderer*, Fiorenza knew for several years that Holley had sexually abused minor males and that recurrences of "his past problems" finally prompted Fiorenza to expel Holley in 1984.

Bishop Fiorenza acted properly by expelling Holley; but a look at Holley's career illuminates the problem Dallas attorney Sylvia Demarest raised in the Kos case – of bishops ordaining men with severe sexual problems, allowing them to act on them, and then transferring them from one diocese to another.

Holley joined the Diocese of San Angelo in 1977, two years before Fiorenza arrived, after being expelled from numerous dioceses and undergoing treatment at least three times at different centers for his sexual problems.

In May 1977, Holley was expelled from the Diocese of El Paso. Bishop Sidney Metzger wrote Holley: "...I have come to the painful decision that you will no longer be permitted to function as a priest in the Diocese of El Paso...We do not intend to pass judgment on you or your actions, realizing that many past events have had an impact on your life. It is my suggestion that you remain with your family and seek employment as a layman."

Four months later Metzger wrote to Bishop Steven Leven of San Angelo, who had sent Holley for treatment to Southdown in Ontario, that "you and I also know from our experience with such unfortunate matters that such cases are always a calculated risk."

In 1982, with Holley functioning as a priest in the diocese, Fiorenza wrote to Bishop Bernard Flanagan of Worcester, Holley's ordinary, that he knew of Holley's "past difficulties" but that "with our priest shortage, I am willing to risk incardinating him."

In a June 2, 1982 letter to Flanagan, Fiorenza wrote:

"I am grateful for your letter concerning Fr. David Holley. He has been working in the Diocese of San Angelo for four years and, as far as I know, there has been no serious problem with his ministry here. I am aware of some of his past difficulties yet I do not know the extent of his problems.

"With our shortage of priests, I am willing to risk incardinating him unless you would advise me against it, since you know him far better than I do. During my time as bishop here, he has not given me any serious reason not to accept him into the diocese. If I do incardinate him, I will urge him to continue some sort of therapy in order to guard against a relapse.

"He is very sensitive about his past and becomes most emotional in talking about it or if he thinks any of the priests are too inquisitive about his past ministry before coming to West Texas..."

Less than two weeks later, on June 14, 1982, Bishop Flanagan sent a letter to Holley formally excardinating him from the Diocese of Worcester:

"...I write to inform you that, since it is apparent that there is a greater need for your services in that diocese for the good of souls, I hereby excardinate you by this letter permanently and unconditionally according to Canon #112 that you may be incardinated in the Diocese of San Angelo.

"Your excardination will take effect upon your receiving letters of incardination from the Bishop of the Diocese of San Angelo..."

Six months later, on December 22, 1982, Fiorenza wrote to Flanagan to advise him that Holley had relapsed and he had no plans to incardinate him, but that he would give him a "fair chance":

"Dear Bishop Flanagan:

"In June you were kind enough to issue a letter of excardination for Fr. David Holley. Since that time some of his past problems surfaced again which made it advisable for me not to incardinate him. In fact, at this time I have no plans to incardinate him. I communicated this to him last October. He understands completely my position on his incardination.

"For the past several months Fr. Holley has been studying Spanish in San Antonio and Mexico in order to more efficiently minister to the people of this Diocese. I have made it clear to him that I will give him a fair chance to exercise his priesthood here, but if there is one more lapse I will ask him to leave. This, too, he fully understands..."

On May 25, 1984, Fiorenza wrote to the new bishop of Worcester, Timothy Harrington:

"Dear Bishop Harrington:

"One of your priests, Fr. David Holley, has been working in the Diocese of San Angelo for the past several years. During this period of time on a few occasions his past problems surfaced. On Dec. 22, 1982, I informed Bishop Flanagan that I would give Fr. Holley one more chance. It is with regret that I write now to say that Fr. Holley has made it impossible for us to keep him in this diocese...As a small missionary diocese we are unable to continue our association with him..."

One month later, Fiorenza advised Harrington that Holley was living at a parish in the Diocese of Amarillo, but had already been told by Bishop Leroy Matthiesen that he could not be incardinated in Amarillo.

On August 13, 1984, Fr. Holley wrote to Bishop Flanagan to inform him "I am now working at St. Joseph Church [in Amarillo]. My plans are to remain in this diocese and, God willing, to be incardinated."

Flashback

Let's look now at David Holley, born in 1928 in Pennsylvania, and ordained a Benedictine priest in 1958. His first assignment was in Reading, Pennsylvania, where he was unable to get along with the other priests, and so he applied to Bishop Flanagan to be incardinated in the Worcester Diocese in May 1962.

In 1962, according to a deposition filed by Holley, his "psychosexual disorder began to manifest itself," though medical reports indicate his homosexual problems and addiction to pornography began at age 20 while serving in the Navy.

According to Holley's own deposition, filed in response to a 1992 lawsuit:

"Before I became officially incardinated to the Diocese of Worcester, Bishop Flanagan had received reports that I had sexually molested boys in the above-referenced [three parishes: St. Philip's in Grafton, St. Mary of the Hills in Boylston and Our Lady of Fatima in Worcester]. On at least two occasions, Bishop Flanagan called me in to discuss the allegations, cautioned me against causing scandal in the Church, but he expressed no comments about my victims."

In 1968, Flanagan sent Holley to priest-psychiatrist Fr. Jerome Hayden for treatment; and assigned Holley to be associate pastor at St. Anne's parish in Southboro. In 1969, Flanagan sent Holley for treatment of his psycho-sexual disorder to Seton Psychiatric Institute in Baltimore.

In Dec 1970, he was discharged, had his faculties restored, but was refused an assignment by Flanagan, who then began trying to find a place for Holley in a different diocese. Holley was rejected by Boston and Wilmington, Delaware.

In March 1971, Flanagan sent Holley to the Servants of the Paraclete in New Mexico, where he was placed in a house in Albuquerque and worked as a priest for the Archdiocese of Santa Fe. According to his deposition, "I participated in no therapy or treatment programs offered by the Paracletes... Additionally, I believe Paracletes obtained faculties for me from the Archdiocese of Santa Fe since I performed all the holy sacraments in these Albuquerque churches…"

In 1972, Holley was posted to Alamogordo and remained in that diocese until 1977, when he moved to San Angelo and began efforts to become incardinated there.

According to *Wanderer* sources in Texas, Holley, now 74, received his 275-year prison sentence in 1993 for abusing "hundreds of boys" while stationed in New Mexico, though the civil lawsuit filed against him was brought by only 16 of his victims. Unconfirmed reports from reliable sources indicate that the Diocese of San Angelo settled several claims against Holley while Fiorenza was bishop, though all records remain sealed.

Apart from Fiorenza's unfortunate involvement in the case of Fr. Holley, Holley seems to signify an ecclesial "meltdown."

To begin with, why were the Benedictines in Pennsylvania unable to discern that the troubled young man who applied to be a Benedictine priest – who had manifested effeminate traits, had homosexual experiences and had already become addicted to pornography – should not be ordained a priest?

What does this say about the Benedictine formation process?

Second, why would Bishop Bernard Flanagan incardinate a known child abuser in his diocese and continue to reassign Holley to parishes even though he knew of his compulsive addiction to both pornography and sexual experiences with young males?

Third, why did Church authorities fail to return Holley to the lay state when they knew that's where he belonged?

In a 1970 letter, the late Bishop Timothy Harrington, then auxiliary bishop in Worcester under Bernard Flanagan, wrote to Dr. Louis Cleary, clinical director of the Seton Psychiatric Center in Baltimore, that "Bishop Flanagan and I have had such serious doubts about Fr. continuing in his priesthood that, at one time, it was suggested that he seek a dispensation and return to the lay state…

"People have been so greatly disturbed by his behavior that we would wonder whether he can avoid his reputation going before him in any area of this compact diocese. We also question whether we can chance the possibility of his having another relapse."

Fourth, when bishops talk about "calculated risks" they are speaking falsely: they are not the ones exposed to the real risk. The ones whose lives are put in jeopardy, who are really at risk, are the families and young people put at the disposal of these predators.

Fifth, the Holley case illustrates the refusal of the Catholic hierarchy to understand that pedophiles are not curable and, if clerical pedophiles have a claim on the Church, they should be permanently isolated from the Catholic community and confined to maintenance centers for the rest of their lives.

Sixth, most unfortunately, the Holley case provides an insight into the episcopal mind-set that Catholic lay people and families are not to be respected or in any significant way included in problems of this sort. Not to inform the laity that a problem priest is coming into their parish shows a profound disrespect for the laity, especially parents of children.

Bishop Ryan resigns

On October 19, 1999, Bishop Daniel Ryan of Springfield announced Pope John Paul II had accepted his resignation, becoming the second U.S. prelate to resign within four months following public allegations of homosexual misconduct.

Ryan's resignation was a vindication for Stephen Brady, founder of Roman Catholic Faithful (RCF) in Springfield, who had been publicly demanding Ryan's resignation since November 1996 after receiving reports from priests about how Ryan sexually abused them.

Ryan and his aides had denied RCF's allegations of homosexual misconduct, and engaged in smear attacks on Roman Catholic Faithful.

But the lurid details of his sexual misconduct had circulated for years among clergy and laity in Springfield, among readers of RCF's newsletter, *Ad Majorem Dei Gloriam (A.M.D.G.)* and on the Internet website double-cross.com, which posted the signed affidavit of a male prostitute whom Ryan paid handsomely for sexual favors for 11 years, from 1984 to 1995.

The male prostitute, Frank Bergen, said he spent the large amounts of money Ryan paid him for "cocaine, pot, LSD and alcohol," and that Ryan knew "as I confessed this to him many times, and he continued to give and give, never even offering to help me with treatment or counseling."

"Obviously we are delighted at the announcement of Ryan's resignation," Brady told this reporter at the time, "but we are very sad that it took the Holy See almost three years to act. The damage that Ryan has done since we first notified the Holy See of his homosexual activity with prostitutes and others is monumental," and he added, "I also hope that the American hierarchy will find some way to honestly address the issue of abuse and homosexual activity by members of the hierarchy."

The news of Ryan's "retirement" was released at 5 a.m. October 19 in a curiously-worded statement issued by Springfield's vicar general, Fr. John Renken, which began: "Below is the statement of Bishop Ryan, former Bishop of Springfield in Illinois, made public at 5 a.m. today...More details will come as they are available."

In his statement, Ryan, who was dogged by demonstrators carrying signs whenever he showed up for a public appearance, said:

"I am grateful to our Holy Father for allowing me to retire and for sending a very fine priest, whom I know and esteem, to be ordained bishop as my successor. Monsignor Lucas is a person of keen intelligence, devoted to Christ and His people, kind and pastoral in outlook. I will be in the front line to welcome him and to assure him of my full cooperation and support.

"I have felt for some time that I should step aside and have an opportunity for another type of service to our Lord's people than that of being 'where the buck stops.' My next birthday will be my seventieth. While I want to discuss details of my retirement with Bishop-elect Lucas, I look forward to spending it here in our diocese, which I have come to know and love as my home..."

Ryan, a native of Minnesota, was ordained a priest for the Diocese of Joliet, Illinois, in 1956 and an auxiliary bishop for Joliet in Sept. 1981 (two years after his mentor, Joseph Imesch of Detroit was appointed Bishop of Joliet). He was appointed Bishop of Springfield in Nov. 1983.

On the day of his consecration as bishop, Joseph Cardinal Bernardin of Chicago, the metropolitan, proclaimed Ryan's consecration as "a joyful day in Springfield...

"Today there is excitement and joy because we are installing Bishop Ryan. It signifies a new era...Ryan has already earned the respect of fellow bishops and is a long-time friend and collaborator of many local clerics."

After fourteen years of Ryan's reign, in which the diocese deteriorated in every measurable way, Steve Brady founded Roman Catholic Faithful after an outpouring of support from *Wanderer* readers following a report in this newspaper documenting the layman's efforts to oppose rotten sex education programs in public and Catholic schools supported by Ryan's chancery bureaucrats.

Once the establishment of RCF was announced in May 1996, Brady started receiving reports from priests in the diocese, from priests across the Midwest, and laity in the region about Ryan's homosexual activity.

Provided compelling information, Brady's first step to effectuate Ryan's removal was to write to Cardinal Bernardin asking for a meeting, which Bernardin denied, saying it was not appropriate for him to intercede in another diocese.

In November 1996, with the assistance of attorney James Bendell, who had successfully litigated pedophile cases in the Archdiocese of Seattle, Brady wrote a letter to Ryan asking him to resign within five days or he would make the information about his strange sexual proclivities public.

One day after Brady sent the letter, his attorney, Bendell, received a response from the diocesan attorneys, Graham and Graham, declaring, in part: "…We know there is absolutely no truth to these baseless claims made in the Brady letter and know that you would, with an absolute minimum of investigation, find these claims are utterly fantastic…

"We must advise, however, that should Mr. Brady proceed with any further threatened publication of these false, unsubstantiated defamatory allegations, we will advise the Diocese and this Bishop Ryan, to respond and assert their legal rights against Stephen G. Brady, Roman Catholic Faithful, his or its counsel, and others so involved, to the fullest extent of the law."

One month later, Brady contacted Fr. John Hardon, SJ, and provided him with documentation from priests of the diocese who claimed Ryan had sexually propositioned them. Fr. Hardon personally interviewed those priests, and possessing their statements, visited the Apostolic Nuncio in Washington, Archbishop Agostino Cacciavillan, to relay that information to the Holy See.

Subsequently, Fr. Hardon made a visit to Rome, with one of the priests from Springfield, to personally deliver the documentation to the prefect of the Congregation for Clergy, Archbishop Darion Castrillon Hoyos.

Nothing was done.

In February 1997, Brady called his first press conference in Springfield to publicly accuse Ryan of homosexual misconduct, charging Ryan had "physically harassed priests" and had "consensual sex with priests," though he would not disclose their names, leaving himself open to the charge that his claims were not credible.

Ryan, himself, said the charges were "vague" and "unfounded," adding, "I categorically deny his accusations."

Nearly a year later, in December of 1997, with the help of private investigators and laity, RCF contacted several male prostitutes who had been paid by Ryan for their services.

"The information they gave, about Ryan's anatomy, the inside of his rectory, his eating, drinking and spending habits, was compelling," said Brady.

At that point, Brady announced another press conference to release this new information.

Just days before the scheduled event, however, Brady was contacted by the Archdiocese of Chicago, now headed by Francis Cardinal George. During that contact, Brady was asked to postpone the conference to give the Vatican some time to effect Ryan's resignation. Brady agreed to postpone the press conference for one month.

Cardinal George sent Jimmy Lago, executive director of the Catholic Conference of Illinois, a Bernardin appointee, to meet with Brady and determine what information Brady possessed.

"What was extremely puzzling," Brady recalled, "is that Lago did not want some of the information we had, claiming they had other sources for this information.

"I assume Lago discussed the matter with Cardinal George, because shortly thereafter I received a phone call from the cardinal, who asked us to remain silent. He promised us a 'relationship with the hierarchy' if we were obedient. I asked him what obedience meant. I was told, essentially, obedience means remaining silent, and to let the hierarchy work to remove Ryan – but he couldn't promise anything. He made that very clear."

Fully aware that neither the Vatican nor Ryan's fellow bishops in Illinois would work to remove Ryan, RCF began an intensive public relations campaign to expose Ryan, publishing information about him in its newsletter, picketing him at public events, even outside the hotel where the National Conference of Catholic Bishops met in Washington.

Brady held his second press conference in January 1998, at which he provided members of the press with the affidavit of Frank Bergen, then in prison on a theft charge.

Local media attended the conference, but provided little coverage.

As Brady's efforts to expose Ryan continued, he began receiving more information pertaining to Ryan's friends in the hierarchy, notably the "Detroit mafia," established by the late John Cardinal Dearden, which included, among others, Cardinals Hickey and Bernardin, and Bishops Imesch, Kenneth Untener, Thomas Gumbleton, and other bishops originally from the Midwest, who were by then posted elsewhere.

"We especially received information from some prominent Midwest attorneys regarding the pedophilia problem in the Church – particularly in the Midwest – and how the victims were treated as the enemy by diocesan attorneys," said Brady.

"The attorneys told us court documents were sealed, but that we were on the right track and should proceed."

One of those who contacted Brady was attorney Mark Bellow of West Bloomfield, Mich., who successfully litigated cases of sexual abuse against Detroit priests.

He told Brady directly: "Imesch, Dearden and Gumbleton: all of them lied under oath. Dearden and Gumbleton were professional and respectful; Imesch was sarcastic and nasty."

(Imesch, incidentally, was named an auxiliary bishop in Detroit under Dearden, in 1973.)

Despite Brady's constant efforts to expose him as a sexual predator, Ryan continued his homosexual cruising around Springfield.

"The most recent information we have," Brady said the day Ryan announced his retirement, "is his sexual contact with prostitutes continued up to Christmas 1998."

In his signed affidavit, mentioned above, male prostitute Frank Bergen describes in abundant detail the nature of his homosexual relationship with Ryan, beginning when Bergen was 16, and ending in 1995, when Bergen was 27.

Not only was Bergen sexually abused by Ryan, but also by a number of other priests in the diocese, which he named, and whose names he gave to Ryan.

Bergen also described Ryan's residence:

"I also was taken to his personal residence above the Cathedral of the Immaculate Conception at 6th and Lawrence St. I was always taken to his apt. there thru the garage entrance which was past a huge walk-in vault, like the ones in a bank, then up the stairs to the elevator which led to his top floor apt. The frontal room of his apt. looked down over 6th St. It also served as a library and study. There was a long hallway. His personal bedroom was right next to his personal bathroom, which was very beautifully done in black and white marble and gold faucets…

"I dated him until he went into treatment [for alcoholism], and even a few times after…"

Bergen also identified other male prostitutes Ryan hired, who also submitted affidavits detailing their relationship with the bishop.

Possibly, one of the most suspicious circumstances surrounding Brady's investigation of Ryan was the untimely, and as yet unsolved, brutal murder of Fr. Alfred Kunz, pastor of St. Michael's parish in the Diocese of Madison, Wisconsin.

At the urging of Fr. Hardon, Brady contacted Fr. Kunz, a well-known and reliable canon lawyer with contacts in Rome, at his home in Dane, Wisconsin in March 1997, approximately one year before his murder.

"Fr. Hardon suggested that Kunz would be a good individual to guide us regarding canon law," said Brady, "and it was Fr. Kunz who told me, 'in ordinary times, you'll find justice in the Church, but these are extraordinary times and you'll not find justice in the Church.'" Brady remained in regular contact with Kunz throughout the year, right up to his death.

Prior to Kunz's murder, Brady contacted Kunz about Jimmy Lago's visit.

"I asked Fr. Kunz if there was a reliable person in Chicago, close to Cardinal George, that I could contact, and it was shortly after Kunz gave me that individual's name that he was murdered," Brady said.

Following Kunz's murder, Dane County investigators traveled to Springfield and spent three days there, talking to Brady and Ryan's prostitute, Frank Bergen, and even Bishop Ryan, along with several other priests in the diocese.

Investigators also went to Detroit to talk with Fr. Hardon.

"I don't know the outcome of that investigation," Brady said, "but I can tell you the investigators wanted to know what files I had sent him, so they could check to see if they were still in his home after his murder."

The irony of all this unpleasantness is that Ryan's homosexual misconduct would never have come to light had he and his apparatchiks shown even a little respect to those faithful Catholics in his diocese such as Stephen Brady.

When the laity objected to liturgical abuses, abuses of their children through so-called "sex education", and the modernist catechetics imposed on children and their families in parish religion programs, they were dismissed by the diocese and the local press as "dissident" cranks.

If Ryan had shown himself to be a Catholic bishop, aware of his duty to uphold the faith, his personal problems would have remained hidden.

But his commitment to modernism and self-gratification unleashed a flood of revelations from different sources that coalesced into serious and credible accusations of grave abuse of ecclesiastical power and the resources of the faithful.

Nine days after Ryan announced his retirement, a lawsuit was filed against him. "It is specifically averred," the suit declared, "that Bishop Ryan ignored his oath and obligation of celibacy by virtue of multiple homosexual relationships with then, now former, male prostitutes and other priests or deacons to wit: John Doe X, John Doe Y and Reverend Fr. John Doe Z (the identities of whom are known to the Defendants), among others, during his tenure as bishop to such an extent that an atmosphere of tolerance to the sexual abuse of minors was thereby created, facilitated and perpetuated by Defendant Ryan."

Brady's investigation into Bishop Imesch's background, especially his close ties to Detroit Auxiliary Gumbleton, in the Spring/Summer 2001 edition of his newsletter, *A.M.D.G.,* shed a great deal of light on the ecclesial gangsterism that is the operative in Amchurch, and that gangsterism's relationship – so to speak – with the spread of homosexual agit prop in Amchurch structures and the protection of pedophile priests.

Gumbleton and Imesch, both of whom were ordained in 1956 for the Archdiocese of Detroit, were groomed in gangsterism by the late Cardinal Dearden, and both were pretty much running the archdiocese in Dearden's last days. In the late '70s and early '80s, when Gumbleton was promoting Dignity in Detroit, Imesch and Dearden were trying to frustrate a Vatican investigation into St. John's Seminary where homosexuality was rampant, and all three were working hard to get fellow priest Ken Untener, St. John's rector, appointed as Bishop of Saginaw – even after his role in showing seminarians pornographic videos was publicly exposed.

The most fascinating revelations Brady offered concerned Imesch and his relationship with priest-pedophile Fr. Gary Dennis Berthiaume, who was arrested and convicted in 1977 (criminal case # 77-34652-FY). At the time of Berthiaume's troubles, he resided at Our Lady of Sorrows Church. Then Fr. Joseph Imesch was pastor. After Berthiaume's conviction, he was conveniently welcomed into the Diocese of Cleveland, then run by future Washington Cardinal James Hickey, formerly of Saginaw, and another of Dearden's gangsters. After Imesch was appointed Bishop of Joliet, he brought Berthiaume to Joliet, aware that there were allegations of misconduct against him in Cleveland.

Another tell-tale episode involved Fr. Lawrence Gibbs, another pedophile whom Imesch transferred from parish to parish – even though Catholic parents in the diocese were aware of Gibbs' background and alarmed Imesch would appoint a pedophile to a parish with a school.

Brady prints Imesch's responses to a number of these letters. Typical of Imesch's attitude are these three sentences, from different letters:

"There is no reason to believe that Fr. Gibbs cannot minister effectively in a parish situation."

"[H]is ministry at Christ the King was very well received by a great number of people."

"I believe that Fr. Gibbs is an excellent priest and has served the people of your community extremely well."

What's interesting about Gibbs – in addition to the fact that he went into the priesthood from Holy Name Cathedral, Chicago, under the tutelage of now-retired Auxiliary Bishop Timothy Lyne, is that the chancellor for the Joliet Diocese who handled all of the ordination paperwork for Gibbs was none other than the retired Bishop of Springfield, Daniel Ryan, whom Imesch advanced into the episcopate even though he was widely known to be an alcoholic (among other things) at the time.

Another interesting insight on Imesch was presented by Detroit priest Monsignor Clifford F. Sawher in *An Autobiography of a Grateful Priest*. This really wonderful book details the trials and tribulations of a priest ordained in June 1952, who lived through the ethnic cleansing or "urban renewal" of Detroit in the post-war period, and then the autodemolition of the Church in the post-conciliar period.

In addition to being pastor of the justly-famous Assumption Grotto parish, Msgr. Sawher served as the Chairman of the archdiocese's Family Life Bureau, and he chronicles in considerable detail how the revolution unfolded in the archdiocese once Cardinal Dearden returned from the Council, how the presbyterate quickly polarized between "liberals" and "conservatives," and how the revolutionaries came to power. He has offered many vignettes of fellow priests including this of then-Fr. Imesch. Recalling how the priests of the chancery would often dine together after a long day of work, Sawher relates:

"...Dinner was always a delight...It was a great time to relax. We dined in shirt sleeves, leaving our collar and jacket in our room...Fr. Joseph Imesch who later became monsignor, and then bishop, was often the life of the conversation. He was so serious all day long as secretary to the archbishop that he really let loose at dinner whenever he was with us. One of the most belittling experiences of all my life took place at one of these dinners. I do not recall the occasion, but it was not unusual for someone to dare another to do something. We were laughing about something silly, and then Msgr. Imesch picked up a full pie, creamy, perhaps a banana pie, and said, 'Sawher, I think I'll put this pie right in your face.' I said, foolishly, 'You wouldn't dare.'

"'You dare me?' he said. 'Yes,' I said, 'I dare you.' Before I could take it back he was up and the pie was in my face. I couldn't believe it. Who would believe a grown man would do such a thing? But I should have known better. Joseph Imesch was not yet grown up. We were both embarrassed, but I had the pie on my face…"

After telling that story, Msgr. Sawher described the battles between clergy over *Humanae Vitae*, and the ridicule he endured for staunchly defending Pope Paul VI's encyclical. Most in the chancery rejected it, he says, as did most of the professors at the archdiocese's seminary. He also recalls how Detroit priests became enamored of Carl Roger's self-fulfillment psychology, and like lemmings, left the priesthood to marry or whatever else might have felt good at the time.

Sawher, himself, was edged out of the Family Life Bureau, and assigned to Assumption Grotto by Dearden, where he had the near-impossible task of maintaining the parish amidst the parishioners' flight to the suburbs. But at a time of tremendous social and ecclesial change, Sawher realized the key to a successful parish was running it according to the Church's precepts – and for that he suffered more ridicule.

When the nuns wanted the "new catechetics," he stood up to them and told them to teach the *Baltimore Catechism* or leave. When liturgical innovations and abuses were the norm, he gave his parishioners the fullness of the Roman Rite of the Mass. When his fellow pastors were "renovating" their churches and discarding statues and hiding the tabernacle, he beautified his parish, and promoted Adoration of the Blessed Sacrament and Novenas. When other priests were abandoning the Confessional, he extended the times he spent hearing confessions, and promoted frequent confession in his parish.

The Ziemann case

On July 21, 1999, Bishop G. Patrick Ziemann, a former auxiliary bishop of Los Angeles under Roger Cardinal Mahony, resigned as Bishop of Santa

Rosa, just days after Fr. Jorge Hume Salas, then 41, filed a complaint in Sonoma County Superior Court accusing Ziemann of sexually abusing him since 1996.

Ziemann, then 57, was appointed bishop of Santa Rosa in 1992, after having served as vice-rector and dean of studies at Our Lady Queen of Angels Seminary in Mission Hills.

There are a number of bizarre improprieties to this case that again raised the question more and more Catholics were asking: had a homosexual clique in the Church become so powerful and arrogant that they could use and abuse anyone and anything that came within their orbit? Not only did Ziemann force an illicitly ordained priest to commit sex acts with him, he drove the Santa Rosa Diocese to the brink of bankruptcy, all the while grooming his reputation as a national leader of "youth ministry."

Jorge Hume Salas, a Costa Rican native, was recruited by Ziemann to work in "youth ministry" among Hispanics. Ordained by Ziemann in 1996 at an outdoor fair, without ever going through seminary training or receiving the standard psychological evaluations, the lawsuit claimed that Ziemann began pressuring Salas for sex as soon as he learned that there were financial irregularities at the parish to which Salas had been assigned.

The lawsuit stated: "Ziemann summoned Salas to his home under pretense to talk to about how Salas was feeling. During this private meeting, Ziemann grabbed Salas and began to kiss him, to remove his clothes, and fondle his genitals."

After the sexual abuse began, Ziemann sent Salas to a treatment center for priests in St. Louis for psychological evaluation. Ziemann visited Salas there, took him to a hotel for sex, and then "bought him an ice cream and tucked $80 in Salas' pocket."

The lawsuit also alleged that after Salas returned to Santa Rosa, Ziemann would summon the priest by cell phone or beeper once or twice a week for sex. The lawsuit also claimed that Salas "often would cry when forced to perform acts on Ziemann, and he begged Ziemann to stop calling him for sex." Salas also claimed that Ziemann gave him a venereal disease.

While "Bishop Pat" pretended to be a great reformer of abuses, wrote Bob Klose and Mike Geniella in the Santa Rosa *Press Democrat* in an August 23, 1999 report on the crisis in the diocese, "since Ziemann's financial mismanagement came to light following his resignation, he was, in reality, a master of deceit."

However Ziemann responded to cases involving sexual abuse of minors, the reporters wrote, a review of his record dating back to 1980 appears to indicate that his actions – in cases of sexual misconduct within the priesthood, financial irregularities, or even questionable credentials of some priests and religious school administrators – were meant to discourage public scrutiny.

In 1992, shortly before his arrival in Santa Rosa, Ziemann and other Church leaders in Southern California were criticized by Simi Valley police for resisting filing criminal charges against a priest who faced accusations of embezzling $60,000 in church money. In another case, a former seminary student in a 1994 sworn statement claimed that Ziemann in 1980, while an instructor at an Orange County seminary, ignored his complaints that seminary and high school students were being sexually abused by priests.

In Ziemann's own case, Hume's explosive charges were hidden from public view for months after his lawyers and Hume's – beginning in September 1998 – attempted to negotiate a financial settlement and keep the sexual allegations quiet. When the talks broke down for the last time in April, Hume went public by filing a lawsuit...

For Ziemann, his own scandal has attracted attention to his earlier roles in the sex investigations in Orange and Ventura counties before he was appointed bishop of Santa Rosa. Ziemann had been an auxiliary bishop in Santa Barbara, and before that, a seminary instructor.

In the Orange County case, Richard Nason, a former seminary student, signed a sworn affidavit on Oct. 24, 1994, in support of a lawsuit filed by two friends who accused a former principal at a Catholic high school of sexually molesting them while they were students. In the statement, Nason said he told Ziemann in May 1980 not only about numerous incidents of sexual abuse at the seminary, but also about cases involving students at the Catholic high school.

Nason said he didn't learn until years later, when another former student filed a claim against the church, that church leaders, including Ziemann, had taken no action. 'I felt let down by Fr.

Ziemann, and was very distressed that the abuse had continued,'
he said…

The youth ministry scam

Because of all the publicity about Ziemann at the time of his outing, often
neglected was contemporaneous news about Santa Rosa priest Fr. Don
Kimball, considered a "national leader" in youth ministry, who was facing
charges for molesting both boys and girls in the late 1970s.

"The Kimball case keeps the focus on sexual crimes and misconduct by
diocesan priests; allegations of cover-ups and looking the other way by
diocesan officials; and the potential for more payouts that already have cost
diocesan members more than $6 million," wrote Santa Rosa *Press Democrat*
reporters Bob Klose and Roger Digitale back in November 1999.

Kimball became well-known in the youth ministry circles for his book, *The
Wedge*, which adapted the teachings of Abraham Maslow, founder of
"humanistic psychology," to the destruction of Catholic youth in Church-
sponsored programs through sophisticated mind-altering and mind-
controlling techniques.

"The suit against Kimball," Klose and Digitale continued, "filed two years
ago, claims that between 1976 and 1981 Kimball sexually abused the four
young people while he was an associate pastor at Resurrection Parish in
Santa Rosa and later administrator of the diocese's High School Youth
Ministry. The plaintiffs are Neil and Ellen Brem, a brother and sister;
Lorraine Brunz and Chris Ovard, who claim they were abused by Kimball
during the four-year time period. The alleged abuse, ranging from fondling
and massage to sodomy, began when Neil was 12, Ellen was 8, Lorraine
was 17 and Chris was 17, according to the lawsuit…"

Since Kimball's arrest, there have been a number of very-high profile cases
of "youth ministers" and sexual abuse of minors, the most notorious of
which involved Christopher Reardon, in the Archdiocese of Boston, and
two youth ministers in the Diocese of Phoenix, both of whom were
involved in LifeTeen Masses.

The whole notion of "youth ministry," some have argued, is based on a
false premise, that "youth" need to be reached "where they are" and
enabled to "open up" and speak about their emotional needs and desires. It
is the program of Church bureaucrats who have nothing of substance to

offer, and it provides them with the opportunity and the subjects for their own theories and desires.

A sick minister

Perhaps the sickest "youth minister" to ever serve the Church in this country was Christopher Reardon, religious education director at St. Agnes Church in Middleton, in the Archdiocese of Boston, who was arraigned on June 16, 2000 for sexually abusing as many as 250 young people.

Essex District Attorney Kevin Burke said the Reardon case may be the "largest single child abuse case in Massachusetts history."

"Burke," reported *The Boston Globe* on June 17, "said that while searching Reardon's home this week, investigators found a list of 250 names of boys ranging in age from 5 to 14. Burke said that notes were found next to the most of the names, offering detailed descriptions of the children's genitalia and how Reardon had allegedly molested them.

"In addition, Burke said police found a video at the suspect's home showing Reardon and one of his alleged victims masturbating. The district attorney said the tape was recorded using a camera in the ceiling of the rectory of St. Agnes Church in Middleton, where Reardon was youth ministries coordinator."

Among the dozens of charges against Reardon, he not only secretly videotaped his abuse, he saved the boys' semen in Styrofoam cups in a closet in the home he shared with his wife.

A year later, at his August 17 trial, Reardon's defense was that he was just trying to give his young charges sex education, a defense the judge found ridiculous before sentencing him to 50 years in jail.

At sentencing, Judge Isaac Borenstein was stern, telling Reardon:

> This was sexual molestation. In the face of overwhelming evidence to the contrary, claims that this was sexualization are incredible…Mr. Reardon, I've got to tell you, you did not perform oral sex on four boys, repeatedly, or had them perform it on you, to educate them…You did not indecently touch a number of other boys or had them touch you, to educate them. You did not, sir, masturbate with them in, in front of them, or had them masturbate in front of you, to provide sexual education. You did not, sir, use paraphernalia of a sexual nature,

and toys, with these boys, to educate them. And you did not have in your possession a significant amount of child pornography, to educate any of these boys. I'm convinced beyond a reasonable doubt Mr. Reardon that you did these things for your own sexual gratification, for your own selfish needs, and with a callous disregard for the impact that your actions were going to have on these victims...

The short-and long-term harm may be worse to these children from having been violated by someone they trusted than from someone who may have caused them harm on the street.

The Reardon case is not likely to disappear soon, since there seems, at this writing, no limit to the number of lawsuits against the Archdiocese of Boston filed by his victims, and there are credible allegations that archdiocesan officials were repeatedly warned that Reardon was engaged in felonious activities, and his supervisor – the pastor of the parish – was himself so engaged in sexual affairs he looked the other way.

Less than a year after Ziemann's resignation, reporter Eric Reslock of the *San Francisco Faith* (June 2000) interviewed Dr. William Coulson, a former colleague of Carl Rogers, with whom he transformed the minds of hundreds, if not thousands, of California priests, religious and seminarians in the years after Vatican II, and got them focused on sex.

This interview sheds enormous light on the nature and root causes of the sexual dysfunction that has plagued thousands of Catholics since the outbreak of the sexual revolution in the early 1960s.

"Coulson and Rogers," wrote Reslock, "found their legacy as humanistic psychologists to be the dismantling of many convents and seminaries throughout California and elsewhere. By the mid-70s, both Rogers and Coulson had retracted their beliefs. But Coulson still believes that their ideas, and the ideas of Abraham Maslow, in particular, sowed the seeds for the moral crisis in religious life that is clearly evident today...

"But the passing of time also caused Coulson to search out his own answers to what went wrong with the American Church in the late 60s and 70s. His research has lead him to believe that, more than the work of Carl Rogers, the influence of humanistic psychologist Abraham Maslow on the American Church is under-acknowledged and poorly understood.

"This was partly confirmed when Coulson examined the journals of Maslow – not released to the public until 1979 – which show the diabolical nature of his enterprise, and the contempt he had for religious people, some of whom, ironically, swallowed his ideas with little resistance...

"Coulson said, 'Maslow was always the revolutionary...' [I]n1965, [Maslow was] working on a radical idea about children-and-sex into his book on the psychology of management, *Eupsychian Management: A Journal*:

> [I]t always struck me [Maslow wrote] as a very wise kind of thing that the lower-class Negroes did, as reported in one study, in Cleveland, Ohio. Among those Negroes the sexual life began at puberty. It was the custom for an older brother to get a friend in his own age grade to break in his little sister sexually when she came of a suitable age. And the same thing was done on the girl's side. A girl who had a younger brother coming into puberty would seek among her own girl friends for one who would take on the job of initiating the young boy into sex in a nice way. This seems extremely sensible and wise and could also serve highly therapeutic purposes in various other ways as well. I remember talking with Alfred Adler about this in a kind of joking way, but then we both got quite serious about it, and Adler thought that this sexual therapy at various ages was certainly a very fine thing. As we both played with the thought, we envisaged a kind of social worker, in both sexes, who was very well trained for this sort of thing, sexually, but primarily as a psychotherapist in giving therapy literally on the couch, that is, for mixing in the beautiful and gentle sexual initiation with all the goals of psychotherapy.
>
> I suppose that for these days this is a wild thought, but ...there's no reason why it shouldn't be taken quite seriously, especially for youngsters and maybe also for the very old people. I guess what I'm trying to say here is that these interpersonal therapeutic growth-fostering relationships of all kinds which rest on intimacy, on honesty, on self-disclosure, on becoming sensitively aware of one's self – and thereby of responsibility for feeding back one's impressions of others, etc. – that these are profoundly revolutionary devices, in the strict sense of the word – that is, of shifting the whole direction of a society in a more preferred direction. As a matter of fact, it might be revolutionary in another sense if something like this were done very widely. I think the whole culture would change within a decade and everything in it.

As offensive and presumptuous Maslow's theory about blacks' sexual initiations is, the point to be grasped is that Maslow, who became the guru for many among the Catholic intelligentsia, understood that early sex education is the key to deconstructing the moral foundations of both Church and society.

Coulson continued: "Too much damage has been done, not least among Catholics, and now even a bishop. I say this because Maslow and Rogers came to Santa Rosa to lecture in August 1962, when the Santa Rosa diocese was being launched, and Maslow said some equally unfortunate things about the meaning of life. For one, he thought therapy could replace churchgoing...I think some of the problems of the Diocese of Santa Rosa date from that occasion and others like it in the seminaries, when TMP – Too Much Psychology – came to call."

One of the prime examples of "youth ministry" gone totally off kilter is the LifeTeen Mass, promoted in dozens of dioceses around the country, which began at St. Timothy's Church in Mesa, Arizona, under the leadership of Fr. Dale Fushek.

Not only are LifeTeen Masses sacrilegious and hyper-sexually charged, but anyone involved in their promotion or celebration should be viewed with suspicion. After all, any priest or leader who is willing to treat the Mass as a night club act has more problems than just his theology.

That priest or leader is deeply involved in highly subversive work on a number of levels: most importantly, he is leading youth into a Maslow-type experience of hyper-sexuality and emotionalism that is designed to smash to smithereens any notions of what the Mass is and what sacred ritual is supposed to be.

And the youths attracted to such events can easily be lured into others, as a banner headline over the top of the *Arizona Republic's* Dec. 11, 2001 B section blared: "E.V. Man Faces Sex Charges, Church Worker Accused in 24 Counts."

Reporter Jim Walsh's story was about 32-year-old Marc Gherna, a former youth program volunteer at St. Timothy's Church, where LifeTeen Mass began 1985. He showed pornographic videos to minors in a "church-owned building," and is charged with "touching" and "sexually assaulting" at least two boys while he was on the "Life Teen staff," and more charges are anticipated.

"The Church had no idea he was seeing juveniles outside of church functions," said a spokesman. Fr. Fushek had no comment. Six weeks later, another "youth minister" involved in LifeTeen, Kevin Alexander Monelli, 24, was accused of engaging in sex acts with minor girls.

Archbishop Patrick Flores

On March 11, 2002, a canonical petition seeking the removal of Patrick Flores, Archbishop of San Antonio, was sent to Pope John Paul II and the Holy Roman Rota. The petition charged Flores with gross negligence in the exercise of his episcopal office, failure to protect the temporal goods of the archdiocese, and endangerment of the faith of the people entrusted to his care by allowing the free reign of sexual predators within the clergy.

The canonical suit was filed by Houston attorney J. Douglas Sutter. Sutter represents two women, along with several minors, in several pending civil actions against Flores, the Archdiocese of San Antonio, and two priests who are accused of sexual abuse. Flores was installed as Archbishop of San Antonio in October, 1979.

Included in the documentation sent to the Holy See against was yet another indication that an American bishop went out of his way to recruit, train and ordain a known pedophile. In this case, the priest was Fr. Javier Ortiz-Dietz, who is now serving time in a Texas penitentiary for numerous crimes against young males.

The two Catholics petitioning the Holy See for Flores' removal were sexually abused by Fr. Michael Christopher Kenny. Kenny testified in his depositions for civil suits that he fathered an illegitimate child, that he had sexual intercourse with both adult and minor girls after taking them out to bars to drink and dance. Throughout this 27-year pattern of behavior, his pastor for much of the time was Fr. Thomas Flanagan, now Auxiliary Bishop of San Antonio, who never instructed Kenny that this behavior was inconsistent with that of being a priest.

Kenny also stated under oath that he "never" heard Archbishop Flores tell him or other priests that priests were not to engage in sexual activity at clergy meetings and "never" heard Flores speak about any rules concerning clerical conduct.

"What these documents show," attorney Sutter told *The Wanderer* (April 4, 2002) "is the breathtaking ignorance of the Church's canon law and Church doctrine by Archbishop Flores, his vicar general and his canon and civil lawyers. It is clear that no one involved in running the archdiocese has any idea of what a priest does or is supposed to do, or what a priest is not supposed to do. Over and over again these Church leaders profess ignorance about the most basic things. It blows my mind.

"Essentially," Sutter continued, "the archbishop's view is that any Catholic – priest or lay – can do whatever they want, as long as they don't interfere in the archbishop's jurisdiction – which means financials, how they make their money."

In his deposition, taken April 16, 1998, Fr. Ortiz-Dietz, a native Mexican who was ordained for the Archdiocese of San Antonio in 1978, claimed Fifth Amendment privileges against self-incrimination nearly 350 times, and refused to answer any question after being asked his name.

One particular excerpt illumines the plaintiffs' charge in the canonical action that Flores is grossly negligent:

Q: 'Do you deny, Fr. Deitz, that you suffered from pedophilia prior to your ordination as a priest by the Catholic Church?"

A: "I invoke the Fifth Amendment, sir."

Q: "Do you deny that you were a child molester before you ever came to San Antonio [and were ordained]?"

A: "I invoke the Fifth Amendment, sir."

Q: "Do you deny that you had been provided with medical care for pedophilia prior to July of 1992?"

A: "I invoke the Fifth Amendment, sir."

Q: "Do you deny that you have been counseled by employees of the Archdiocese of San Antonio regarding allegations of child molestation prior to July of 1992?"

A: "I invoke the Fifth Amendment, sir."

Q: "Do you deny having been counseled by Archbishop Flores himself regarding allegations of having made sexual advances towards young boys in your parishes prior to July of 1992?"

173

A: "I invoke the Fifth Amendment, sir."

Q: "Do you deny, Fr. Dietz, that after you resigned as a priest within the Archdiocese of San Antonio, that you were subsequently diagnosed as a pedophile?"

A: "I invoke the Fifth Amendment, sir."

Q: "Do you deny that after being diagnosed as a pedophile or an ephebophile that you wrote a letter to Archbishop Flores dated April 21 requesting that he reassign you to another parish?"

A: "I invoke the Fifth Amendment, sir."

Q: "Do you deny that you wrote Archbishop Patrick Flores a letter on April 27th of 1993 requesting that he reassign you to another parish?"

A: "I invoke the Fifth Amendment, sir."

Q: "Where did you ever get the thought, Fr. Dietz, that you would be eligible to be reassigned to another parish after being diagnosed as a pedophile?"

A: "I invoke the Fifth Amendment, sir."

Q: "Fr. Dietz, do you believe the truth will set you free?"

A: "I invoke the Fifth Amendment, sir."

Flores Grilled

In his December 18, 1997 deposition for the lawsuits against Dietz, Flores pled complete ignorance on how Dietz was accepted as a seminarian for the archdiocese at the precise time he was in the process of being expelled from a Mexican seminary for a number of personality problems, especially sexual problems, and had been accused of molesting two boys.

Dietz's "final evaluation" from the Mexican seminary in Oaxaca stated he has "distortions of reality, obsessive mania, delusions of grandeur, paranoid risk, vanity, narcissism....[is] hypocritical and not in touch with reality....and [suffers] accented sexual conflict."

Flores maintained throughout his deposition – both as an auxiliary bishop and archbishop – that he had no responsibilities over the recruitment, evaluation, supervision or training of seminarians, that the archdiocese has no input whatsoever in who is accepted as a seminarian, has no responsibility for doing background checks, and that the archbishop has no input on whether a seminarian is ordained or not.

During the course of the deposition, however, Flores had his memory "refreshed" a number of times. Plaintiffs' attorneys showed him a letter he wrote to Dietz dated November 22, 1973, after he met Dietz while on a pilgrimage to Mexico and after he had been expelled from the seminary, inviting him to study at Assumption Seminary – though Flores said he didn't recall writing the letter.

Plaintiffs' attorneys also produced a letter written by Flores to the vocations director, Fr. Jose Lopez, recommending Dietz's admission as either a first or second year theology student – but Flores did not recall writing that letter either.

In a letter dated July 26, 1974, written while Fr. Lopez was doing a background check on Deitz, Flores told Dietz not to worry about any "negative evaluations" Lopez might receive. He even said that if the bishop of Oaxaca advised against admitting him, that would not be "treated as an invalidating document."

He closed the letter by encouraging Dietz to start making plans to come to San Antonio.

After Dietz was ordained by Bishop Raymundo Pena of Brownsville, in Puebla, Mexico, in 1978, (while Flores was serving a year-long stint as Bishop of El Paso) he became somewhat of a celebrity in Pentecostal and charismatic circles, and created a public stir by performing exorcisms on his radio program.

During his tenure as a priest of the archdiocese, the indescribably vicious Dietz sodomized numerous altar boys, and as parents reported the abuse to archdiocesan officials, Flores simply moved Dietz from parish to parish.

Reginald Cawcutt

Contemporaneous with the publication by the Kansas City *Star* of a week-long series on the number of Catholic priests who have died and are dying of AIDS, in January 2000, *The Wanderer* published a report, "Homosexual Clerics' Web Site Indicates Deep Influence in Church," a revelation on a network of gay clergy and bishops who were operating a homosexual email list on the Internet where they bragged of living openly homosexual lifestyles and their animosity toward the Catholic Church.

While the web site only had about 50 regular visitors, the information members disclosed to one another suggests homosexual influence in areas of the Vatican, and indicated the existence of a web of homosexual clerics in the United States and abroad who are in constant communication with one another, sharing intelligence most Catholics will never have access to, and coordinating efforts to promote a radical homosexual agenda for the Catholic Church.

One of the most notable threads on the site reported how the Los Angeles contingent of bishops was so alarmed about a document being prepared at the Congregation for the Doctrine of the Faith, which would bar the ordination of homosexuals as diocesan priests or for religious orders, that they approached Pio Cardinal Laghi to express their opposition.

Laghi, then prefect of the Congregation for Catholic Education, allegedly told the Los Angeles bishops not to worry because Joseph Cardinal Ratzinger's proposed document would never get through the Vatican vetting process.

This information appeared on an Internet web site titled "St. Sebastian's Angels." It opened with an image of a young man, pierced by arrows that seem to provoke languorous pleasure rather than pain. Beneath this "St. Sebastian," there was a small cartoon character licking the icing off a cake. Until recently, that spot was filled by an animated member of the male anatomy.

"Ok! Let's see who we are and where we're from! (Couldn't You Just Kiss Them!)," read the next heading, beneath which one finds the photographs and web addresses of a dozen male Catholic religious, one of whom is a bishop.

Identified as from South Africa, the bishop's caption reads: "A SHARP dresser!!!" The caption for the photograph of "Joe from the UK" asks, "Is that a RED edging we see on that Cassock??" Steve, in his final formation year for the priesthood, a "Benedictine fella," "Bill from Mexico," and the "Dominican" are clearly identified as religious.

When one of the players on the St. Sebastian's web site realized the site was under observation by Roman Catholic Faithful (RCF), he shot off this message to RCF founder Steven Brady, who provided a tip to this reporter on the website:

> Dear anonymous cowards,
>
> You are such a sad, pathetic bunch of small-minded creeps. Wake up and smell the coffee will ya? There is NOTHING wrong with homosexuality, and any Bible scholar worth his salt can more-than-adequately prove that to you!
>
> You are trying your damning damnedest to ruin good men who have only sought out some support and a little fun. And, big wow, there's a little fantasy content on this site - what does it 'prove' of the people who may enjoy it? I think it proves far more of the people who find it 'sinful.' You guys and gals should get help. You judges of morality are the ones with problems. Talk to a sex therapist, get some counseling ... maybe you just need to jerk off!! Whatever you need, get it and quick. Deal with your own problems. Your pure hatred, which you try desperately hard to disguise with lots of loving platitudes, is gonna get you all one-way tickets to Hell if you're not careful!
>
> Love thy neighbor and stop spying on him.
>
> Love thy neighbor and stop investigating him.
>
> Love thy neighbor and stop trying to disgrace him.
>
> Love thy neighbor and stop coveting his personal freedom.
>
> Love thy neighbor and keep your own house in order..."

Brady told *The Wanderer* that the conversational threads show that these gay clergy are not only networking in cyberspace, but also meeting, in the flesh, so to speak – at various retreats, including the October 1999 meeting of the National Association of Catholic Diocesan Lesbian and Gay Ministries in Chicago.

The "spiritual moderator" for the site was Cape Town, South Africa Auxiliary Bishop Reginald Cawcutt, then 61, and chairman of the South African Bishops' Conference AIDS Department.

The e-mails exchanged by the 50 or so men on the list are full of personal detail. Many reveal the priests are frank about rejecting celibacy. One wishes he would get a new assignment "near an urban setting where there is a chance for some gay socializing and support. I would also like to be openly gay so that I do not have to hide anymore."

The bishop teases one of the correspondents about spending the night with him and imagines "walking around St. Peter's all in drag." There's a great deal of adolescent sexual humor and the exchange of nude shots, including one "St. Sebastian's Angel" at his Ordination with the South African bishop "still keeping an eye on me."

The men on the list waffle between bravado and fear. They devote many of their e-mail exchanges on the "witch-hunts" and "sexual pogroms" they fear may lie ahead, when actively homosexual persons may no longer be permitted to enter into religious life or serve as Roman Catholic priests.

Bishop Cawcutt joined the discussion to tell about his efforts to sway Vatican opinions. "When I was having my fight with Ratz re[garding] our bishops not opposing gay relationships when it comes up in parliament – one of the documents he sent me to 'read for my requested conversion' was a thing that said gay people should not be appointed as school teachers, PT instructors, and army personnel. I wondered why seminarians were excluded from this prohibition list.

"Now it seems they are catching up. I am wondering what is to happen to those who have sneaked through and got themselves ordained??? Greeley, I think, says 60% of priests are gay. I would be tempted to out myself and ask what I and other gay bishops (cardinals), priests, and religious (male and female) are supposed to do."

Cardinal Ratzinger is a frequent subject for the priests' musings. "Can anything be done to stop this man? He has enough enemies that can bring him down," groans one. "Guys, everyone has a skeleton in their closet and the rat has to have his. It's time the enemies of the rat find his Achilles heel."

And then, there was this important thread, written in the summer of 1999:

"Now for some bad news – Reg do you have any inside on the next 'important document' due from Der Fuhrer's Oberst Ratzinger? I was reliably informed that SCDF and the Congregation for Religious and the thingy for priestly formation are working together on a declaration due in October – and surprise, surprise, it bans homosexuals from entry into religious life or the taking of Orders – what other horrors they contemplate against about 75% of the clergy I shudder to contemplate. I just hope that things become much more toned down than they appear to be at the moment. I am reliably informed that Herr Josef's secretary is as flaming as they come (silence on the good [cardinal] though), if this idiocy gets through then the queens on the Vatican hill are piercing their own insteps with their stilettos..."

An east coast priest responded (as also noted above): "It bans homosexuals from entry into religious life or the taking of Orders? Well, if it is going to happen, I say GOOD! Then these despots will have unwittingly signed the execution warrant for the present anachronistic, medieval expression of 'presbyter' and force it to reform in ways that are consistent with the Gospel.

"The straights are CERTAINLY not going to come forward under present conditions...and with 'gay rights' being so 'out there,' I would imagine that it is more and more difficult for youth to remain in denial about whether they are gay or not.

"(Oh wait! But the straights ARE coming forward! In their 60s and 70s. After they have lead a decently human life...and have reached the age where wisdom is possible – that is, the 'hormones' have died down! Nice, safe, sexually tame, old men. Eunuchs, by virtue of age!) Once, when asked to list my occupation on a form, I wrote 'Medieval Lord' – and *I* don't even wear French Cuffs!!! (Ever notice that the guys who are DYING to wear the purple usually wear French Cuffs?) Unfortunately, in the coming sexuality pogrom, I fear many of us will be casualties in one way or another – if we insist on saying 'We are here!' I've noticed that the idea of 'activism' among the older gay clergy is a rather foreign idea. They feel no urge to slit their own throats in the name of Truth, Justice, bla, bla, bla. They simply go to plush old-gay-men piano bars in Boston and sit around the piano singing show tunes and wishing...they were young..."

The hatred for Rome

The hatred for "Rome" expressed on the site goes to the extreme of wishing the Pope would die, as this comment shows: "Tony's comparison to a Disney visit vs. a Vatican visit reminded me that a while ago I was

179

walking around St. Peter's all in drag and so many people wanted to take my pic and have one of themselves with me – I thought it would be a good idea to have someone walking around all dressed up (like Mr. Mouse does at Disney) for the pics. Ratz could make some money out of it no doubt. Talking about the Vatican – JP is in Poland at the mo - mebbe he will die there? I shall listen to the news broadcasts in hope!"

What also comes through from some of the exchanges is the liturgical acumen of the site members, as this post indicates: "Has anyone else noticed that the interlude between verses of 'Bread of Life' is also the first phrase of 'O, Dem Golden Slippers'? Or am I just not sufficiently focused on the Sacred Mysteries? At the Abbey we had what I called the 'Diamonds Are a Girl's Best Friend' entrance antiphon (no kidding it was identical as far as 'A kiss on the hand may be quite …') The Abbey was also home of the 'Sweetheart Tree' offertory. One of OCP's psalms is a dead ringer for Brahm's Lullaby. Anyone else notice other similarities?"

And there were unique insights into Vatican intrigue, as the South African bishop disclosed:

"Indeed, FUCK!!! Bloody Ratz – Martin gives us this bad news. I am a bit reluctant to believe it – have not heard anything of it from other sources – and it's surprising that the news guys have not got onto it yet. I was amused to hear JPII's supposed comment that Ratz does things without asking him. I was reminded of JP's comment when we had lunch with him during our ad limina. We asked him if he was going to watch the soccer game between Germany and Poland on TV that night (he is not supposed to be gay, so he should have been watching) and his reply was that he could not 'because Ratzinger is coming to check up on me tonight'."

Another post verified the bishop's alarm, because, apparently, the letter was discussed by the bishops of Los Angeles during their ad limina visits to Rome.

"Greetings to one and all. I read with great interest Martin's note about rumors of another letter coming from the Vatican. Actually, this is not the first time I have heard of such. When the Los Angeles bishops, et al., went to Rome for their official visit late last fall, they came back talking about that very letter. Apparently Ratz's office was very proud of it, and was telling all those who were visiting that the next official letter would in fact ban gays from religious orders and priesthood. When the LA crew mentioned the letter to the more sympathetic Pio Laghi, he told them not to worry, that the rest of the congregations would never allow such a letter to get through. So, in spite of Pio Laghi's best intentions, it appears as though the letter might have made it through…"

Called to Rome

In an October 1999 message, the Cape Town auxiliary wrote:

"I suppose the issue really is celibacy and not gay sex. I am of the belief that we have all been screwed up by holy mother church…"

After *The Wanderer* disclosed Cawcutt's participation on the web site, the news quickly spread via the Internet and became an international scandal, making newspaper headlines from Cape Town to Edinburgh, and across North America. Just as quickly, Cawcutt's defenders in the hierarchy and the official Catholic press came to his defense.

The papal nuncio to South Africa reassured Cawcutt of his support; Cawcutt's archbishop, Lawrence Henry, defended his "ministry" to homosexual clerics and refused to consider the idea of Cawcutt's resignation; the Washington-based Catholic News Service dished out a sympathetic story that cast the blame on Roman Catholic Faithful, and the *National Catholic Reporter*, along with Catholic newspapers in England and South Africa, rallied to Cawcutt's defense.

On September 25, Cawcutt was informed by the papal nuncio to South Africa that he had been summoned to Rome for a meeting with Ratzinger on October 9. But when he showed up at the cardinal's office, he learned that Ratzinger was refusing to meet with him.

"I went to Rome, I kept my appointment, but it had been canceled since our spy had sent them a note in which I said I have been called to the 'lion's den,'" Cawcutt wrote to fellow priests on the St. Sebastian's email list for homosexual clergy, in a message posted October 17.

The "spy" referred to by Cawcutt was Stephen Brady.

"Ratz did not appreciate the humor", Cawcutt wrote, "saying that if that was my attitude, they were wasting their time seeing me – and so called off the meeting and repeated to our president that it had to be sorted out locally."

The message Cawcutt is referring to, which Brady forwarded to Cardinal Ratzinger on September 25, the same day Cawcutt sent it to members of the St. Sebastian's list, read:

"Sebs – yeah I guess everyone feels as I do at present – bashed, bashed, bashed. I heard Saturday night from the Nuncio that I am to appear at the front door of the CDF at 1000 on October 9 to meet the boys – not only for an explanation of the St Sebs things, but my whole attitude to homosexuality…"

Still up to his tricks

Cawcutt remains incorrigible, and a symbol of the power of homosexuals in the Church. In the summer of 2001, he again made headlines around the world, when he said the Catholic Church should not oppose the burgeoning sex trade. The major Catholic newspaper in South Africa, *The Southern Cross* reported in its June 6-12 edition:

"Christian, Muslim, and Jewish figures in Cape Town have warned that the Mother City could end up like the notorious sex-for-sale districts of South East Asia, according to local newspaper reports. The alliance has demanded an urgent clampdown on the city's burgeoning prostitution and child sex industry. The Catholic Church is not part of the group… Bishop Cawcutt, auxiliary in Cape Town said: 'The Catholic Church had no comment to make in the context of this particular campaign and some of the role-players involved in it.' This should not be about political point scoring, he added. He said the sex trade in particular, and the choices involved in it, is very complex, requiring integrated strategies that are well thought out and sensitive to the personal issues affecting sex workers. Until such a campaign occurs, the Church, he said, will reserve its judgment. Moreover, Bishop Cawcutt stressed that human sexuality on the whole is complex, requiring sensitive consideration."

CHAPTER NINE

The Show Must Go On

In January 2000, the Kansas City *Star* published the results of a four-year investigation into homosexuality in the Catholic priesthood, a book-size series of a dozen articles over three days announcing the fact that the Catholic priesthood in the United States has suffered a disproportionately large number of deaths from AIDS.

While that may have been news in Kansas City, what this reporter found deeply disturbing in reporter Judy Thomas' series was the news that the U.S. bishops had selected Fr. Jim Gill, SJ, – the priest and psychiatrist who counseled Fr. Dennis (now Denise) Brennan into having a sex change operation (*The Wanderer,* Jan 27, 2000) – to train sex counselors to work in seminaries.

In the last installment of her series, Thomas revealed cheerily that the American bishops are finally starting to address the sex ignorance crisis of its seminarians, clergy and bishops by consulting such "sexperts" as Gill and the prominent homosexual activists Frs. Jim Schexnayder and Rodney DeMartini from San Francisco and an AIDS activist with AIDS in Miami, Fr. Dennis Rausch.

The investigative report by Thomas, under the direction of *Star* editor and vice-president Mark Zieman, who identified himself as a Catholic, showed that Catholic seminaries in the 1960s joined in the sexual liberation frenzy of the decade; that many seminarians and priests embraced an active homosexual lifestyle in and out of the seminary; that many of these homosexual seminarians went on to ordination and were groomed for and entrusted to high positions by their superiors; and in the late '70s and early '80s, the onset of AIDS served as a means to bring these facts to public attention.

As sensational as Thomas' report was – and it was serialized in newspapers from coast-to-coast – it was also fundamentally dishonest, because Thomas did not disclose the backgrounds, connections and careers of the key figures in her story which she presents to the public as knowledgeable expert commentators, such priests as Schexnayder, DeMartini, Rausch, Gill and others who – as *Wanderer* readers had known for the better part of a decade – are the intellectual and clerical elite working for the homosexualization of the Catholic Church in America.

While the report drew attention to the high proportion of homosexuals in the priesthood, estimated by the *Star's* survey at 15 percent, plus another five percent who identify themselves as "bisexual," it did not try to explain how so many homosexual men were recruited for the priesthood, preferentially retained or advanced through the seminary process, or approved for ordination.

The *Star's* report particularly focused on the Jesuits' St. Stanislaus Seminary in Florissant Missouri, which closed in 1971, and was clearly dominated by homosexual students, several of whom have died of AIDS, while others, like former student Joseph Kramer, have gone on to become high-profile promoters of homosexuality.

(Kramer is founder of The Body Electric, Ero-Spirit and other businesses which produce homosexual pornography; advertisements for his businesses appear regularly in the *National Catholic Reporter* in large paid display ads.)

Thomas informed readers that AIDS had claimed such dazzling stars as the late Jesuit priest, Fr. Thom Savage, "a beloved man, an energetic, fun-loving soul who made an impression on Catholics and non-Catholics alike."

In 1988, Savage, then 41, became the youngest Jesuit college president after his appointment to Rockhurst College, and "over the next eight years, he became a highly respected community leader. When he unexpectedly died last May at age 51, he was eulogized as 'a meteor that burned itself out in the service of others.'"

Thomas' report also showed how comfortable many prominent Church leaders, such as Washington's James Cardinal Hickey and Kansas City's Bishop Raymond Boland, are with giving public honors to homosexual priests, such as the late Fr. William Peterson, founder of the St. Luke's Center in Suitland, Maryland, whose funeral at St. Matthews' Cathedral – after dying of AIDS – was a grand ecclesiastical spectacle attended by some seven bishops and 180 priests.

But while the *Star* mentioned Peterson and his close friends in the hierarchy, it did not try to explain how Peterson worked his way into the priesthood and episcopal favor and became the U.S. bishops' "expert" on sexual issues.

The *Star*, however, did expose the fact that many priests and at least one bishop, Emerson Moore (a New York auxiliary) who have died of AIDS had other causes listed as the cause of death on their death certificates. In Moore's case, his job occupation was even denied: he was described as a "laborer."

The libertine agenda

The underlying premise of the *Star's* lengthy series of articles is that seminaries and monasteries for an exclusively male priesthood are the equivalent of homosexual bathhouses, and the only way to prevent AIDS from spreading among this population is more sex education and easier access to "safe sex" information and devices, and, of course, more resources devoted to finding a definitive treatment and cure for AIDS.

According to the *Star's* survey of 3,000 priests, which elicited 800 responses (which often confirm or validate previous surveys by other organizations), nearly two-thirds of priests blamed faulty, insufficient, inadequate sex education in the seminary for the prevalence of the disease among clerical ranks.

"Sexuality still needs to be talked about and dealt with," said Fr. Dennis Rausch, who has AIDS and directs an AIDS ministry program for Catholic Charities in the Archdiocese of Miami.

"I've been trying to get into the seminary here for the last several years to do an awareness course for the guys, so when they come out, they at least have some knowledge," he added.

Rausch is typical of those interviewed by Thomas over the 18 months she worked on the story.

Thomas' story lacked the authentic Catholic voices of those priests and laity who accept Church teaching, who had true vocations, and who have faithfully – by utilizing the Church's sacraments and prescriptions for living a moral life, and the graces Jesus Christ makes available through the Catholic Church – lived as Catholics.

Instead, almost everyone quoted from the survey and interviewed assumes that the Church's position on homosexuality and on sex in general is wrong, archaic, irrelevant, punitive and primitive – compared to the modern sexual enlightenment espoused by such prominent Catholic figures as Fr. Schexnayder in Oakland, Fr. Liuzzi in Los Angeles, and their patrons, Bishop Cummins and Cardinal Mahony, respectively.

In one installment, Thomas quotes Fr. Schexnayder, who "developed" the Diocese of Oakland's policy of *not testing* applicants for the priesthood for AIDS, saying: "One [reason] was that it is limited in terms of what it is trying to communicate." He went on to say, "You'd have to test regularly, because one test at one time would not necessarily resolve the question."

Others quoted frequently include Bishop Thomas Gumbleton, the Detroit Auxiliary who openly advocates a change in the Church's teaching on homosexuality. "I think this [clerical AIDS] speaks to a failure on the part of the Church," Gumbleton said at one point. "Gay priests and heterosexual priests didn't know how to handle their sexuality, their sexual drive. And so they would handle it in ways that were not healthy.

"How to be celibate and to be gay at the same time, and how to be celibate and heterosexual at the same time, that's what we were never really taught how to do. And that was a major failing."

Reporter Thomas' voices also include former priest John Hilgeman of St. Louis, who spends his time making panels memorializing dead priests for the AIDS Quilt; Augustinian Fr. Tom Casey of Boston, who blames Church officials for clerical AIDS because they have "created a tremendous amount of homophobia," and ex-Jesuit Robert Goss, author of *Jesus Acting Up*, now chairman of the Department of Religious Studies at Webster University in St. Louis.

More disinformation

Thomas' reporting that the Church is finally coming to grips with its deficiencies in the sexual education of seminarians, and rectifying past problems, as mentioned above, is the most significant part of her story.

Kansas City's Bishop Raymond Boland is quoted explaining in an early installment of the series:

> I do feel today that a lot of our men get many opportunities –
> the standard of spiritual direction, the standard of formation is

much higher…And in all of the seminaries, we have people who are trained counselors.

"Seminary education on sexuality has been slow to evolve," continues Thomas, "but so has the acceptance of homosexuality and the understanding of AIDS in the general population. Many of today's priests, whose average age is about 60, entered the seminary in the 1960s, the age of 'free love' and sexual experimentation – not HIV awareness."

In the third day's installment, Thomas wrote: "Church leaders say they are now searching for ways to prevent the spread of AIDS, including more sex education in the seminaries and HIV tests for priest applicants.

"Among the more radical suggestions are eliminating the requirement that priests be celibate, changing Church doctrine on homosexuality or even banning gays from the priesthood."

After quoting Frs. Rausch, Schexnayder and DeMartini as "experts" on the problem, Thomas turned her attention to priest/psychiatrist Gill:

> Distressed at the lack of education on sexuality at the seminary level, the Rev. James J. Gill, a Maryland priest and psychiatrist, founded a program for those who teach prospective priests…

> Participants in the Rev. James J. Gill's program learn how to counsel prospective priests about sexual issues…

> For years, the Rev. James J. Gill watched as priests came to him for treatment of sexual problems long after the "acting out" had begun. The priests told Gill they were scared to talk about their sexual inclinations while in the seminary.

> "They were afraid they'd get thrown out if they brought up something sexual, or else they said there was nobody they could talk with," said Gill, a senior consultant at the Institute of Living in Hartford, Conn.

> For Gill, a Jesuit priest and psychiatrist, that raised a question. "Who trains, who educates the faculty members, the spiritual directors, the teachers, to be able to deal with the sexuality of the young people who come under their care?"

> The answer, he discovered: Nobody.

In 1994, Gill started The Christian Institute for the Study of Human Sexuality. Gill and his 10-member faculty train those who teach prospective priests.

Based in Silver Spring, Maryland, the program runs 30 days and costs $3,000.

Students participate in role-playing to gain experience in counseling priests about sexual issues.

To date, about 400 have been through Gill's program. What baffles him is that more haven't attended.

(Simple math calculates this as a $1.2 million cash cow!) Nor did Thomas inform readers that it was Fr. Gill who counseled Albany priest Dennis Brennan to become a woman.

Promoting institutional pedophilia

While the U.S. bishops are, allegedly, intensifying their efforts to teach seminarians about sex, militant homosexuals in the Church were intensifying their efforts to promote homosexuality among America's Catholic school children, as a Sept. 7-10, 2000, NACDLGM conference in Oakland demonstrated.

As their secular counterparts in the homosexual movement accelerated their aggressive program to implement so-called "safe school" programs, "tolerance" education and "stop the hate" campaigns which teach acceptance of the homosexual lifestyle and promote homosexual behavior, Catholics affiliated with NACDLGM are pursuing a parallel track to complete the seduction of Amchurch youth.

The NACDLGM conference, held at Oakland's City Center Marriot, drew some 140 representatives from dioceses across the United States to hear, among others:

- Cincinnati Auxiliary Bishop Carl Moeddel explain how he has tried to convince all principals of Catholic schools in his archdiocese to establish youth support groups for gays and lesbians;

- Oakland Vicar General, Fr. Paul Vassar, say that homosexuals and lesbians are specially blessed by God and they have a special

188

commission from God to tell the Magisterium the truth about homosexuality;

- Casey and Mary Ellen Lopata, from the Diocese of Rochester, New York, explain that activists must explain to parents of gay and lesbian children that those children are, in a special way, "God's love revealed."

Here, again, was proof that NACDLGM's agenda is nothing but institutional pedophilia: the targeting of those weak and dysfunctional dioceses headed by ineffectual or functionally absent-or-abdicated bishops which are dominated by radical feminist nuns, priests, and lay bureaucrats who leave defenseless the Catholic children in parishes, schools and families.

To extend the analogy of a pedophiliac syndrome in Amchurch, just as a pedophile has to deceive or seduce a parent, and frequently uses pornography and small gifts to groom his child victims to accept his sexual molestations, so the institutional pedophile desensitizes individuals through institutionally imposed K-12 sex education programs in schools and catechetical programs, leaving them easy prey for a perverse movement whose motto is "Recruit, Recruit, Recruit" or "sex before eight or it's too late." (Most chilling is this motto-borrowing from NAMBLA, the North American Man Boy Love Association; NAMBLA's sole mission is to advocate the legalization and acceptance of grown men having sex with young boys.)

NACDLGM's September 2000 program, held at the same time parents in California and across the country were mobilizing to stop a Gay Lesbian Straight Education Network/Anti-Defamation League-sponsored "Toward A Hate Free Millennium" program in public schools, can also be seen as a deliberate Amchurch project to undercut any organized Catholic opposition to the promotion of homosexuality in government schools.

Less than one month after NACDLGM's Oakland conference, California Governor Gray Davis signed two bills, A.B. 1931, which provides $150,000 in taxpayer money to establish a "tolerance" organization to monitor public schools for any nascent signs of homophobia, and an additional $2 million to fund "tolerance" field trips, and A.B. 1785, which promotes homosexual and bisexual behavior to children in public schools through "human relations" education.

189

NACDLGM's seventh annual conference, entitled "A Life of Favor from the Lord," (a parody on the Jubilee Year motto, "A Year of Favor from the Lord") was held in the home base of its founder, Fr. Jim Schexnayder, who used Catholic Charities of the East Bay as a host and resource for his agenda to homosexualize all Catholic institutions, under the patronage of Bishop John Cummins.

In his welcoming remarks, Fr. Schexnayder, who is now officially retired from the diocese, lamented that his years of work in this field had not yet led to the Church approving same sex marriages, but he acknowledged the small steps he and his group have made.

"We're just trying to help people live their whole Christian lives," he said. "Chastity is one virtue, but it's not the only virtue. We don't put a spotlight on (the sex lives of) heterosexuals, and it's not productive to do that with gays and lesbians. We're not negating Church teaching. We're just trying to put them in context."

The conference's co-chairs were Michael Harmuth, of Oakland, a retired Air Force officer and father of a lesbian daughter, and Margaret Roncalli, chair of the Diocese of Oakland's Task Force for Outreach to Gay and Lesbian Communities and their Families. Roncalli also serves on the Ecclesial Lay Ministers Council formed by Bishop Cummins.

Indeed, this conference showcased the successful inroads gay and lesbian activists have made in Oakland, across California and into dioceses around the United States. It is clear, just from reading the program, that homosexual activists now have thoroughly infiltrated the American Catholic Church, and are able to manipulate and use its institutions, resources and facilities to rapidly consolidate and extend their grip – not only the Church, but the country's institutions as well.

Among the speakers from California:

- Terrie Iacino, Episcopal Director for Pastoral Ministry for the Diocese of San Jose, chaired a discussion on "Exploring the Challenges of Ministry to Gay and Lesbian Catholics in a Multicultural Setting," with panelists Belinda Dronkers-Laureta, a Filipino involved in school and family gay and lesbian projects and Kyle Miura, a Japanese-American and a graduate of the Graduate Theological Union in Berkeley.

- Fr. Dan Danielson, pastor of "the Catholic community of Pleasanton," [ed. note: in California, it is increasingly the case that parishes identify themselves as "communities," eschewing the traditional Catholic vocabulary] who was told by Bishop Cummins to stop blessing homosexual unions after *The Wanderer* publicized his officiating at homosexual marriages, spoke on "welcoming parish ministry."

- Julie Lienert, head of the Safe Schools Project at Catholic Charities of the East Bay, joined Joan Kral of the Livermore School District in Livermore, California, to discuss how area public and parochial schools "currently address sexual orientation and diversity issues," particularly through teacher training programs and parent and student workshops.

- Diane Berry, from Fr. Danielson's parish; David Dezern, from the Newman Center at Berkeley; and Victoria Forester of Our Lady of Lourdes in Oakland held a workshop on how they have successfully brought gays and lesbians into parish study groups.

- Fr. Ben Owens, OSB, a teacher at Bishop O'Dowd High School in Oakland led a workshop on the "experiences and challenges of ministry working with students in a Catholic high school around homosexual issues," with particular attention to helping homosexual students become comfortable with their homosexuality, and on "educational efforts to combat prejudice among students, faculty and staff."

- Rita Billeci, director of the Office of Family for the Diocese of Oakland; Gus and Stella Roemers, a "deacon couple" at Our Lady of the Rosary Church in Union City, California; and Amity Pierce Buxton, director of the Straight Spouse Network, discussed "ministry with families" in light of the U.S. bishops' document *Always Our Children*.

- Fr. Richard Gula SS, professor of moral theology at the Franciscan School of Theology, Berkeley, a noted "proportionalist," who attempted to "retrieve a vision of the moral life that gives priority to being a good person over figuring out the right action."

- Toni Tortorilla, a professional counselor and spiritual director, currently an M.Div. student at the Jesuit School of Theology, Berkeley, on "ministering to ourselves."

- Fr. Chris Ponnet, director, St. Camillus Center for Pastoral Care, Archdiocese of Los Angeles, who promotes homosexuality in the Spanish-speaking communities.

- Bishop Moeddel from Cincinnati, whose imprimatur appears on the pro-homosexual propaganda distributed by St. Anthony Messenger Press to parishes, especially in its publication *Catholic Update*.

- Casey and Mary Ellen Lopata, from Rochester, New York, charter members of NACDLGM and co-directors of the Catholic Gay and Lesbian Family Ministry in Rochester.

- Fr. Eugene McCreesh, S.J., pastoral minister and spiritual director, St. Peter's Parish, in the Diocese of Charlotte, North Carolina – which hosted last year's NACDLGM conference.

- Fr. Richard Rohr, OFM, who was celebrating lesbian marriages in Albuquerque until he was told to resist the impulse to perform such "blessing ceremonies" by Archbishop Michael Sheehan;

- Fr. Ken Hamilton, SVD, a "minister in liberation theology," based in Cincinnati. His specialty is conducting "rites of passage" rituals for "at risk" youth; and

- James and Evelyn Whitehead, long-time sex educators who now advocate "coming out" rituals parents and their offspring can celebrate when a child announces he or she is gay.

Among the most revealing talks was Bishop Moeddel's "Diocesan Ministry: Built on Compassion and Fidelity," in which the bishop told how homosexual ministry in Cincinnati is an outgrowth of Dignity, and spoke about his role as one of six bishops charged with producing *Always Our Children*.

Moeddel said his main work in the archdiocese over the next year will be approaching high school principals to attend "in-service days" to persuade them to promulgate *Always Our Children*, to be followed by a similar program for elementary school principals. He complained, however, that the Archdiocese of Cincinnati still does not have a formal policy on promoting homosexuality, so principals and teachers are somewhat reluctant to become involved in his program.

Moeddel also complained that his "Youth Support Group idea for gays and lesbians at the secondary school level was torpedoed" by the Director of Catholic Social Services after he left Cincinnati.

Once news of Moeddel's talk traveled around the country, some Cincinnati Catholics wrote to the bishop, expressing their concerns. Moeddel responded in the typical episcopal fashion: by denying the truth of reports that appeared in *The Wanderer* and elsewhere. So Cincinnati-area Catholic Michael Rose, publisher of an independent Catholic monthly, the *St. Catherine Review*, did some investigation, obtained a tape of the talk, and published his findings in the March/April 2001 issue of his magazine.

"Just what is Bishop Moeddel up to?" Rose asked.

"No doubt, many of our readers have expressed their concern to Bishop Moeddel, auxiliary bishop of Cincinnati, about his personal interest in 'targeting' the local Catholic high schools and then the elementary schools as the 'top priority' of the new ministry to lesbians and gays.

"A few readers have sent us copies of the bishop's response to their inquiries. While he admits to having addressed this conference, he denies certain claims made in the articles. It is opportune then that SCR finally obtained a tape and transcript of the bishop's talk so that we might clarify the issues in these pages.

"To one *SCR* reader, the bishop wrote, 'It is not true that I am supporting or promoting youth groups in our secondary schools for gays and lesbians. I am not doing so.' However, in his Oakland talk, delivered last September 8, he said, 'I was pretty proud of the fact that we were starting a youth support group for gays and lesbians at the secondary school level,' which was 'being done under the auspices of our Catholic Social Services and the counselors there.'

"On a second issue, Bishop Moeddel has responded to readers that 'it is not true that I said that I was going to promote my agenda with elementary school principals.' Yet, at the conference, the bishop told his audience: 'Our priority in the coming year is to try to get into all of our high schools. Talk to all of our teachers. Hopefully to move from there into our elementary schools, but starting with our high schools.'"

After explaining his role in the production of *Always Our Children*, Moeddel told how he traveled around the archdiocese promoting the document, how he, along with Cincinnati Archbishop Daniel Pilarczyk, formally established the ministry to lesbians and gays.

The audio tape of the conference reveals that Moeddel, who usually speaks in a deep, strong voice, effected a queer lisp for his audience. "The only other public program offered by the ministry group thus far," Rose continued, "was a day of reflection which attracted, in Bishop Moeddel's estimation, about forty people. Although two more days of reflection were advertised, they were canceled due to 'lack of interest,' he added regretfully.

"But the bishop explained that days of reflection for gays and lesbians isn't the primary focus of the new ministry. The 'top priority,' he clarified, is to 'change the environment' in the Catholic high schools in order to make them 'safe places' for gay and lesbian students. The complaints he's been hearing, he told his Oakland audience, is that high schools are 'hostile environments' for those attracted to members of the same sex."

After elaborating on his successful project to create "safe" high schools, he went on:

"Hopefully," he said, the program needs to expand "into touching our elementary schools."

"Thus," concluded Rose, "the bishop is implying that the environments in our Catholic elementary schools, which serve 5- [to] 13-year-olds, may also be 'hostile' to gays and lesbians. What Bishop Moeddel is talking about here is indoctrination of the youth in Catholic schools to accept homosexuality as normal, while painting the propaganda as 'tolerance' and 'anti-discrimination' education. Do our children really need such indoctrination, especially when most Catholic schools can't even teach the Catholic faith to their students?"

The fact is, homosexuality is the new faith for men like Moeddel.

Queer alliances

The year 2000 also saw the emergence of the nine year old National Catholic AIDS Network, headquartered in the scandal-plagued Santa Rosa Diocese, as a lead agency promoting AIDS education in Catholic parishes. NCAN enjoys official recognition by the National Conference of Catholic Bishops, and has Bishop Howard J. Hubbard of Albany as its episcopal moderator.

At 1999's NCAN annual gathering, Bishop Hubbard praised Cape Town South Africa Auxiliary Bishop Reginald Cawcutt as an exemplar of progressive leadership on AIDS issues in the Catholic Church.

While most Catholics who learn of the Network through their parish bulletins or diocesan newspapers, or, perhaps, at a special AIDS Mass, will perceive the organization as an association of altruistic and compassionate caregivers ministering to the sick, suffering and marginalized, a deeper investigation reveals the organization as a well-funded front for homosexual activism and agit-prop in league with other activists, both secular and religious.

According to its 1998 IRS tax return, obtained by Roman Catholic Faithful and provided to *The Wanderer*, NCAN is a $331,267 a year tax-exempt organization which exists "to provide networking opportunities and continuing education…and specialized workshops for people with AIDS." Its director, Fr. Rodney DeMartini, draws compensation of $34,500.

Fr. Rodney J. DeMartini, according to information provided on the homosexual web site thebody.com, on which he provides spiritual advice, "is a native San Franciscan and an ordained Roman Catholic priest. After a close friend was diagnosed with AIDS in the early 1980s, Rodney began his involvement in early community-based and Church efforts to respond to the epidemic. Since 1991 he has been National Catholic AIDS Network Executive Director. He believes that the Catholic Church and all churches and faith communities should be welcoming and healing places for all those living with and affected by HIV/AIDS."

IRS documents, along with Sonoma County real estate and property tax records, make it appear that Fr. DeMartini is in some type of a "domestic partnership" with retired businessman Frederick Kasl, who owns the property at 12500 Dupont Rd in Sebastopol, which is the official address of the National Catholic AIDS Network.

That residence, for which Mr. Kasl claims a home owner's exemption, sits on a 26.80 acre site, and has an assessed valuation of $688,273. The property is also listed as the official residence for both DeMartini and Kasl. In addition, both Kasl and DeMartini share a post office box, 960, in Occidental, about two miles away from their rural residence. A nearby estate belongs to the former U.S. Ambassador of Luxembourg, James C.

Hormel, the prominent San Francisco philanthropist who is a major funder of the homosexual agenda.

The Wanderer asked Fr. DeMartini what his arrangement is with Kasl, and he replied that Kasl "assists around the office. He's one of the volunteers here."

DeMartini also owns a home he inherited in nearby Guerneville on the Russian River, which is one of the most well-known homosexual enclaves in the world.

Also resident at Kasl's home is Fr. Edward Kilianski, SCJ, who is listed in the 1999 Kenedy Directory under the Archdiocese of Milwaukee's directory as residing at the St. Francis Residence for Priests in Franklin, Wisconsin, though it lists Kilianski's address as "P.O. Box 960, Occidental, California" – i.e. it is shared with Kasl and DeMartini.

DeMartini described Kilianski as "another volunteer."

(For the record, there are some other strange Milwaukee connections: In June 2000, Fr. DeMartini celebrated a special AIDS Mass at St. Pius X church in Milwaukee – the former parish of Fr. Dennis Pecore, a convicted pedophile. And on Pentecost, when DeMartini preached at the AIDS Mass at St. Lawrence Church in Sacramento, he was the guest of Fr. Steven Avella, a history professor at Marquette University who was on a one-year sabbatical.)

In his brief interview with *The Wanderer*, DeMartini also described the sources of NCAN's funding as "individuals, religious orders, dioceses, and others who believe in what we do."

California's most prominent pro-homosexual priests tend not to be shy about their living arrangements. For example, about the same time as *The Wanderer* publicized DeMartini's arrangement, it also published a report on Fr. Rod Stephens, the Diocese of Orange's Director of Evangelization, Liturgy, Music and Adult Education, and head of the diocese's catechumenate office, who, at the time, had just taken a 23-day cruise on the Royal Princess "love boat" with his long-time companion, Howard Sellers, around South America. Fr. Stephens' itinerary included several extras, including a pre-cruise tour of the Chilean wine country, a post-cruise tour of the Iguauzua Falls in Brazil, a flight over Antarctica, penguin watching, glacier cruising, and cost in the neighborhood of $10,000-plus per person.

Stephens, who sent out copies of the itinerary to his and his companion's friends before embarking, with phone numbers for each leg of the trip, also sends out Christmas greetings of himself and his partner, Howard Sellers, a professor of English at Fullerton College.

Fr. Stephens denied he was in a "domestic partnership" with Professor Sellers, although a Lexis-Nexis search for their addresses indicates they share the same residence, 55 Fabriano, Irvine, CA, 92620.

Stephens said he resides at the diocese's cathedral rectory. Stephens, however, has admitted that his liturgical design business, Sacra Forma, is based in Sellers' residence.

A greeting card he and Sellers sent out to friends at Christmastime, showing him and his partner standing together on a ladder, read, "from our digs to yours, Howard and Rod" and wished recipients a Happy Christmas, Chanukah and New Year.

Fr. Stephens, who first came to the attention of *Wanderer* readers in the late 1980s in a report on a Good Friday liturgical dance he performed in skin-tight black leotards, is also active in the local homosexual lobby's AIDS Walk, and other trendy publicity stunts; but he is known primarily as one of the southwest's premier liturgical design consultants, having designed "worship spaces" and furnishings for numerous old and new churches in Orange, Los Angeles, and other dioceses.

Educating the faithful

Back to NCAN: its website declares:

"We maintain a relationship with the National Conference of Catholic Bishops and the United States Catholic Conference through Bishop Hubbard of the Archdiocese [*sic*] of Albany, New York who serves as Moderator Bishop and liaison with the NCCB"

The Catholic Conference website, in turn, refers to NCAN in the list of "Background Sources" it provides for the media.

The president of NCAN's board of directors is Fr. Robert J. Vitillo, a longtime AIDS activist who argued in a March 23, 1994 speech at Boston

College that the Church's moral teachings are not "reality-based" (see *The Wanderer* January 9, 1997). Vitillo is also the executive director for the Catholic Campaign for Human Development.

In addition, NCAN was included as a "Planning Organization" and gave a workshop for the 1999 NCCB/USCC Jubilee Justice Gathering.

The "relationship" with the NCCB/USCC opens other doors for NCAN: it is referenced as a "Catholic" resource by other Catholic agencies, such as The Catholic Health Association of the United and the National Catholic Educational Association. (DeMartini was a member of the NCEA task force that produced its AIDS education curriculum.) The Diocese of Richmond's Office of Justice and Peace directs Catholic AIDS activists to the NCAN website.

Among the many articles posted on this website is "HIV/AIDS in the United States" (Reprinted in the NCAN newsletter *Connections* from the World AIDS Day Resource Booklet – undated).

The article speaks of "alarming statistics about the growing [HIV/AIDS] crisis" and says: "One of the best ways to prevent the spread of HIV is to promote open communication and greater honesty about the issues of postponing sex, using safer sex practices, and avoiding the sharing of needles and other injection equipment…"

Like his friend Vitillo, who also has promoted Church approval for condom use, DeMartini is using his episcopally-approved organization to lobby for a change in Church teaching.

Among the books recommended by NCAN on the website is Kevin Kelly's *New Directions in Sexual Ethics: Moral Theology and the Challenge of AIDS,* which asserts the Church should learn from the gay experience and give it approval.

At the bottom of the NCAN home page, there is the following note: "NCAN's Executive Director, Fr. Rodney DeMartini, offers spiritual counseling on AIDS/HIV related issues on TheBody.Com…and AIDS and HIV Information Resource."

The NCAN website then links directly to thebody.com (which in turn, refers the web surfer to NCAN), which, according to the Medical Library

Association, is the most frequently visited HIV/AIDS-related site on the Web and one of the dozen most visited health sites.

If the NCAN website is "fuzzy" about sexual morality, thebody.com is openly "alternative." While the site does give valuable information about HIV and AIDS, it also openly promotes "safe sex" activities.

One writer exhorts: "There is no reason why we have to let AIDS stop us from celebrating ourselves as sexual beings, as long as each of us continually reinforces our commitment to safe sex." [Michael Shernoff, MSW "Some Reflections on Relationships and Sexual Intimacy for Gay Men with AIDS/HIV," People with AIDS Newsline, Issue 69, September 1991 – reprinted on www.thebody.com]

Rick Sowadsky, a Senior Communicable Disease Specialist, hosts a question and answer section on TheBody.Com. Questions include such topics as "HIV risk from sex toys" and "Tooth cavities, oral sex, and AIDS transmission." A number of Sowadsky's articles are also on the site, including "Latex Condoms For Oral Sex? You Gotta Be Kidding!" "So Many Condoms, So Little Time" and "Barebacking in the Gay Community."

This last article discusses the relative benefits and drawbacks of "unprotected anal intercourse," explores why gay men will risk "unprotected" intercourse, provides a glossary of pertinent slang terms, and sends the reader to several graphic gay sites with the warning that they are "adult-oriented" and "should only be viewed by adults who are not offended by graphic sexual materials."

One section on thebody.com website directs the surfer to activist organizations, including five local chapters of ACT UP, the radical gay organization that made headlines in the late 80's when it disrupted a New York City Mass by shouting obscenities at its celebrant, the late Cardinal O'Connor, and throwing condoms about the church and desecrating the Blessed Sacrament.

NCAN also sponsors an annual national conference at Loyola University in Chicago, runs local workshops, and disseminates its ideas through a number of publications. *Many Threads, One Weave: A Resource Program to Assist Parish Communities in Responding to the HIV/AIDS Pandemic*, released earlier this year, was a collaborative project of NCAN and Catholic Charities.

Many Threads, One Weave bears no imprimatur, but is given "official" blessing through an Introductory Letter signed by Bishop Howard Hubbard, Moderator Bishop of NCAN and Bishop Joseph M. Sullivan (auxiliary bishop of the Diocese of Brooklyn), Moderator Bishop of Catholic Charities, USA.

The AIDS "resource" sees the parish as providing an opportunity to "bring the light of the Gospel and Church teaching into the darkness of fear, judgment, and isolation…" but explains that "The 'Good News' is that there is evidence that parishes across the country are offering…outreach to those living with HIV/AIDS…"

The material stresses the importance of being nonjudgmental in many places, emphasizes the diversity of people affected, and encourages Catholics to overcome stereotypes and assumptions: "Sexual orientation, in particular, has suffered many misrepresentations and generalizations. As 'sex' and 'sexuality' have been equated, so 'orientation' has often been reduced to 'genital behavior.' New infections continue to decline among gay white men…" The material then asks how a parish can become welcoming for gay and lesbian persons.

The factual material presented by *Many Threads, One Weave* spins the facts: "The most common means of transmission is through sexual contact…by means of insertive vaginal or anal intercourse." By lumping together all the various ways HIV may be sexually transmitted, the material is delicately able to avoid stating plainly that the most common means of HIV/AIDS sexual transmission is through homosexual anal intercourse.

Many Threads, One Weave does mention that delaying sexual intercourse until marriage and mutual fidelity are ways to prevent infection.

However, a boxed "Note" (and therefore the emphasized bit) on the same page, however, takes away the power of this statement by saying: "Scientific evidence has demonstrated that consistent and correct use of good quality latex condoms can significantly reduce the risk of sexually transmitted diseases…for serious moral and ethical considerations, the Roman Catholic Church and many other churches, groups, and individuals stress the need to abstain from sexual activity before marriage, and to limit sexual relationships to a lifelong commitment to one faithful partner within marriage."

If anything, it appears *Many Threads* is the late Joseph Bernardin's *Many Faces of AIDS* brought back from the grave.

Bear in mind as you read this that this program is *designed for parishes!* Included with *Many Threads, One Weave* is a worksheet titled "Values Clarification Exercise." It contains the moral query: "If someone insisted on using a condom during sexual intercourse with me…" The reader is invited to finish the sentence. Another worksheet called "A Cultural Sensitivity Self-Assessment" asks a number of ambiguous and loaded questions, lulling the reader into taking a privatized religious position, where everyone has his own values, attitudes and beliefs and there are no objective, external and eternal values.

The section that discusses "Factors which Promote Change in High Risk Behavior" includes knowledge of the risks and "acquisition of the skills to change," but ignores completely spiritual motives. The section on "Creating an HIV Education Program for Youth" says "don't preach," "use culturally sensitive educators" and use "educators who understand the benefit of harm reduction." Harm reduction? The materials have said that condoms reduce risk of infection – is that "harm reduction?"

The Chicago connection

Another book NCAN collaborated on is *HIV/AIDS: The Second Decade.* Published with the Communication Ministry, Inc. in 1995, the book is a collection of essays, including NCAN's Fr. Rodney DeMartini's "Learning about Living in the Midst of the HIV Pandemic."

DeMartini writes that failure of the Church to talk openly about sexuality and addictions is "behavior" that "contributes to the spread of this HIV/AIDS pandemic" (as opposed to placing responsibility for disordered behaviors on the persons committing them). "Let the Church, then, be at the forefront of a cure for AIDS – by accepting healing ourselves for our own fears and silences, for our anger and blame."

Another essayist is Robert Nugent's "Homophobia, AIDS-Phobia and Pastoral Care." Nugent is a cofounder of the Vatican-censured New Ways Ministry, and lecturer for the Baltimore Center for Homophobic Education.

"Homophobia," Nugent writes, "can affect the quality of HIV/AIDS education and services…it can generate feelings of discomfort and raise questions about beliefs and values." Nugent describes a variety of attitudes on the "continuum" of "homophobic" responses: "homonegative" is a coined term to describe those who, while holding that heterosexuality is normative, view "committed, faithful gay relationships as morally good."

Nugent talks about the developing "theology of AIDS" and, like DeMartini, writes that "some gay activists have claimed that the absence of any official ethical or moral guidance about responsible expressions of gay sexuality, the churches are in some way responsible for aggravating the epidemic."

He notes that "some Catholics in HIV education even in official positions do not hesitate to recommend and even distribute condoms privately although they realize that this activity can put their jobs in jeopardy." Nugent appears to find this commendable.

Rev. Robert Vitillo, MSW, currently the Executive Director of the Catholic Campaign for Human Development, co-authored "Gathering, Teaching, Serving." Quoting John Paul II's remarks about God's love for those with AIDS, Vitillo says: "Here it might be respectfully suggested that the Church has a very long pilgrimage ahead of itself…many members of the Church…still try to distinguish between the 'innocent' and the 'guilty' persons with HIV or AIDS." They "close the doors" of the community to "those they consider to be too 'unorthodox', or 'sinful', or 'unnatural' in their behavior or orientation."

Though the article then goes on to describe some wonderful examples of Church-supported generosity to those who have AIDS, the point has been made: once a person contracts AIDS, he is an innocent victim, not a sinner. Fr. Richard D. Young, a member of Communication Ministry's national Board of Directors, contributes the following scriptural exegesis: "The prophets were extremely outraged when referring to the residents of Sodom and vehemently condemned their deadly insensitivity. That was holy anger. Obviously, this inhospitality is the same sin of those who hate gay and lesbian persons with AIDS. The tables have been turned: the sin of Sodom is committed by the very ones who have been most inhospitable to the people they wrongly condemn as sodomites."

Sr. Mercedes Reygadas, writing "An Invitation to Compassion, At the Service of My Brothers and Sisters with HIV/AIDS," offers that illness is a time when we want someone near us who is "full of compassion who would affirm in us the belief that God, whatever name we give Him/Her: Buddha, Universe, Energy…God is also with us and gives us strength and the courage we need…"

This publication comes, remember, from an organization that is "in a relationship" with the National Conference of Catholic Bishops.

CMI's *Communication* newsletter began after the 1977 Dignity National Convention in Chicago and at least one of the original board members was a speaker at an early Dignity conference. (For a full history of CMI, see Fr. Enrique Rueda's 1982 book, *The Homosexual Network: Private Lives and Public Policy* (Devin Adair Company, Old Greenwich, CT), which described Communication and the work of Communication Ministry, Inc. (CMI) in its early days. The ideology of the organization, he writes, "offers as an alternative the possibility of rationalizing homosexual behavior within the confines of Roman Catholicism." (p. 349)

Despite Rueda's exposure of the organization, CMI continued unchecked. Fr. Rodney DeMartini of NCAN served as a CMI Co-Director from 1997-98. The CMI monthly newsletter, *Communication*, continues to flourish, boasting a readership of hundreds of gay priests and religious.

Its substance is still as rebellious as ever. The March 2000 issue carried an article on "Merton and Gay Spirituality." Quoting Tim McFeeley, the author (who is anonymous) writes: "Gay people and homosexuality are essential components of creation – for the religious part of God's plan – and concealing these components dishonors the creator and shrouds the fullness of creation itself…Merton's words about the creation of new human values seem to speak of this mission [to move beyond binary systems and dualism, such as male-female]…Scripture says the stone that was rejected has become the cornerstone. The gay communities are being called by God to play this 'cornerstone' role. The only way, however, that gays can play that role is to overcome their fears and have the courage to come out of the closet."

The issue also has a book review by "Bob, OFM, CMI Co-Chair." Robert Pawell (the CMI Co-Chair) gives days of recollection and renewal for priests, religious, and laity on the Enneagram, archetypal spirituality, male sexuality, and masculine spirituality and working with people with AIDS.

He is also on the staff of Our Lady of Mt Carmel, Chicago, which holds the Archdiocesan Gay and Lesbian Outreach Mass every Sunday night. His review on *Spiritual Direction and the Gay Person* (by Fr. James A. Empereur, SJ, Continuum, New York, 1999) ends: "I am sure, that once the thought police on Tiber's banks get wind of this [book] they'll be gathering faggots for the fire."

Letters to *Communication* include one from a "first year (lesbian) novice" who has "been battling with what the vow of chastity actually calls me to, other than 'giving up sex.'" She confides that she is coming 'to religious life with 13 years of experience living as an active lesbian…I was in a long-term monogamous relationship where I was a chaste lover…everything gets complicated for me when celibacy is added to the vow of chastity. I have no idea how to be a chaste celibate!…the biggest challenge for me is to honor the sexuality that Goddess blessed me with in gift by being a chaste lover with all whom I am in relationship with."

An article titled "Thomas Merton and Gay Spirituality (part IV)" discusses the "liberation of gay people" and asks the question "What, if anything, is unique about the soul of a same-sex oriented person?" The author suggests that "gays can help 'deconstruct the rigid definitions of masculinity and femininity and social constructions based on these definitions.' [quoting Robert Goss, *Jesus Acted Up: A Gay and Lesbian Manifesto*, San Francisco, 1993, p. 3] In Jung's terms, this involves the reconciliation of the animus (the masculine spiritual energy) and the anima (the feminine spiritual energy) in each person's soul, creating a sacred marriage within each person."

In the April 2000 *Communication* newsletter, referring to the Vatican's censure of Gramick and Nugent, one author writes "…For me these expressions of asking forgiveness and calling them mistakes is not enough. What about calling them sins, which they are, and including the present sins being committed against religious, priests and lay people who are still being discriminated against and persecuted by the Vatican because they're homosexual."

The details concerning NCAN and CMI's member activities begin to create a chilling picture of how deeply entrenched these anti-Catholic positions are within "Catholic" institutions.

One California provincial on the CMI Board of Directors was a participant in the scandalous "St. Sebastian" website and email list for gay priests, where he confided that he is not celibate and recommended CMI to other members of the group.

Roman Catholic Faithful first learned of the existence of low-profile Communication Ministry, Inc. (CMI) from a message posted on the e-mail list St. Sebastian's Angels (SSA) by Fr. James Mott, OSA of San Diego. Mott, a board member of CMI, was also of member of SSA, which was the email list previously mentioned, that was restricted to homosexual priests and brothers. Mott was recently removed as pastor of his San Diego parish after his involvement with St. Sebastian's Angels became public – although there were rumors that his removal from the diocese is due to a far graver scandal.

Reaching the kids, again

If, by now, the reader is wondering: "What more can our Church leaders in the United States do to promote homosexuality?" thinking the possibilities have been exhausted, now is the time to understand that the agenda goes on, and on, and on, as the recent publication of a new "catechetical" series called *Growing In Love* indicates.

The authors of *Growing in Love* are James J. DeBoy, Jr., formerly of Time Consultants, now executive director of the National Center for Pastoral Leadership; Toinette M. Eugene, formation director for the Pastoral Leadership Placement Board and director of the African-American Pastoral Center of the Diocese of Oakland, and a self-described expert in "womanist and feminist ethics," and sexologist Fr. Richard Sparks, CSP, currently chaplain at the Newman Center at Berkeley, California.

At his February 2001 appearance at the Los Angeles Religious Education Congress, Sparks identified himself as the ghostwriter of the U.S. bishops' 1990 sex document *Human Sexuality: A Catholic Perspective for Education and Life-Long Learning*, and named his theological mentors, all of whom are noted dissenters, including Sister Margaret Farley, RSM, who is an advocate for same-sex marriages and the Church's most prominent dissenters against Pope Paul VI's anti-contraception encyclical *Humanae Vitae*: Fr. Charles Curran, Bernard Haring, CSSR, Rick Gula, Fr. Richard McCormick, SJ, and Lisa Sowle Cahill.

Sparks' admission that he was *Human Sexuality's* ghostwriter is important in the context of his new sex series, *Growing in Love*, because it illustrates how that document will cover the most vile, intrusive, invasive and corrupting sex information imaginable to be imposed on children.

Twenty years ago, the sexology conveyed to little children, beginning in Kindergarten in *Growing in Love,* would have been graduate level course material for professional sex therapists, nurses, doctors, biologists and sex educators.

Sparks' sexual catechesis programs children to accept all the vices which have become current in Amchurch and the society at large. The sexual information conveyed to children, ages 5-12, constitutes an extreme form of psychic rape, in which children are taught the most private and intimate behavior reserved to married people, as well as the bizarre and self-destructive abuses of the sexual faculties by sexual perverts.

It is not incidental that Sparks' so-called "ethics of perplexity" and "ethics of compromise" sanctions the homosexual practices of gay activists who have been pressuring the Church to change its sexual ethics and its condemnation of sodomy.

This new catechetical series, which carries the imprimatur of Archbishop Jerome Hanus, OSB, of Dubuque, Iowa, is a "homo-erotic" sex program intended to indoctrinate Catholic children into the homosexual lifestyle, said the U.S. Coalition for Life's Randy Engel, a leading expert on "Catholic sex education" in the United States for decades.

Growing in Love, Engel observed optimistically, "is so utterly disgusting and depraved in its explicit description of perverted sex acts including oral sex techniques for male and female heterosexuals and homosexuals, and so in-your-face with 'gay and lesbian agit-prop,' that it just might spark enough public outrage to force the American hierarchy and the Vatican to bring this fifty-year anti-life, anti-child, anti-family and anti-God experiment to a merciful end."

Engel asked Hanus to remove his imprimatur from the program in a letter dated Feb. 22, 2001. Archbishop Hanus acknowledged the letter in a Feb. 27 letter to Mrs. Engel, and said her critiques would be "taken under consideration." One year later, of course, nothing had been done.

Growing in Love immediately engendered significant public controversy, most notably in the Diocese of Syracuse, where parents in Syracuse, Binghamton, Utica and Rome, New York have protested the introduction of the textbook series into Catholic schools.

As usual, parents opposing the program have been maligned as "a small group of very vocal and highly critical parents...[who] have used misinformation to try to convince our own parents, as well as parents from other local Catholic schools, that its way of thinking is the *only* way" – as Anna Pastore, chairman of the Holy Family School Advisory Board wrote in a guest editorial published in the Syracuse *Post-Standard* Feb. 20, 2001.

From the other side, Paul Marek wrote in a letter to the editor of the same edition of the paper: "...Shame on you, Church and school leaders, who deliberately expose these innocent children which focuses on and stimulates the sexual function... Make no mistake that this diocese is in disobedience to the Vatican. This diocese is causing scandal. Parents have a right to know this before this series is introduced into their parish schools..."

The U.S. Coalition for Life's second objective was to bring *Growing in Love* to the attention of three Roman Curia dicasteries, the Congregations for the Doctrine of the Faith, Catholic Education and the Pontifical Council for the Family.

"The situation is so grave," said Engel, "that nothing less than a public declaration from the Congregation for the Doctrine of the Faith signed by the Holy Father confirming the traditional total ban on classroom sex education as enunciated by Pope Pius XI in his encyclical *On the Christian Education of Youth* on December 31, 1929 will do. This declaration must be accompanied by severe sanctions for hierarchical, clerical, religious and lay teacher offenders.

"Words must be backed by action and effective sanctions. Simply removing the offending program, will, as experience has shown, be a futile effort. *Growing In Love* will simply be replaced by another sex program so that the last state is worse than the first."

In her letter to Archbishop Hanus, Randy Engel outlined the two major problems with the series: its publisher and its content:

> The following two-part report on catechetical materials produced by Harcourt, Inc. and its acquisitions is being forwarded to your office as the first step in obtaining the removal of the Nihil Obstat given by Rev. Richard L. Schaefer Censor De Putatus and your Imprimatur as the Archbishop of Dubuque from all Harcourt catechetical materials including Brown-ROA's new sexual catechesis *Growing In Love*.

Once the facts have been laid before you I trust you will act affirmatively and judiciously in this matter so as to minimize the occasion of public scandal should this grave matter become public.

The first part of this complaint involves Harcourt, Inc. itself. As you are no doubt aware, in 1994 Harcourt acquired Brown-ROA, a major publishing house for Catholic religious instruction materials. Harcourt is a global multi-media corporation with fiscal revenues of more than $2.41 billion.

Since 1994, Catholic dioceses and their secondary and higher educational institutions throughout the United States have, by their purchasing of such Brown-ROA Catholic texts and study/instruction which bear your Imprimatur, have become a core asset to Harcourt's overall financial success.

In addition, given the ecclesiastical meaning of the Imprimatur and Nihil Obstat, Brown-ROA/Harcourt Catholic catechetical publications have acquired a semi-official Church-approved status without which the publishing house would find it difficult, if not impossible, to compete in the multi-million dollar catechetical market.

In 1999, Mr. Matthew J. Thibeau, the President of Brown-ROA, informed Catholic religion teachers, that in keeping with the realities of the 1994 acquisition, Brown-ROA was changing its name to Harcourt Religion Publishers. It is clear from his statement that Mr. Thibeau, at least publicly, is satisfied with the acquisition But then again, it is your Imprimatur that appears with the Brown-ROA/Harcourt Religion Publishers identification and not his.

Now, to cut to the chase. Harcourt, Inc. is a multi-national cartel with a large stable of notorious anti-life publishing houses. May I draw your attention to the fact that in May 1999, Churchill Livingston, a Harcourt Health Sciences Company, publicly announced the publication of *A Clinician's Guide to Medical and Surgical Abortion* – "the first clinical reference on abortion practice to be published in the United States in over fifteen years." This "how-to-kill unborn children" guide features multi-extermination methods of abortion, at all stages of fetal development, including RU 486, manual aspiration, and late abortion techniques using prostaglandins. It provides a list of resources for abortion providers. Harcourt tells us that the book carries the imprimatur of the National Abortion Federation.

In October 1999, another Harcourt company, W. B. Saunders, published *Contraception and Office Gynecology*, with clinical details related to contraceptive, abortifacients and "therapeutic termination of pregnancy."

In November 1999, Churchill Livingston published *Contraception: Your Questions Answered*, complete with a philosophical Malthusian introduction on "The Population Explosion and the Importance of Fertility Control." Abortifacient information including updates on the Pill and "postcoital" [read abortion] methods are provided.

In October 1997, still another Harcourt sister company, Bailliere Tindall, published the *Handbook of Contraception and Family Planning*, which includes the application of all forms of contraception and abortifacients and sterilization.

As its contribution to the Homosexual Movement, in October 1995, Harcourt published *The Lives of Lesbians, Gays and Bisexuals* for use in undergraduate and graduate courses in gay, lesbian, and bisexual "studies" designed to confirm homosexuals in their death-style – physically [AIDS], psychologically and spiritually.

As early as 1988, Harcourt Brace and Jovanovich published Bioethics which promotes virtually every eugenic medical practice condemned in the Vatican's *Instruction on Respect for Human Life in Its Origin* issued with the Holy Father's approbation by the Congregation for the Doctrine of the Faith in 1987.

Clearly, Harcourt is neither a friend of the Roman Catholic Church or to the unborn child. Your Imprimatur on any Harcourt catechetical material is as inappropriate as a Jewish good-housekeeping seal would be for I.G. Farben.

Now, let me take up the specific case of your Imprimatur on Brown-ROA/Harcourt Religion Publishers' new sexual catechesis for grades K-6, *Growing in Love*.

As the Archbishop of Dubuque, successor to the Apostles, and the promoter and guardian of doctrine on faith and morals you possess both the duty and right to exercise vigilance in order that the faith and morals of the members of the faithful entrusted to your care, most especially the souls of innocent children, may not suffer harm...

Sexual catechetics such as Brown-ROA/Harcourt Religion Publications' *Growing in Love*, designed for Kindergarten - 6th grade students, ages 5 to 12, constitute a direct spiritual, emotional and psychological assault on the very souls of Catholic children – dare I say – a demonic rape of innocence. So-called "sex-education" is sexual abuse in its worst form because it directly affects the immortal souls of thousands of Catholic school children (and their parents) and is carried out under the auspices of the Roman Catholic Church itself.

This communication does not lend itself to a full review of *Growing in Love* from a Catholic perspective. However, I should be remiss, in not bringing to your attention, the aggressive manner in which the ideology and practices of the Homosexual Movement/Church in the United States are advanced in the texts of *Growing in Love*.

Interestingly, it is Harcourt Religion Publications itself which alerts us to the homosexual overtures to be found in *Growing In Love*.

On its Catechetical Research web site promoting *Growing in Love*, Toinette M. Eugene, Ph.D., in an essay titled "Relationships that Make a Difference: The Importance of Including Culture and Scripture in Family Life and Human Sexuality Education," states that in the program [*Growing In Love*], "racism, sexism and *homophobia*, and other socially isolating evidence of social sinfulness are addressed thoughtfully, explicitly, and carefully." [Engel's emphasis].

Now the term "homophobic" is a gay political homosexual verbal construct. In the homosexual manifesto *Jesus Acted Up*, ex-Jesuit and self-proclaimed homosexual Dr. Robert Goss defines "homophobia" as "the socialized state of fear, threat, aversion, prejudice, and irrational hated of the feelings of same-sex attractions" which can be held by "individuals, groups, social institutions, and cultural practices." According to Goss, the most influential purveyor of the "sin" of "homophobia" is the Roman Catholic Church...

In the Family Resource Book of *Growing In Love* for parents of kindergarten children ages 5-6, the authors also use the politically-loaded homosexualist term "gay," and grossly misrepresent the nature of homosexual acts to parents by stating that "A man who is gay loves another man. A woman who is gay, or lesbian, loves another woman." What a debasement and defilement of the word "love"...

In the 5th grade Student Activity Book, students ages 9-10 are informed that while the majority of men and women have a "tendency" to be heterosexual, some have the "tendency" to be homosexual. The fact is that heterosexuality is a biological norm not a "tendency." Same-sex attraction is a psycho-sexual aberration related to a complex set of familial disturbances in the formative years, combined with opportunities for initiation into sodomical practices.

Moving on to the 6th grade Family Resource Book for parents of children ages 10-12, parents are treated to a dissertation on oral sex including fellatio, commonly employed by male homosexuals and cunnilingus employed in lesbian acts. The authors of *Growing in Filth* assure parents that "Both homosexual and heterosexual couples engage in oral sex" and the text provides a detailed description of the perverted acts. Given this acceleration in erotica one wonders what further explicit information on perverted sex lies ahead for parents and students.

Growing in Love is all the more offensive because it attempts to hide explicit sexual materials including descriptions of perverted acts behind a religious facade.

I shuddered when I was advised that in your letter of November 9, 1999 to Brown-ROA/Harcourt Religion Publishers, you chose and approved as the Imprimatur date for *Growing In Love,* January 8, 2000, the feast of St. Thomas Aquinas!

In December 1995, the Congregation for the Doctrine of the Faith withdrew the Imprimatur given to a Scottish sex instruction text by Archbishop Keith O'Brien of St. Andrews and Edinburgh, which advocated the use of condoms as a way of avoiding AIDS. The removal of the Imprimatur led to the "sex education study pack" being banned from all Catholic schools in Scotland.

I hope that you will take the initiative yourself without an order from the Congregation for the Doctrine of the Faith and agree to remove your Imprimatur from all Harcourt publications beginning with *Growing in Love*. Further that you will publicly disassociate your person and the Archdiocese of Dubuque from any direct or indirect association with Harcourt and its sister companies. And that you immediately inform the Congregation for the Doctrine of the Faith, the NCCB/USCC, all the American bishops, and all Catholic schools administrators of your actions…

Judy Ammenheuser of the Maryland-based Mothers' Watch evaluated the entire program. Each grade level of *Growing in Love* consists of a student text, a Teaching Guide, a Family Resource, and a Program Resource. One set of the entire K-6 program costs more than $500, including an Implementation Manual and two videos.

"By just looking at the children's text and Teaching Guide," she told *The Wanderer*, "parents will not see the explicit material contained in the Family Resource book and the Program Resource. The Program Resource is the book that teachers also use in the classroom.

"What is so devious about this program is that the Implementation Guide, which school officials will use to convince parents of the worthwhileness of the program, only gives parents 15 minutes to look through the entire program during the parent meeting. Parents are not likely to see the Program Resource, nor the reference to this resource in the lesson extension in the Teaching Guide. If they should see the objectionable material in the Family Resource, it is likely that the content will be explained away as for 'parents' eyes only' and to be used at their discretion," Mrs. Ammenheuser said.

"The Implementation Resource suggests one of three ways to implement the program: one is at home, using the "appropriate" Family Resource; the second is in the joint parent-child session, with a teacher or catechist in a school or parish; and the third is by the teacher in the class with parental permission.

"The third, one would expect, will be the routine effort, by the teacher in the classroom who, obviously, after obtaining parental permission, has an interest in exposing his students to the entire sexual liberation agenda.

"Anyone who approves this program in any way has to have a perverted sexual interest in children.

"This program should make the homosexual pedophiles in our Catholics schools joyful," she added.

Ammenheuser also stated that this program is guaranteed to destroy religion in a child's life, and sex will become the child's new religion, putting the child keenly in tune with all the sexual messages in society today, especially those on television, music and in advertising.

No end in sight

One wishes for a reprieve, but the homosexual propaganda machine shows no sign of slowing down, as an event last fall in the Diocese of Joliet – hardly a unique occurrence – illustrates.

"When young gay people ask about the appropriateness of an open relationship, I can help them evaluate their decisions by reviewing what conditions would allow them to find casual sex outside of a primary relationship to be honest and faithful."

That is the kind of advice one finds in the recommended reading material for "Scriptural Guidance Regarding Homosexuality," offered by Bishop Joseph Imesch.

Despite numerous complaints from Joliet area Catholics, Imesch persists in inviting pro-homosexual speakers to his chancery who promote sex between two men as something loving, holy, and completely acceptable, all the while assuring area Catholics that everything being said and promoted at his chancery is "orthodox."

Last September 4, Roman Catholic Faithful's founder and president, Stephen Brady, sent a letter to Imesch informing him that:

"According to a flyer distributed by the Joliet chancery to all priests, on October 13, 2001 a Mr. David Schimmel [an ex-priest] will be giving a lecture at the St. Charles Pastoral Center from 9 a.m. to 3 p.m…The cost to attend is $15.00 and the event is sponsored by the Catholic Family Network (CFN). The Catholic Family Network is an official support group/ministry of the Joliet Diocese, 'for parents and friends of gays and lesbians and their children.' The title of Mr. Schimmel's talk is 'The Bible tells me so / Scriptural Guidance Regarding Homosexuality.'

"Upon learning of Schimmel's forthcoming appearance at the Pastoral Center," continued Brady, "I did some research and obtained several copies of his (Schimmel's) newsletter *Passion*. It is clear from his writings that he

213

does not accept Church teaching regarding the sinfulness of homosexual activity and the disorder that the homosexual orientation represents.

"In his July 2001 Issue of *Passion* titled 'Queer Justice,' in an attempt to explain away the sin of Sodom as nothing more then a sin against hospitality, Schimmel refers to the 'simplistic association of Sodom with homosexuality' and accuses the Church of 'the misuse of scripture, perpetuated by ignorance and blinding self-righteousness,' which 'causes Christian lesbians and gays to question divine justice as they protest, It's not fair!' He then goes on to quote ex-priest Daniel Helminiak's book *What the Bible really says about Homosexuality*: 'those who oppress homosexuals because of the supposed sin of Sodom may themselves be the real sodomites, as the bible understands it.'

"Unfortunately, Mr. Schimmel is not the first speaker sponsored by the CFN whose apparent beliefs deny the truths of the Catholic faith. There has been a clear pattern of pro-homosexual speakers brought into the diocese under the guise of 'Ministry to Gays.' This is not something one would expect from a celibate bishop who accepted Church teaching. On the other hand, this is something you would expect from a bishop with a disordered sexuality who was/is possibly living a lie…"

Brady continued his letter by reciting a long litany of official, diocese-sponsored events and speakers, a litany which he can surely continue well into the foreseeable future.

CHAPTER TEN

Trying To Make
Sense Of It All

In late March, 2001, the *Sydney Morning Herald* reported that the Vatican had "banned" a recent book by Australian Christian Brother Dr. Barry Coldrey, an historian, that attempts to give a broad overview of clerical sexual abuse scandals in the English-speaking world.

That book, *Religious Life Without Integrity: The Sexual Abuse Crisis Within the Catholic Church*, offers detailed and abundant documentation on the "sexual underworlds" that have grown up in dioceses and religious orders in Australia, England, Ireland, Canada and the United States and the complicity on the part of religious superiors, including bishops, who have nurtured them and enabled them to flourish.

Coldrey's book stems from an assignment he was given in the early 1990s to produce a report on sexual abuse scandals involving his order, the Christian Brothers, in Australia, and a subsequent, more detailed report he was asked to write for the Congregation for Religious Orders and Secular Institutes in Rome.

The book began circulating privately in April, 2000, and in December the Congregation asked him to withdraw it; but copies began circulating on the Internet, and it is now available as a download on the Internet site of the Chicago-based Linkup (thelinkup.com), an association of individuals who have been sexually abused.

In light of Pope John Paul II's exhortation to the cardinals of the Catholic Church at last year's special consistory, that they must pay more attention to the training of priests, it is more timely than ever to take a look at what Coldrey calls "the elephant issue in the Catholic Church in the English-speaking world," which, the most recent evidence indicates, is an issue the English-speaking bishops still cannot confront.

Citing various studies, Coldrey establishes the number of priests and brothers in Australia who have sexually abused minors at 7%-10% of the total number, and that in the United States, approximately 12%-15% of

Catholic clergy indulge in homosexual sex acts, about 5%-7% are pedophiles and 20%-28% are involved sexually with women.

On the positive side, this means the majority of Catholic priests are faithful to their vows of celibacy. On the other hand, as the trial of Dallas priest Rudy Kos showed, as well as the recent trials in Boston of former priest John Geoghan, the typical priest-pedophile will abuse hundreds of boys before he is exposed – if ever.

Coldrey explores the myriad reasons why Church leaders are reluctant to deal decisively with the problem of its sexual-abusing priests, but the strongest reason that emerges is that too many bishops and religious superiors are, themselves, part of the problem.

For example, Coldrey reveals that at least 20% of seminarians report they have "experienced" homosexual activity in the seminary, and he has numerous reports of priests testifying that they have been pressured by their bishops to join their homosexual networks, members of which typically receive the plum chancery and parish assignments, while those who refuse the bishop's advances are exiled to remote or undesirable parishes, or, in some cases, exiled from their own dioceses.

The major obstacle

"This [clerical] infidelity," he writes, "has become a major obstacle to preaching the gospel in the English-speaking world. Priestly 'zippergate' has become to the Church what 'Watergate' was to U.S. President, Richard Nixon. As Bishop Geoffrey Robinson told the recent (December 1998) Synod of the Bishops of Oceania in Rome: 'Victims of abuse and the whole community demand that the Church do everything possible to ensure that no one else will be abused in the future. They demand that all aspects of the life of the priest and the religious be studied and that all attitudes to power and authority be carefully reviewed'…

"Meanwhile there is the frustration of the dedicated Catholic laity faced with increasing evidence of the infidelity of many of their priests to the most public of their vows. It is the laity who have to face the ribald humor and coarse innuendo of their non-Catholic friends and acquaintances at each new revelation of priestly infidelity, child molestation or personal shortcomings, the more so since Catholic priests have rarely been slow to lay down the law on what the community ought or ought not to be doing…Our reputation has declined seriously, and it may sink further

216

before things improve. Catholics ache with a sense of innocence lost or destroyed, of the dangerous allure of evil: criminal behavior, vows ignored, the squalid efforts to cover-up."

Coldrey gives credence to some of the standard boilerplate excuses that some bishops have used when responding to the public when sexual abuse issues arise, such as "We didn't know how to handle it"; "We didn't know how much the victim suffered"; "We didn't know that the condition isn't treatable", etc.

"However, there is still a downside, a shadow side which includes widespread denial among ordinary Brothers and priests of the extent and dimensions of the problem; an empathy with the perpetrators which confronts the victims with at best, sympathy-fatigue, and a defensive attitude to discussing the situation with any degree of frankness or detail. There are attempts to silence in-house critics.

"There is evidence, also, that some Religious Superiors, their lay advisors and solicitors have skirted the edge of illegality by paying hush money to complainants to withdraw their allegations after criminal proceedings have started against priests or Brothers...

"Rhetoric remained pious, generalized, evasive; some meetings to discuss the issue were stage-managed, sterilized and carefully orchestrated to avoid confronting sexual problems too directly. Individuals who work, or have worked to bring the abuse issue to the attention of authorities can find themselves marginalized, subject to continuing lying and character assassination, a sort of low-level verbal terrorism, while offenders are readily excused and integrated, and either are, or give the appearance of being protected.

"There is the toxic mixture of brotherhood and betrayal, high belief and low cunning. Sin is congenial; jail a novelty; 'promotion' is based on sexual experience."

Abundance of evidence

Coldrey's book is, by and large, simply a compilation of material published in the United States, Britain, Canada and Australia by the so-called "mainstream" secular and Catholic publications; conspicuously absent from his hundreds of sources are any references to the groundbreaking, extensive reports that have appeared in *The Wanderer* since the early 1980s, when Paul

Fisher and Fr. Charles Fiore began exposing the extent of the "homosexual network" in the Church in the United States and the initiation of the first sexual abuse lawsuits.

Nevertheless, his study, conducted over an eight-year period, is undoubtedly the most comprehensive collection of horror stories pertaining to the most serious crisis the Church is facing – for not only are the homosexuals and pedophiles violating their vows, emotionally, physically and spiritually damaging their children-victims and the rest of the Catholic laity by their acts, but the homosexual network in the Church continues to do irreparable damage by its influence in and control over liturgy, education, especially sex education, and social justice operations.

Unfortunately missing from Coldrey's investigation, also, are figures such as former Honolulu Bishop Joseph Ferrario, one of the first bishops in the United States to be charged with sexual abuse, and his protector Archbishop John Quinn of San Francisco, whose closest associates were implicated in numerous sexual scandals.

After presenting a sociological analysis of the consequences of the "sexual revolution" that erupted in the 1960s, and the gradual unraveling of the shroud of secrecy covering clerical sexual abuse (a consequence of the episcopal policy of assigning pedophiles from parish to parish, from diocese to diocese) that began with the Gauthe affair in Lafayette, Louisiana, Coldrey discusses the bishops' benign neglect of a document prepared for them, the famous 1985 Doyle-Mouton report, "The Problem of Sexual Molestation by Roman Catholic Clergy: Meeting the Problem in a Comprehensive and Responsible Manner," and their initial efforts at establishing treatment centers for offenders.

In the years immediately following the Doyle-Mouton report, Coldrey writes, the bishops probably hoped the issue of clerical pedophilia would quietly disappear, and it seemed to, until it burst into the international press with a number of high profile cases in Newfoundland, Worcester and Dallas.

"The new wave of scandals," writes Coldrey, "broke first in Newfoundland (1988) with criminal prosecutions for repeated molestations committed by two parish priests. Over time other priests were implicated until some ten per cent of the diocesan clergy were tainted by allegations, arrest, trial and commonly conviction. In the spring of 1989 attention shifted to the long history of both physical and sexual abuse committed by members of the

(Irish) Christian Brothers Congregation against teenage boys in the Mount Cashel boys home in St. John's. In this case, allegations had surfaced originally in 1975 and in a widespread state-church cover-up certain Brothers had been permitted to leave the Province without facing criminal proceedings when investigations were closed. The story remained in the headlines for several years, with a Royal Commission, an internal investigation by the Catholic church, a series of criminal trials and highly-publicised civil actions and negotiations for compensation for the numerous victims...

"The year 1990 marked a watershed as confused Church authorities began to lose their damage-control efforts to the rising tide of the voices of the victims."

When the news revolving around the Mt. Cashel situation reached Australia, it produced an avalanche of similar allegations against the Christian Brothers in that country, and the subsequent publicity generated even more reports of clerical sexual abuse in England, Ireland and the United States: no longer were the long-suffering Catholic victims and their families willing to be intimidated into silence.

The grim details

Coldrey coldly recites the grim details: the numbers of priests arrested, charged and convicted; the number of accused priests who have committed suicide; the number of priests and bishops who have resigned from the offices upon exposure; estimates of the number of victims, etc.

But a deeper problem than the clerical shortcomings, hypocrisy, scandals and crimes is the sexual network and underground. Coldrey explains:

"A sexual network is a small group or circle of priests, Brothers or lay workers who are living at variance with their vows on sexual matters – two's and three's who support one another by supportive silence and covering for each other. A sexual underworld is a larger, more amorphous state-within-a-state inside a diocese or Religious Congregation, where there is a substantial [group of] people who are not living their vows (or have not for periods in the past) and who co-operate to hide one another's extracurricular activities..."

"Bad apples attract more bad apples. 'I have secrets about you; you have secrets about me. I won't fink on you; you won't fink on me.' Blackmail and extortion are the ways things are kept quiet in the Church. They were one way to build trust. It's 'I know this about you and you know this about me, so I'll take you along with me.' People go through stages in their lives. They may no longer be active sexually, but they have a sexual history and have to deal with people from their past.

"There is an ironic parallel here with the sexual underworld in some dioceses and provinces of Religious Congregations. Priests/Brothers/ church workers who abuse minors and commit criminal offences have been (are?) able to hide within a sympathetic underworld of other clergy and church workers who are merely breaking their vows by having heterosexual or gay sex with consenting adults. All are doing the wrong thing and have a similar incentive to provide mutual support. They share an unstated capacity for mutual blackmail. Each has friends."

Chapter 12 of Coldrey's book begins with an account reported by A.W. Richard Sipe in his 1995 book, *Sex, Priests and Power: Anatomy of a Crisis*:

> A weeping young American priest struggled to absorb an experience that threatened his idealism and tells his story: "I had completed graduate schools and was flattered when my bishop asked me to accompany him to a high-level meeting attended by a large number of the hierarchy. During my time there, I was approached and asked for sex by a bishop from another diocese. I declined, and the bishop remarked: 'You know, Father, if you want to progress in this organisation, you are going to need friends.'" The young priest was to find out later that some men on the bishop's staff were themselves connected sexually to the gay network…he witnessed priests who won promotions based on sexual involvement, was offered pornography and endured sexual advances from a number of highly-placed fellow clergy.

Coldrey continues:

> …here are four key features of a sexual underworld in a religious organisation: a shared guilty secret based on illegal or immoral sexual activity in breach of either criminal law: a priest's vows of celibacy; mutual support in seeking positions of responsibility; in good-mouthing one another; bad-mouthing perceived critics and supportive friendships permitting a toxic cone of silence over mutual shortcomings, more profound than the mafia code of *omerta…*

The following could be the sequence of growth of a sexual underworld in a province of a Religious Order or diocese.

a) Occasionally, a rogue staff member of a training college, juvenate or seminary (or a Vocation Director) has used his position to molest student(s), as occurred on a wide scale in the now-suppressed "Brothers of St. Gerard Majella"...

(b) More often...and sometimes quite often...some seminarians get involved in peer sexual activity. These activities are not criminal but are extremely embarrassing when viewed from the vantage point of later life...

(c) Occasionally (some) seminarians show one another porno-movies, visit brothels or gay bars...maybe seek an affair or a "one-night-stand". The stated motive is along the lines of "seeing what it's like before signing on the dotted line"...

(d) In due course, Brother is professed and seminarian ordained. However, the heterosexual attraction proves stronger than anticipated in the freer atmosphere away from the college. There a loneliness...a certain bitterness as the priest or Brother observes family life. He drifts into an affair with one of the ladies' committees, the housekeeper or a woman who comes for counseling.

(e) There can be a parallel development in the case of a gay relationship. The young man may have had some doubts as to his sexual orientation but not pursued the matter...

(f) Then there is, for a small minority, behavior with sexual connotations: obscene 'phone calls, curb-crawling, hanging around in the Red Light area for the vicarious thrill of the unsavory.

(g) Finally there are the 5% to 7% who have really molested minors, i.e. committed serious sexual offences according to the criminal law.

Many priests or male religious who have molested children were themselves molested or propositioned at some stage of their development, occasionally by priests or Brothers.

(a) Between 1964 and 1987, dozens of teenage boys were molested by Franciscan friars at St. Anthony's (Junior) Seminary in Santa Barbara, California.

(b) Between 1968 and 1992, many former students at the Wisconsin (Junior) Seminary of the Capuchins (Franciscan) were molested by six of the friars…

The gay profession

Coldrey also discusses at length the problem of the homosexualization of the priesthood and religious life, observing:

> [G]ay activists in Religious Congregations or in dioceses are likely to draw other men into their activities. There is, after all, safety in numbers. Moreover, such men will always have around vulnerable characters who for one reason or another are 'down on their luck' and easy prey for genuine or apparent kindness and interest, even if the one offering the friendship has a quite different agenda.

> This drift to a gay lifestyle may be accentuated by the fact that many of the seminarians in a given seminary at a specific time maybe of gay orientation. Gay orientation does not mean sexually active homosexuals. This reality was not understood until fairly recently and when first realized was desperately covered up as a taboo subject. One of the reasons why the traditional seminary was isolated, often secluded in pastoral serenity, was to separate heterosexual candidates from the presumed temptation of female company.

> 'All' the seminarians were presumed to be 'normal', i.e. heterosexual in their orientation even if few adverted to the fact. All had chosen to be trained for the priesthood which involved taking a vow of celibacy. What were taboos until quite recently were a cluster of interrelated facts with which the Church now must come to terms:

> - Some seminary staff in the past (not many) have molested or propositioned students; (more commonly) there has been sexual activity between certain seminarians. This can form the basis for a sex underworld in a diocese or Religious Congregation.

> - If the number of men in the community whose sexual orientation is gay are around 10-15% of the age cohort, the percentage of such men in the seminary is higher than in the population as a whole. Studies overseas seem definite.

- In some seminaries at some times, men of homosexual orientation could be in the majority. While many men with gay orientation can, and do make excellent and celibate priests, there can be extra problems if many or most of the men training in a given seminary are of gay (orientation)…

- Thus a covert gay sub-culture can develop in a seminary. This does not mean that all such seminarians are sexually active, but if some are, and some are predatory (i.e. actively seeking partners) they can subvert the goals of seminary training, especially if the active gay seminarians are the humanly-speaking strong personalities.

- The modern seminarian is normally older than was customary and usually commences training in his early twenties. It is likely that some seminarians are sexually experienced. The mix of the sexually experienced, gay and straight, the virgins (gay or straight orientation) and the merely confused does provide problems for the seminary staff. These need to be recognized by staff.

The solution:
Light & Noise

If the Church's leaders ever become serious about addressing the problem of the homosexual underworld in the ranks of diocesan priests and Religious, two things are necessary, writes Coldrey: light and noise.

> Noise and light draw attention. Perhaps there is a parallel situation in the case of sexual networking that can exist in the diocese or the Province of a Religious Order.

> If relevant authority makes it clear in various ways – hints, explanations to key people – with the idea that the word will spread – then those involved may take the big hint that 'the game is up' and s/he will either regularise his situation or leave the consecrated life.

Coldrey also offers some concrete suggestions to re-orient the vocation screening process, suggesting that aspirants to the priesthood or consecrated life should sign a document stating that he has done nothing for which he is liable for prosecution and that he should swear that he has never been abused sexually by a priest or religious.

Seminary staff need to be aware that cases of abuse of seminarians (by rogue staff) have occurred, with devastating results all around when all is revealed as in the modern world it is likely to be.

A scary fact

In Appendix 4 of his study, Dr. Coldrey informs his readers that the Brotherhood of St. Gerard Majella, disbanded in December 1994, was founded in 1958 by John Sweeney, quite possibly as a club for pedophiles.

"Whether John Sweeney founded the society with the deliberate intention of perverting its young members is not known – and is not pleasant to contemplate," he reflects; but nevertheless the order, which was committed to the education of youth, quickly became just that – and the consequences were enormous.

In December 1993, the secrets came out when a Melbourne-based, sexual abuse survivors support group, Broken Rites, publicized its national telephone hotline and "several former Brothers of the Society of St. Gerard Majella called to tell of systematic sexual abuse while they were members. There were three senior-priest-members of the Society and each and all were sexual abusers, pedophiles…

"Meanwhile, Frs. Sweeney, Pritchard and Robinson were arrested in early 1995 and their several court appearances spanned three years. A week before Fr. Sweeney's sentencing for sex offences, Bishop [Bede] Heather took early retirement. The three priests' convictions were reported widely in the media…All three priests, the entire leadership of the small congregation, were jailed – for sex offences against trainees over many years…"

A plausible theory

It is now time to ask the question: How could all this happen? How far back must we go to find the root causes? All the way back to Adam and Eve in the Garden of Eden?

I believe the case can be made that the Protestant Reformation was a milestone event leading to the homosexualization of the Church in the United States. The great English historian Hilaire Belloc in his 1920 work, *Europe and the Faith,* wrote that the most evil effect of the Reformation was the "isolation of the soul."

To claim this is not to exclude other factors that have contributed to both the Church's and the larger society's problems with sexual predators, of which mention must be made of the social and psychological trauma of the World Wars, which left so many men permanently disabled and millions of boys fatherless; of seventy years of systematic propaganda for the sexual revolution; of a hundred years of radical feminism that poisoned, like mercury in the food chain, the natural relationship between men and women, husbands and wives, parents and children, and worked an even-more noxious effect on the Catholic clergy; the psychotherapeutic revolution which replaced the concept of sin with guilt, to be resolved by therapy; the social dislocation of Catholic ethnics from their neighborhoods in the great Catholic cities from Boston to Buffalo, from Cleveland to Chicago, through an intentionally anti-Catholic "urban renewal" and racial politics, their dispersal into the suburbs, and their homogenization into the liberal, consumerist milieu of contracepting, working mothers – all issues the U.S. bishops have either cooperated in facilitating or ignored.

"The isolation of the soul," Belloc explained, "means a loss of corporate sustenance; of the sane balance produced by general experience, the weight of security, and the general will. The isolation of the soul is the very definition of its unhappiness…

"[T]he new isolation of the soul compelled the isolated soul to strong vagaries. The soul will not remain in the void. If you blind it, it will grope. If it cannot grasp what it appreciates by every sense, it will grasp what it appreciates by only one…" A new stage in humanity's brokenness is approaching, predicted Belloc, and the isolated soul will "breed attempted strange religions: witchcrafts and necromancies."

Writing in the chaotic aftermath of World War I, Belloc prophesied the coming New Age religions, driven by new psychological and psychiatric theories popularized in the mass media.

In his 1933 classic, *Essays of a Catholic*, Belloc predicted that "when the gods of the New Paganism come they will not be merely insufficient, as were the gods of Greece, nor merely false; they will be evil. One might put it in a sentence, and say that the New Paganism, foolishly expecting satisfaction, will fall, before it knows where it is, into Satanism."

In that same period, the 1930s, Swiss psychologist Carl Gustav Jung began sending out his anointed disciples from Zurich to Britain and the United

225

States to spread his Jungian doctrines and establish what historian and psychologist Dr. Richard Noll described as "an anti-orthodox Christianity cult of redemption or Nietszchean religion," finding fertile ground especially among disoriented Catholics.

Dr. Noll, a student of the history of science (then at Harvard), explained in his 1994 work, *The Jung Cult: Origins of a Charismatic Movement* (Princeton University Press), Jung's entire life and work was motivated by a desire to overthrow the Catholic Church, whose religious doctrines and moral teachings he considered the source of all the neuroses which afflicted Western man. In short: Jung hated the Catholic Church, and by his experience with occult forces, he believed he could destroy it by unleashing the power of disordered sex.

With the financial backing of some of the wealthiest Americans, including the Rockefeller family, and the support of Marxist ideologues, eugenicists and sexual libertines in the media, universities and government, Jung's program to deconstruct orthodox Christianity became the playbook for the managerial elite of the new planned society that came into being in the western world in the 1930s.

Jung's influence cannot be underestimated. With the help of such disciples as the CIA's first director, Allen Dulles, Jung's new psychological theories helped support the research and work of CIA-funded Dr. Ewen Cameron, former president of the American Psychiatric Association, who conducted horrific experiments on thousands of Canadian children in the 1940s and '50s. In addition to testing all sorts of mind-altering drugs on children (often at the behest of the giant pharmaceutical companies), testing the limits of abusive physical punishment (such as beatings and torture), sexual abuse and sexual experiments, Cameron used to pipe into the cells of his subjects for days, sometimes weeks, on-end, repeated messages such as, "I am worthless," "I am a nobody," etc. – the same message drummed into the heads of Catholics all through the '60s and '70s by the pop-theologians in the "new catechetics."

Cameron, who also headed the Canadian Psychiatric Association and founded the World Psychiatric Association, was the world's leading expert on "deprogramming," and "de-patterning" – wiping a mind clean through sensory deprivation techniques.

CIA director Dulles once referred to Dr. Cameron's Allan Institute at McGill University as "a good source for human guinea pigs," and it is worth noting that the Rockefeller Foundation funded both Cameron and his pedophile colleague in the United States, Alfred Kinsey, the famous "sex researcher" whose well-publicized, but fraudulent, studies were promoted by the Rockefeller Foundation and their publicists in the major media and especially in Catholic institutions, particularly through Notre Dame University.

Cameron's story is told by Gordon Thomas in his book *Journey into Madness: The True Story of the Secret CIA Mind Control and Medical Abuse*. The untold story is the cumulative effects of physical, emotional and sexual abuse on tens of thousands of children – mostly Catholic – under the auspices of the Canadian and American governments, at a time when the CIA, apparently, was giving the Church's intellectual leaders LSD to develop a new sense of religiosity ("LSD: Trip Through The Looking Glass To God," Mark Bowden, Baltimore News-American, January 18 and 19, 1976)

Jung was born July 26, 1875, to Paul Achilles Jung, a Protestant minister, and Emilie Prieswerk, both of whom were the thirteenth children born to their parents. On both his parents' sides, Jung was descended from a long line of interesting Swiss and German characters: his grandfather Jung the Elder was weaned away from the Catholic Church by Friedrich Schliermacher, and was alleged to be the illegitimate child of Goethe – to whom Carl Jung attributed his own genius. On his mother's side, wrote Noll, there was "significant evidence of hereditary degeneration."

By 1912, Jung was totally absorbed by eroticism and entranced by the occult, particularly the ritualistic liturgies of Mithras. That year, he announced he could no longer be a Christian, and that only the "new" science of psychoanalysis – as he defined it – could offer personal and cultural renewal and rebirth.

To Jung, honoring God now meant honoring the libido. Indeed, observed Noll, after quoting from Jung's *Wandlungen*, "Jung offers the psychoanalytic term 'libido' as a mystical substitute for 'vital force' or even 'God.' Just as we feel the surge of vital power within us as living biological beings, so then are we also experiencing the god within.

"…The experience of the god within was always a key promise of Jung, and his method of psychotherapy…and it is indeed a central part of Jung's repudiation of traditional Christianity that offered a God that was distant, transcendental and absolute. In the pages of *Wandlungen* we see the first liturgical exegesis for these core Jungian concepts.

"Having a god within could lead to the experience of becoming one with God, or merging with this God-force in some way. It is clear from his many statements in *Wandlungen* that Jung felt that the central experience of transformation in the ancient mystery cults of the Hellenistic world involved just such a process or experience of self-deification."

"Two thousand years of Christianity," wrote Noll in summing up Jung's belief, "makes us strangers to ourselves. In the individual, the internalization of bourgeois-Christian civilization is a mask that covers the true Aryan god within, a natural god, a sun god, perhaps even Mithras himself...In society, too, Christianity is an alien mask that covers our biologically true religion, a natural religion of the sun and the sky..."

What Jung was searching for

As Dr. John Kerr showed in his important book, *A Most Dangerous Method: The Story of Jung, Freud and Sabina Spielrein*, Jung's drive to formulate a new religion was the result of trying to justify his own sins: the betrayal of his wife and the betrayal and seduction of his patient Sabina Spielrein. He needs to conceive a "better" religion, wrote Kerr, one that wouldn't condemn him for his sins.

At bottom, Jung betrayed his father, his wife, his patient, and, of course, Christ, in trying to ease the rebukes his conscience delivered.

Another early important influence on Jung was the German physician and psychoanalyst Otto Gross (1877-1920), from whom Jung picked up his ideas on the "life-enhancing value of eroticism," which, wrote Gross, "is so great that it must remain free from extraneous considerations in laws, and above all, from any integration into everyday life...Husbands and wives should not begrudge each other whatever erotic stimuli may present themselves. Jealousy is something mean. Just as one has several people for friends, one can also have sexual union with several people at any given period and be 'faithful' to each one...Free love will save the world."

According to scholar Martin Green, quoted by Noll: "Otto Gross was familiar with every kind of heresy" and "his teachings attacked not just

Christianity but the whole complex of secular faiths that had grown up around Christianity in the West, and had largely stifled and supplanted it."

Gross and Jung spent a considerable time together, sometimes analyzing each other for twelve-hour stints, from which Gross would have to flee to feed his drug habit. But until his suicide, Gross was very much Jung's mentor, and Jung could write approvingly of Gross' use of sex orgies to promote pagan spirituality, as he did when he wrote: "The existence of a phallic or orgiastic cult does not indicate *eo ipso* a particularly lascivious life any more than the ascetic symbolism of Christianity means an especially moral life."

"The revolutionary of today," wrote Gross, "with the help of the psychology of the unconscious, fights oppression in its most basic form: the father and patriarchy. The coming revolution is the revolution for matriarchy."

In 1912, Jung published his *New Paths in Psychology*, which wrote Noll, was the equivalent of Lenin's *What is to be Done?*

In this work, Jung "calls for an intrapsychic overthrow of custom, a revolution in the internalized European traditions that enslave the individual personality." The only way to overthrow the neuroses-inducing Judeo-Christian religion and its sex-fixated ethics, said Jung, was to establish a new religion – the religion of psychoanalysis.

Today, writes Noll, "for literally tens of thousands, if not hundreds of thousands, of individuals in our culture, Jung and his ideas are the basis of a personal religion that either supplants their participation in traditional organized Judeo-Christian religion or accompanies it."

Moreover, Jung is fueling the widespread fascination with all areas of witchcraft and the occult and is a "source of inspiration and affirmation for the neopagan religious movements... (which) have adopted Jung as a prophet."

Jung has been the driving force of the "Quiet Revolution" in the Catholic Church for the past sixty years, at least. His teachings long ago replaced those of Jesus Christ, St. Paul, St. Augustine and Thomas Aquinas in the "mainstream" of Catholic teaching in seminaries, convents, Catholic colleges and universities, retreat programs and spiritual formation courses in

Western Europe and the United States – a revolution which most Catholics have not yet noticed.

Even more peculiar is the fact that Jung, an "apostle for adultery," who believed in (and practiced) polygamy, who devoted his life to overthrowing patriarchal society and reviving the ancient pagan gods of the libido, should have his "insights" into masculinity, femininity and sexuality upheld by a woman – Dolores Leckey – who headed the U.S. bishops' marriage and family life office in their national conference for 20 years!

Two years after publishing *The Jung Cult*, which demonstrated that Jung deliberately founded a new religious movement, Noll returned with even more explosive revelations detailing Jung's obsession with overthrowing orthodox Christianity in *The Aryan Christ: The Secret Life of C.G. Jung* (Random House).

After this book appeared, this reporter interviewed Noll, and asked about Jung's view that "sexuality is the sine qua non of spirituality – one only exists through the other," and what that means, and what its implications are in the real world?

Noll's answer speaks directly to the crisis in the Church today, especially Cardinal Law's predicament in Boston:

"What it meant to Jung was that to fully individuate – i.e. to become a whole or complete person – one must fully explore the sexual realm, even if it goes against societal values and moral constrictions. One of the reasons Jung advocated polygamy, particularly for men, is that he thought if one lived that kind of free instinctual sexual life then one was getting in touch with the archaic manly men – that is, plugging back into the ancient spiritual and biological energies. One thing I cannot stress enough is that Jung believed, at least for the first 60 years of his life, that spirituality was rooted in biology and race.

"The real world implications are this: In the Jungian community of today most analysts refuse to stand up publicly and just say no: that certain things are wrong. Some Jungian training institutes do not have codes of ethics. Boston, as of today, is planning one but does not have one as we speak.

"For their patients, the problem is that some analysts, like John Hule, say it is okay to have sex with your patients if the self demands it. Self is just a Jungian code word for God, a word that is invoked. The self must be obeyed, even if the law says it's wrong. Essentially, it is spiritual seduction as a way of enacting sexual abuse, and it is condoned by Jungian analysts."

This reporter also asked Dr. Noll to interpret and analyze a statement in a book written by Dolores Leckey, while she was executive director of the U.S. bishops' Marriage and Family Life Office – a book which carried an endorsement by Morton Kelsey, the prominent Episcopalian Jungian.

Wrote Leckey in her 1987 book, *Laity Stirring the Church* (pp 58-59): "According to Jung the masculine and feminine principles reside in the deepest parts of our psyches, bridging unconscious contents to the soul. Because they are hidden so deep within, the feminine and masculine components remain unknown. Unconsciously, however, we project the animus or anima content onto others…

"Jung's is not only a personal analysis, but a corporate one. In a gender-separate society the conduct of public business, by men, has proceeded out of touch with the feminine principle. With the carriers of the anima at a distance, uninvolved and not easily influencing the policies of public institutions, the feminine (in both men and women) which Jung calls the soul, the spark of divine energy, is missing. Some call this the intuitive reality, the non-rational way of knowing, the artistic-mystic vision. And some assume that women are closer to this reality than are men, simply because the anima is familiar and not so alarming as it seems to be for men. Can it be that men are running from the lost part of themselves, that part symbolized by and crystallized around women?"

"What do these lines this tell us about the author?" I asked.

Noll responded: "I'm horrified. You have this very prominent woman in the Catholic Church who is essentially espousing a belief which in previous centuries would be considered a heresy by the Catholic Church.

"But she is justifying it by citing Jung as a scientific authority. Those particular ideas of Jung's have no scientific validity. Essentially, Jung borrowed this cluster of ideas from the Aryan spirituality and occultism of his day. That stuff comes directly from books that have been long forgotten on Aryan/racist spirituality.

"People who say such things think they are speaking scientifically, but this vocabulary comes from an occult tradition prevalent at the turn of the century in Germany."

Face the facts

It's certainly one of the most bizarre developments in 20th century Catholicism that Carl Gustav Jung, dedicated to the destruction of the Catholic Church and the establishment of an anti-Church based on psychoanalysis, should have become the premier spiritual guide in the Catholic Church throughout the United States, Canada and Europe over the last three decades.

But that's the case.

Walk into a typical Catholic bookstore and browse in the "spirituality" section, and you'll see the best-selling books of such popularizers of the Jung cult as priests Basil Pennington, Richard Rohr and Thomas Keating.

Read the listings for "spirituality" programs and retreats in many diocesan newspapers, and you will see programs on Jungian dream analysis, discovering the child within, contacting your "god/goddess" or similar such Jungian therapy programs predominate, even though they have nothing to do with Catholic spirituality, and are inherently antithetical to it.

Nearly fifty years ago, wrote the great Catholic psychiatrist Karl Stern in *The Third Revolution* (Harcourt Brace & Co., 1954), most Catholic scholars recognized that Jung and Catholicism were incompatible – irreconcilable – and Stern warned that the Jungian who begins viewing religion as existing on the same plane as psychology ends up viewing all religions as equally irrelevant.

"As a German philosopher friend of mine once remarked with a pun," wrote Stern, *"Das gleich Gultige wird gleichgutig* (that which is equally relevant becomes irrelevant). The curtain of the temple is conjured away with an elegant flourish. The border between Nature and Grace exists no longer, and no longer are you mortally engaged. Matters of the spirit are part of a noncommital therapeutic method; Jacob no longer wrestles with the Angel in a horrible grip which leaves him forever limping – instead he takes his daily hour of gymnastics."

In the years since, however, Catholic scholars, priests, Religious and laity have gone over to Jung with the fervor of Athenians flocking to the Oracle at Delphi.

One of the most important landmarks in the history of the establishment of the Jung Cult in the Catholic Church was the publication of *Jung and Religion*, as a special feature of *New Catholic World*, published by Paulist Press (the same order that produced RENEW), in March/April 1984.

The special feature showed not only how far the Jung Cult had infiltrated Church structures, but now it was being mass-marketed for ordinary parishioners bored with the contemporary, deplorable, state of Catholic spirituality.

Among the contributors (the described credentials were for 1984, when the articles appeared):

- Dr. Wallace Clift, an Episcopalian minister and president of the Jung Society of Colorado, and chairman of the Department of Religious Studies at the University of Denver, predicted that "Jung's notion of religion is…destined to become the most influential development in the psychology of religion in this century." Clift explained Jung was a trailblazer in recognizing that the old form of externalized Christian ritual and belief had given way to a new form of religion: discovery of the Self, or God within, and the technique to discover it.

- Robert T. Sears, S.J., instructor in Pastoral Studies at Loyola University in Chicago, who conceded that Jungian spirituality is at odds with traditional Catholic spirituality, as exemplified by St. Ignatius' *Spiritual Exercises*, but nevertheless recommended Jung's valuable insights on how to "expand to greater inner awareness by accepting our shadow side."

- Fr. Diarmuid McGann, an assistant pastor at a New York church, and described as a "consultant on the USCC-commissioned 30-part TV program on marriage and divorce," offered Jung as a key to understanding oneself. Jung enables one to reach his "inner self" where there is a world of images, messages, symbols, stories and myths that tell us who one is.

- John Welch, O. Carm., chair of pastoral studies at the Washington Theological Union, wrote that Jung was for people who believed God was dead, and Jung could guide them on "their own inner spiritual journey in search for meaning." By searching within, we find the divine. Jung taught that the old religious symbols had become meaningless, and the only way find meaning was to become involved in the on-going discovery of new symbols, which are "on the horizon."

- Elizabeth Dryer, Ph.D., assistant professor of theology at Catholic University, wrote on Jung and the feminine in spirituality. "Jung," she wrote, "has provided a service for us in calling our attention to aspects of human experience that have been overshadowed and even denigrated in our preoccupation with reason and logic…His pioneering work has been seen by many as an invitation to see themselves as persons on the way to psychic wholeness, and to employ the geography of the psyche to assist them on their journey into self-transcendence and union with God."

- George B. Wilson, S.J., former professor at Woodstock College, now an organizational consultant with Management Design, Inc., of Cincinnati, who, it will be recalled, was an active agent in attempting to discredit the late Bishop Joseph Sullivan of Baton Rouge, when his firm was hired (under pressure) to ease the tensions between Sullivan and his dissident priests.

  Wilson shows how Jung's theories on the conscious and subconscious can be applied to organizations, which must constantly be refounded and updated lest their symbols become sterile and lose meaning.

- John Sanford, a certified Jungian analyst in San Diego, compares and contrasts the Church's tradition of the origin of evil and Jung's theories. Sanford argues that traditional or common understanding of the Catholic position would seem to be irreconcilable with Jung's often contradictory theories of evil, but that the Church's position could change and come into line with Jung's, since its position has never been formally defined.

- Morton Kelsey, an Episcopalian minister and certified counselor, observes that Jung offers 20th century citizens the same message Jesus delivered 2000 years ago, only updated to take into account the current psychological condition of modern people. Kelsey wrote that Jung only entered the arena of spiritual counseling because he could find no priests to whom he could refer his patients who needed counseling.

- Thomas Clark, S.J., author of *From Image to Likeness: A Jungian Path in the Gospel Journey* (Paulist, 1983), writes that "we are only at the beginning of the task of utilizing Jungian typology for furthering Gospel purposes" – self-understanding, building community, etc.

The Jung Cult within the American Church is everywhere, from Boston to San Francisco, and entire cadres of priests, Religious and Church functionaries have been initiated into its secrets. It has become an enormous business, too, as the advertisements for books and cassettes in such publications as *The National Catholic Reporter*, and other Catholic publications for Jungian Catholics testify.

This tragedy has enormous institutional and personal consequences. Not only is the Church – the Body of Christ – deformed and disoriented by this cult, but once an individual is initiated, it's almost impossible to break them of their cult addiction, their hunger for self-actualization, individuation and revelation. They think they are alive when they are spiritually dead.

Or, as Leanne Payne and Keven Perotta wrote several years ago for *Pastoral Renewal* magazine, Christian Jungianism is so confusing because "by giving natural psychological drives and images a divine authority and infallibility, it deflects the word of God which comes to 'discern the thoughts and intentions of the heart (Heb. 4:12)'. The notion that fallen man is equipped with a natural drive and center already containing God's purpose and wisdom implies a duty to obey the self, creating a crisis of loyalties when, as inevitably happens, the self's inclinations run counter to the summons to take up the cross and follow Christ...

"Jungians treat supernatural and spiritual realities as psychological realities. Creeds and confessions are regarded as projections of the psyche. Christianity is then valued not for the truths it reveals about man and God, but for its usefulness in mapping and exploring the unconscious. Consequently, Scripture is interpreted subjectively. Christ loses His uniqueness as incarnate Word and mediator between God and man...

"Jungianism, by pushing God beyond the range of human knowledge and beyond good and evil, establishes a god who is both good and evil, a mere projection of the human mind, under whose image spiritual forces come to domineer over human lives. The repudiation of Yahweh invites the return of Baal. The abandonment of the search for holiness and transformation in the Spirit leaves the way open for spirits of sexual bondage, phallic demons."

It's getting worse

To appreciate the horrific descent of Catholic religious orders which have fallen prey to the lures of Carl Jung, consider this report from Australia, where the scandals of sexual abuse by clergy and religious are more widespread – and, until most recently, more publicized – than in the United States.

On November 10, 2001, Brisbane *Courier-Mail's* Jennifer Dudley took a very close, behind-the-scenes look at various programs at the Womenspace Center, where the goddess is worshiped in "menstrual cycle 'moontime' rituals," Spring Equinox and Summer Solstice rituals, Dark Goddess celebrations, etc., even observing that the Womenspace gift shop sells "Wicca'd-wear" and all the rest of paraphernalia of the black arts.

"While such happenings might seem routine at a New Age, pagan or witches gathering," wrote Dudley, "the most startling thing about the Womenspace is the identity of those behind it – some of the most prestigious teaching orders of nuns in the Catholic Church.

> Land titles records show that the Presentation Sisters (who operate St. Rita's College, Clayfield) paid $224,000 in 1999 for an old bakery and shop that have been converted into a series of rooms, or spaces, for rituals, gatherings and meditation…
>
> The Sisters of Mercy, who operate All Hallows School are also involved in Womenspace by way of providing the salary for the co-ordinator…Womenspace chairwoman Sister Judith Murphy is a Presentation Sister and Sister Annette Arnold, the Social Justice coordinator for the Catholic Social Action Office, is a Sister of St. Joseph. (The Social Action Office ran the controversial "marginal seats" campaign during the election, which critics claimed favored the [Australian Labor Party]).
>
> Womenspace newsletters thank a number of prestigious Catholic girls' secondary schools – including All Hallows, Mt. Alvernia College, Kedron, and Mt. St. Michael's College, Ashgrove – for photocopying their literature. They also hold events in some of these schools after hours…
>
> Presentation Sisters Queensland spokeswoman Sister Marlette Black, a former principal at St. Rita's, says mainstream religions need to be more accepting of all people and their religions or beliefs. That, she says, was one of the reasons the Presentation

Sisters voted to buy a property for Womenspace to help fulfill the "spiritual needs of all women whatever their particular religious perspective."

She says the decision to purchase a property for Womenspace, and provide it rent-free, was simply to support a center encompassing all spiritual traditions. She does not believe practices at the center contradict Catholic beliefs.

"The word Catholic by its very nature means something that is open and inclusive and able to encompass a great deal," she said.

Far from being an isolated phenomenon, Womenspace is indicative of a wider trend towards a radical feminist spirituality in some Christian denominations, with Catholic nuns at the forefront.

The website of the Social Action Office (SAO) of Catholic Leaders of Religious Institutes in Queensland, for example, says: "The spirituality which is the foundation for the Social Action Office's vision is centered on Sophia's transformative dream for all creation. Sophia is a feminine image of God often referred to as Wisdom in the Jewish and Christian traditions…"

On October 20, Brisbane's Banyo Seminary hosted between 70 and 80 women and one man, a religious brother, for a gathering called Showcasing Local Feminist Theology. Two of the speakers were Sisters of Mercy, including seminary lecturer and Griffith University academic Sister Elaine Wainwright…

One of the events, which a participant described as "hair-raising," was an "acting-out" of the smashing of the Ten Commandments; another woman said she'd be "damned" if she ever let her grandchild receive Communion from a "man." One "young presenter," a lesbian, led the group in a ritualistic incantation that repeated the "F-word"; one 13-year-old girl told how, when she had her first menstrual period, her "13 mothers" each dipped a finger in a clay bowl holding the blood, and "painted my naked body." Another woman told of a "bread baking" ritual and, as Dudley told the story, "planted handfuls of dough between each other's legs, followed by oral sex…"

Mercy Sister Elaine Wainwright said yesterday, Dudley continued, that the events had been taken out of context. "It was a day in which our research students in the Brisbane College of Theology and the Griffith University School of Theology were

> presenting their research into feminist theology. That's the context in which all of the work was presented. It was all Masters and Doctoral research that had been passed and approved as theological works by competent theologians at a masters level or doctoral level…The theology would predominantly have come out of the Christian tradition. There are students from the University of Queensland who would be working in the Wiccan tradition, but really the tradition would be more on women's spirituality."

This is sheer madness!

After the kids

Jung and his disciple Maslow have completely penetrated the Church's teaching institutions, though most Catholics are abysmally unaware this is so. Some are. Six years ago Scot Mary Kearns addressed the Catholic Headteachers Association of Scotland, on the subject "What Catholic Parents Expect From Their Schools," and focused on a "worrying" phenomenon: the importation of Mallow's theories into Catholic schools:

> …The Humanist manifesto sets out the campaigning atheists' agenda for the secularization of society. Many prominent members of the media and many educationalists are humanists and subscribe to this agenda. The first Director of the World Health Organization promoted this school of thought and set it out like this: "The concept of right and wrong is a barrier to developing a civilized way of life and should be eradicated. Children must be freed from prejudices forced upon them by religious authorities. Parents are dictators and suppressors of the child's better nature…"

> The jargon used is littered with references to children being encouraged to develop "self awareness", "self expression" or "self esteem", (these all being things we want our children to have). These techniques are commonly used in teaching religious and moral education and especially health education in the non-denominational sector. They are insidiously introduced to children and teachers alike.

> The object is to change perceptions and judgments indirectly so that neither adults nor children realize why they feel differently about moral questions. They may think the change is due to "growth" or "liberation" in their outlook and that they are now

more "tolerant" or "caring." Thus they can now tolerate things they would previously have thought wrong.

The methods are based on "the group therapy technique" first developed in America in the 1970's by two psychologists, Carl Rogers and Abraham Maslow. They described how emotional conditioning should be carried out by a group "facilitator." The facilitator does not impart knowledge like the old-fashioned teacher. Instead he/she initiates discussions encouraging children to reveal their personal views and feelings. The facilitator's approach is "value free." There is no right or wrong answer to any religious or moral question. Each person discloses what is right or wrong for them. All choices are equally valid even if they are opposites. Everything depends on feelings or emotions. Reason and conscience are discouraged. If anyone attempts objective evaluation, they are to be treated as an "outsider" and there will be a strong emotional reaction against such "judgmental intolerance".

Writing in the *Catholic Medical Quarterly* (November 1995), "Education or Manipulation", Dr. Helen Davies described the four stages in the behavior modification model, usually labelled "life skills" or "problem solving." Preliminary stage - creating the environment for change. An atmosphere of "openness" and "trust" is encouraged between members of the group using games and/or other "socializing" techniques.

First stage proper – "unfreezing", or creating doubts about previously held convictions. A frequently used method is by presenting the group with various imaginary and difficult situations or "dilemmas", in which they have to chose between various possible solutions presented to them. The terms of reference are strictly limited to the choices the facilitators want the group to make.

Second stage proper – changing or re-modeling of the mental and moral outlook. Whereas the previous stage challenged their existing beliefs, this stage seeks to replace them with different ones altogether.

Flattery is used to make the participants feel they are really the ones who are capable of seeing things clearly and making right decisions, while former generations, parents and religious teachers, are hopelessly old fashioned and out of touch. Another strong factor in producing change is group pressure. The more discussion and revealing of personal views and feelings that take place, the more difficult it is for the individual to maintain their own private views or standards.

The final stage – "re-freezing" or "fixation" of the new ideas and attitudes…

A recent survey of 18-30 year olds found that more than half of them did not believe in right and wrong at all. Not just that they could not tell right from wrong but that they did not believe in the concepts…

Parents expect that in Catholic schools appropriate teaching methods will be used to develop a child's reason and understanding so that they are in control of feelings and emotions. One of the Cambridge dons recently complained that applicants to his University no longer seemed to know how to think or reason things out. They expect that their children will develop a critical faculty and clear orthodox notions of right and wrong against which they can measure what bombards them from the media. We expect that all subjects will be taught consistently with Catholic faith and morals.

Catholics in the United States should expect no less.

After sixty years of the influence of Freud, Jung and their disciples, their overwhelming dominance in Catholic educational and formational institutions, we can see the results in the clerical pedophilia that has cost the Church billions, if not tens of billions of dollars, in the countless ruined lives of perpetrators and victims, in the moral confusion of tens of millions of Catholics, and in the ongoing project to brainwash Catholics into accepting the legitimacy of homosexuality.

Amchurch has come out. It is now time for real Catholics to say, "Get out!"

AFTERWORD

The human malice, human failures and human stupidity documented in the foregoing chapters are not a reason to despair, in terms of the future of the Church. In the Gospels, Jesus Christ points to the wheat and the chaff that will always be present in the Church, and the millstones prepared for those who corrupt the morals of children – and adults – and the accounting that would be expected by prelates, priests, journalists and everyone else at the Last Judgment.

Jesus assured us that the Gates of Hell would not prevail against the Church built upon the Rock of Peter.

Amidst all the trials, tribulations and anguish of the suffering faithful, the Rock has stood firm for two millennia, despite the attacks of unbelievers, unworthy bishops, faithless theologians, and embittered laity. The scandals which have marked Church life in North America since the early 1960s, accelerated by the revolt against *Humanae Vitae* and the sexual revolution, opened a Pandora's Box of evils; but the chief problem that the elites and intelligentsia in the Church have refused to recognize is the inherent evil of Liberalism, an ideology condemned by the Bishops of England and Wales in a Pastoral Letter dated the last day of the 19th century – just one of dozens of similar warnings to the faithful to be on their guard issued by the Church's intellectual giants of the 19th century – Popes, prelates, theologians and laymen – including the Civil War-era American Catholic Orestes Brownson.

When Liberalism infects the Catholic Church, the English bishops declared a century ago, "schisms and heresies arise, take shape and form…Faith becomes tainted, moral virtue becomes relaxed, and, in the process of time, Liberalism in religion invades the whole mind until, like their leaders, many of the faithful are thought to be alive when they are dead."

This Pastoral Letter, titled "The Church and Liberal Catholicism," warned the faithful that as the "storms of persecution have blown over, other dangers of a more insidious character – such as the various forms of rationalism and human pride – confront the Church." The sources of the evils afflicting modern society "consist either in the habit of belittling and

241

despising, or utterly rejecting, the authority of the Church, which presides in the name of God over the welfare of mankind."

The bishops further alerted their people that "a small number of men suffice to infect and unsettle the minds of many, not only by license in private speech; but if they are literary, by use of the press. They take leave to discuss theology and the government of the Church with the same freedom of speech and opinion they are accustomed to use in launching new theories on social science, political economy, art, literature, or any other subject. Being wanting in filial docility and reverence, they freely dispose of doctrine, practice and discipline upon their own responsibility, and with the least adherence to the mind of the Church or to her ministers…

"This is to be Liberal indeed," they observed, and they compared the Liberal Catholic to one who is invited into the royal palace of a sovereign and "who takes advantage of his position to destroy, or dispose of, the royal furniture according to his own caprice of that of friends from outside, and to make even structural alterations, without any kind of warrant for so doing."

The English bishops were under no illusions. Fifteen years earlier, that inveterate foe of Liberalism, Henry Edward Cardinal Manning, Archbishop of Westminster (warmly regarded by his flock as the "Apostle to the Poor") warned of a "pestilent infidel school" that had risen to power in the Press, the State and even the Church, "who, with an audacity never before known in the Christian world, are at this time assailing the foundations of human society and of Divine law. They have talked of late of what they call independent morality. And what do you suppose is independent morality? It means the law of morals separated from the Lawgiver. It is a proud philosophical claim to account for right and wrong without reference to God. And what is the object of this theory? It is to get rid of Christianity, and of God, and of right and wrong altogether…"

Blessed John Henry Cardinal Newman, often claimed by modern Liberal Catholics as one of their own, also addressed the danger of liberalism in his justly famous "Biglietto Speech" upon receiving the red hat of a cardinal:

"…For 30, 40, 50 years, I have resisted to the best of my powers the spirit of liberalism in religion. Never did Holy Church need champions against it more sorely than now, when, alas, it is an error overspreading, as a snare, the whole earth...Liberalism in religion is the doctrine that there is no positive truth in religion, but that one creed is as good as another, and this is the teaching which is gaining sustenance and force daily. It is inconsistent with any recognition of any religion, as *true*."

It is Liberalism, an ideology specifically condemned by name more than 20 times by every Holy Father since Blessed Pius IX, that is the core of the problem facing the Church today, and the reason why a militant homosexual movement has arisen in the Church, captured its most important positions, and moving rapidly to exercise total control.

Three months after the explosive revelations of clerical pedophilia and episcopal complicity in Boston in January 2002, as this book heads to press, a bishop in Florida has resigned, nearly 200 priests nationwide have been "outed" for various sexual crimes, and New Ways Ministry has just completed its three-day convention in Louisville, where it issued a manifesto for an accelerated agenda to homosexualize the Catholic people of this country.

Catholics, who thought that there might be some reticence on the part of gay activists in the face of the Church's current homosexual scandals, can see now how homosexual misconduct and crimes actually advance the homosexual agenda, just as the AIDS disease was exploited, spun and twisted to enormously advance public support for homosexual acts and homosexuals, exemplified by the AIDS activists' slogan, "AIDS Is Our Power!"

On March 10, the conference concluded with the release of a petition, *A Vision for the Future*, a nightmare 12-step program to sodomize the American Catholic Church, demanding:

- "A serious and sustained national dialog with gay/lesbian people" initiated by the United States Conference of Catholic Bishops, so the bishops can better understand the role of gays in the Church.

- The development of "ministry programs" for gays and lesbians and the introduction of these programs and their graduates into every "worshiping community."

- Church support for theologians, bishops and scholars who are engaged in serious research on "the ethics of same-sex relationships. As the world witnesses loving, devoted, and faithful same-sex couples, it is becoming increasingly obvious that scholastic answers are no longer convincing…"

- The development of educational programs and religion and catechetical texts "that reflect accurate images of gay/lesbian people. Homosexuality can no longer be cloaked in lies, stereotypes and jokes. Education about homosexuality should be an essential part of any curriculum that prepares students to follow Christ's command to 'Love one another.'"

- The training of campus ministers, youth ministers and school chaplains to accept, welcome and encourage young homosexuals who are "beginning to experience the gift of sexuality…Educational and spiritual programs on sexuality must include discussions on homosexuality…"

- All church agencies, including chanceries, parishes, schools, etc. must "provide supportive work atmospheres so that lesbian/gay Church personnel – clergy, lay, religious – can disclose their sexual orientation to colleagues and constituents, if they so choose…"

- "Seminary rectors, formation teams, vocation directors, priests' personnel directors, vicars for religious [must] provide educational and personal/spiritual development programs for gay/lesbian priests, religious, seminarians, and candidates…All clergy and religious, regardless of orientation, need to be educated and sensitized to the gifts and needs of their lesbian and gay peers."

- Training of counselors, therapists, confessors and spiritual directors to affirm those with homosexual orientation and to refrain from suggesting or counseling a gay or lesbian person that their "orientation should be changed or reversed by therapy or prayer."

- Training of family life ministers who can support grieving parents to accept their gay/lesbian child's coming out as a time of "grace."

- The training of diocesan and parish social action directors to promote special rights for homosexuals legislation.

- The celebration of homosexual "sexual" activity by "all Catholics and people of good will…We encourage all to reverence the gift of sexuality that helps us share our love creatively and joyously…"

Prior to the release of this statement, New Ways Ministry's leaders defied an order from the Holy See to Archbishop Thomas C. Kelly of Louisville that there be no Mass celebrated at the Galt House hotel, where the conference was held. New Ways denounced the order, with an assertion the Vatican was trying to use "Eucharist as a weapon," and the Holy See had no right to issue the order in the first place!

At the same time, as a result of massive publicity in Boston and other cities on the clerical sexual abuse scandal, real Catholics are beginning to demand that the Church's leaders must revise their seminary admission procedures and prohibit homosexuals from entering the priesthood; they must purge the priesthood of men not faithful to their vows and they must remove from all Church positions, whether in chanceries, outreach programs, or schools and colleges under their control, all those who reject the Church's teaching on human sexuality.

Amchurch Comes Out is one layman's attempt to further this latter cause.

"What then is our duty?" asked Cardinal Manning in an 1849 address to his clergy, in words Bernard Cardinal Law might well recite to his battered priests – "not to lament the past nor to dream of the future, but to accept the present. Dreams and lamentations weaken the sinews of action…We must learn the duty and the necessity of seeing things as they are, in their exact and naked truth" – and act.

Case closed

If January 2002 was a difficult month for Boston's Bernard Cardinal Law, April must have been hell. On April 8, Boston attorney Roderick MacLeish, Jr., representing a man claiming he was sexually abused by the famed "street priest" Fr. Paul Shanley, held a press conference and displayed for reporters, law enforcement officials and area district attorneys copies of documents showing that Law, his top aides and Law's predecessor-archbishops knew Shanley was a "sick" pervert since, at least, 1967.

The documents raised dozens of troubling questions, including suspicions that Law and his predecessor, Humberto Cardinal Medeiros, may have been blackmailed.

One of the documents indicated that Shanley, ordained in 1960 and a founding member of the North American Man-Boy Love Association, claimed – though he didn't say by whom – that he was sexually abused as a teenager, and one of his abusers was a cardinal archbishop of Boston.

Two days after the documents' release, *The Boston Globe's* Eileen McNamara posed "An Obvious Question":

"Was the Rev. Paul R. Shanley blackmailing the Roman Catholic Archdiocese of Boston?

"It is not a frivolous question; it's the most obvious one to arise from the personnel file that Cardinal Bernard F. Law and his high-priced legal team tried so hard to suppress.

"As striking as the revelations of the hierarchy's coverup of Shanley's crimes is the light that more than 800 pages of documents shed on the lengths to which his supervisors went to emotionally appease and financially accommodate a renegade priest they knew to be a serial child molester. Why?"

After displaying some of the most damning evidence that the famed street priest was indeed a very "sick" man who was coddled, protected and promoted by his superiors, McNamara answers her own question:

"Buried in Shanley's personnel file might be a hint. 'I have abided by my promise not to mention to anyone the fact that I too had been sexually abused as a teenager, and, later, as a seminarian by a priest, a faculty member, a pastor, and, ironically, by the predecessor of one of two cardinals who now debate my fate,' Shanley wrote to the Rev. Brian M. Flatley in an appeal for Law's support for his efforts to be appointed director of a church-sponsored youth hostel in New York City.

"Absent blackmail, why would Law recommend to dioceses in New York and California a 'street priest' whose public advocacy of sex between men and boys contradicted Church teaching and whose private behavior violated criminal and canon law?...

"No yardstick can measure the trust betrayed by this cardinal and by the sycophants in clerical collars who have done his bidding during his tenure as archbishop of Boston," McNamara continued. "But if a criminal prosecution of Law and his minions becomes the sole focus of our anger, we will have missed an opportunity to understand the modern history of the Catholic Church in Boston. What we need to know is locked in the files that Law is trying so hard to shield. We should not have to win access to them one plaintiff at a time. Unless Attorney General Thomas Reilly can find a way to subpoena every last piece of paper in the mansion on Lake Street, we will never know the answer to the question that haunts this community: Why?"

If, indeed, Shanley, who was born in 1931, was telling the truth, his abuser would have been the late Cardinal Richard Cushing, the prelate who engineered the election of John F. Kennedy, supported the dissident theologian Fr. Charles Curran (cf. *The Boston Pilot*, April 29, 1969), and who reigned in Boston from 1944-1970.

Whatever the case, according to MacLeish, archdiocesan officials were told by Shanley's pastor in 1967, the same year Shanley was elected by his peers for the new archdiocesan Senate of Priests, that he was a molester – one of a half-dozen priests subsequently exposed as molesters on the archdiocese's first-ever priests' senate.

Ten years later, in a letter dated Oct. 4, 1977, archdiocesan officials learned that Shanley, while addressing a meeting of Dignity/Integrity at St. Luke's Episcopal Church in Rochester, declared that "homosexuality is a gift of God and should be celebrated."

He also said, wrote Dolores Stevens in a letter to Jeanne D. Sweeney – one of the 818 documents released by the Boston chancery – that "it would be a good idea if people thought clergy were gay because it would have a radicalizing effect." He claimed there was no sexual activity that could cause psychic damage, "not even incest or bestiality," and that in most cases where a person is accused of pedophilia, it is the child, not the adult, who is the initiator.

Shanley also revealed that he had been appointed by Cardinal Medeiros to represent sexual minorities on the United States Catholic Conference's Young Adult Ministry board.

247

The documents also show Cardinal Law and his auxiliary bishops, wrote the *Globe's* Walter V. Robinson and Thomas Farragher on April 9, "ignored allegations of sexual misconduct against Rev. Paul R. Shanley and reacted casually to complaints that Shanley endorsed sexual relations between men and boys...

"As recently as 1997 – after the Boston archdiocese had paid monetary settlements to several of Shanley's victims – Law did not object to Shanley's application to be director of a church-run New York City guest house frequented by student travelers.

"Like a priest clad in a Teflon cassock, Shanley received an extraordinary tribute from Law when he retired in 1996, not two decades after Shanley asserted in public remarks that there was no psychic harm from engaging in taboo practices like incest or bestiality.

"In the Feb. 29, 1996, letter, the cardinal declared, 'Without doubt over all of these years of generous and zealous care, the lives and hearts of many people have been touched by your sharing of the Lord's Spirit. You are truly appreciated for all that you have done.'"

After the April 8 press conference where attorney MacLeish released the documents, one of the participants and Shanley victims, Arthur Austin commented: "If the Catholic Church in America does not fit the definition of organized crime, then Americans seriously need to examine their concept of justice."

"This man was a monster in the Archdiocese of Boston for many, many years," MacLeish said. "He had beliefs that no rational human being could defend...All of the suffering that has taken place at the hands of Paul Shanley – a serial child molester for four decades, three of them in Boston – none of it had to happen."

The Law exposés in Boston, mirrored in New York, Brooklyn, Long Island, Cleveland, Detroit, Chicago, Los Angeles, San Antonio and other cities, vindicate charges *The Wanderer* has presented for nearly two decades – that the leadership of the Catholic Church in the United States is fundamentally corrupt – and call for a serious remedial action.

The present crisis afflicting the Church in this country brings to mind the analysis of Fr. Paul Shaughnessy, S.J., published in *Catholic World Report*,

November 2000, "The Gay Priest Problem." "Quite simply," wrote Shaughnessy,

> those entrusted to fix what is broken are broken themselves and are camouflaging their real motives in the fuzzy vocabulary of therapy and pastoral sensitivity. As with every institutional crisis, this one ultimately boils down to the question of accountability...

> The issue of accountability forces us to confront a yet more intimidating crisis, one which is easily misunderstood and which I take up with reluctance, but which must be faced squarely as an unpleasant truth: Why bishops won't act.

> I define as corrupt, in a sociological sense, any institution that has lost the capacity to mend itself on its own initiative and by its own resources, an institution that is unable to uncover and expel its own miscreants. It is in this sense that the principal reason why the action necessary to solve the gay problem won't be taken is that the episcopacy in the United States is corrupt, and the same is true of the majority of religious orders. It is important to stress that this is a sociological claim, not a moral one....

> When the institution is healthy, the gutsier few set the overall tone, and the less courageous but tractable majority works along with these men to minimize misbehavior; more importantly, the healthy institution is able to identify its own rotten apples and remove them before the institution itself is enfeebled. However, when an institution becomes corrupt, its guiding spirit mysteriously shifts away from the morally intrepid few, and with that shift the institution becomes more interested in protecting itself against outside critics than in tackling the problem members who subvert its mission....

> [I]n claiming the US episcopacy is corrupt, I am not claiming that the number of scoundrel bishops is necessarily any higher than it was when the episcopacy was healthy. I am simply pointing to the fact that, as an agency, the episcopacy has lost the capacity to do its own housecleaning, especially, but not exclusively, in the arena of sexual turpitude....

> The Catholic Church, being Christ's bride without spot or wrinkle, is indefectible. She is holy because Christ is holy; she is perfect because Christ is perfect. She cannot teach error. Her

ministers, however, have sinned in the past, sin now, and will sin in the future until the second coming of Christ. She has lost some of her sons to heresy and some to schism, and those who remained have, in various periods, sunk into corruption....

Shaughnessy then proposed a number of actions that must be taken. First, Rome must "require heads on platters." Additionally, no man should be named a bishop, "unless he has a track record as a head-cracker and has cleaned up problems of sexual wrongdoing, by dismissing gay seminarians or seminary faculty, for example, or by getting rid of miscreants at a university chaplaincy."

Secondly, bishops must set an explicit policy that will forbid homosexuals from entering their seminaries.

Third, simplicity must be restored to priestly life. "Physical comfort is the oxygen that feeds the fires of homosexual indulgence. Cut it off. When you enter a rectory, take a look at the liquor cabinet, the videos, the wardrobe, the slick magazines, and ask yourself, 'Do I get the impression that the man who lives here is in the habit of saying no to himself?' If the answer is negative, the chances are that his life of chastity is in disorder as well. It goes without saying that reforming bishops should lead by example in this department and not simply exhort."

Fourth, the lay faithful must demand high standards of their priests, starting with the simple demand that the parish priest always appear in his clericals when he is outside the rectory. Then, laity are to use their checkbooks "as a carrot and stick. Remember that when your pastoral associate flies to Rio during Mardi Gras, you're footing the bill. Don't be silent partners in corruption."

A Partial Bibliography

The following front page headlines are a small sample of news reports on the subject of clerical homosexuality and pedophilia that have appeared in *The Wanderer* over my byline during the decade of the '90s when Amchurch came out:

August 16, 1990: "Byzantine Catholic Diocese Rocked by Homosexual Scandal:

August 30, 1990: "Archbishop's Resignation Offers No Relief to Orthodox Catholic Canadians"

January 3, 1991: "$3.5 Million in Damages Awarded in Sex Abuse Case Involving Priest"

May 16, 1991: "Honolulu Bishop Excommunicates Catholics Who Oppose Him"

July 16, 1991: "Archdiocese and Seminary Hit With $13 Million Civil Suit"

August 22, 1991: "Honolulu Bishop Faces Federal Lawsuit Charging Molestation"

August 22, 1991 "Hawaii's Bishop Ferrario Is No Stranger to Controversy"

September 5, 1991: "Chicago Archdiocese Faces Another Lawsuit Alleging Clerical Sex Abuse"

November 14, 1991: "California's Two Leading Prelates are 'Prisoners' of Homosexual Clergy"

January 28, 1993: "Archbishop's Credibility is At Issue After Priest's Sex Abuse Trial Ends"

November 18, 1993: "Reports Reveal Archbishop Weakland's 'Patience' With Pedophile Priests"

November 25, 1993: "Following Charge of Sex Abuse, Bishops Rally Around Bernardin"

January 6, 1994: "Children's Liturgy Expert Admits Sex Abuse of Children"

January 20, 1994: "$350 Million Lawsuit Filed Against Baltimore Archdiocese"

February 8, 1996: "NCCB Named in Texas Lawsuit for Civil Conspiracy"

February 15, 1996: "The $150 Million Question: Is the NCCB Accountable to Catholic Laity?"

May 2, 1996: "For Seattle Archdiocese, It's Hard to Confess Wrongdoing"

July 11, 1996: "Texas Court Orders Parties in NCCB Lawsuit to Mediation"

August 15, 1996: "Adamec's Arrival in Altoona Coincides With First Major Eruption of Scandals"

August 22, 1996: "Seattle Archdiocese Asks Judge for Gag Order"

September 12, 1996: "Upset Canadian Bishops' Official Ponders Suit Against Magazine"

June 19, 1997: "Diocese's Rotten Underbelly Exposed in Pedophile's Trial"

August 7, 1997: "Were Church Officials Incompetent, Negligent or Just Plain Evil?"

August 7, 1997: "Bishop Apologizes to Victims as Diocese Considers Appeal"

August 28, 1997:

> "The Floundering See: Dallas in the Wake of the Kos Trial"
>
> "How the Kos Annulment Went Through: Just Another Busy Amchurch Day"
>
> "The Wanderer Interviews Attorney Sylvia Demarest"

January 1, 1998: "Amchurch's Homosexual Leader Displays His Lifestyle and Attitude"

February 5, 1998: "Dallas Judge Upholds Jury's Verdict Against Diocese"

March 19, 1998: "Cardinal George to Investigate St. Louis Treatment Center"

June 18, 1998: "Episcopal Scandal, Pedophile Payoffs and the Bernardin Legacy"

May 20, 1999: "Canadian Diocese Implicated As Pedophile Cover-Up Unravels"

June 17, 1999: "Lawsuit Names NCCB President [Fiorenza] For Protecting Alleged Pedophiles"

August 5, 1999: "Bishop [Ziemann] Resigns After Priest Accuses Him of Sexual Abuse"

October 28, 1999: "Springfield Bishop [Ryan] Resigns After Accusations of Homosexual Abuse"

November 11, 1999: "Lawsuit Naming Bishop Ryan Filed"

January 27, 2000: "Greeley Memoirs Refer to Alleged Clerical Sex Ring"

February 3, 2000: "Albany Priest Announces He's Becoming A Woman"

February 10, 2000:

"Homosexual Clerics' Website Indicates Deep Influence in Church"

"KC Newspaper Flacks For Amchurch Homosexualist Advocates"

February 17, 2000: "Canadian Journalist Charges Liturgical Renewal Run By Sexual Liberationists"

March 30, 2000: "Maine Priest Who Created Homosexual Website Put on Leave"

April 6, 2000: "Clerical Pedophile Ring Operated Freely for Decades"

August 24, 2000: "How Seminaries Weed Out Catholics"

November 2, 2000: "Cardinal Ratzinger Snubs South African Bishop After Summons"

Z